The Historiography of Communism

The Historiography of Communism

Michael E. Brown

TEMPLE UNIVERSITY PRESS
Philadelphia

Temple University Press
1601 North Broad Street
Philadelphia PA 19122

www.temple.edu/tempress

Text design by Kate Nichols

♾ The paper used in this publication meets the requirements of the
American National Standard for Information Sciences—Permanence of
Paper for Printed Library Materials, ANSI Z39.48-1992

Library of Congress Cataloging-in-Publication Data

Brown, Michael E.
The historiography of communism / Michael E. Brown.
    p. cm.
Includes bibliographical references and index.
ISBN 978-1-59213-921-7 (cloth : alk. paper)
ISBN 978-1-59213-922-4 (pbk. : alk. paper)
1. Communism—History. 2. Communism—Historiography. I. Title.
  HX36.B75 2009
  355.4072'–dc22
2008011780

2 4 6 8 9 7 5 3 1

Contents

Acknowledgments

I owe a great deal to far more people than I can thank in a short paragraph of acknowledgments. I mention only the few who have been directly connected to the publication of this book and the development of many of the ideas discussed in it. Randy Martin co-wrote two of the chapters and, generously, read all the others. My discussions with him over the years have always been productive, not only because of his vast knowledge of the critical literature but because of the creative way he has of working through difficult concepts and his willingness to help me work through my own ideas. I owe him a special debt of gratitude for having shown me different sides to almost every argument I discuss in this book and for encouraging me to publish it.

Frank Rosengarten and I founded the journal *Socialism and Democracy* more than twenty years ago, when several chapters were originally published. His comments have always been helpful, and I learned a great deal from him about the history of communism in America.

George Snedeker participated with me, Randy Martin, and Frank Rosengarten in editing a collection entitled *New Studies in the Politics and Culture of American Communism*, and he has generously shared his knowledge of critical theory with me.

Bertell and Paule Ollman have patiently read parts of this book and part of a manuscript that lays the foundation for my discussion of the idea of "society," and they have discussed them with me at great length. The theoretical parts of this book have been influenced by our discussions about internal relations and dialectics, and by Paule's willingness to share her considerable knowledge of modern French thought.

I have also had the benefit of discussions with Peter Manning and Michael Meyer. Both helped me to clarify the relationship between key concepts and various theoretical and philosophical literatures with which I was only casually familiar when I undertook this project, but which turned out to have been important to its completion.

Finally, Marie-Annick Brown took precious time from her preparation of a forthcoming exhibition of her drawings to read the final manuscript and help me edit the prose. Our discussions about art have been instructive and contributed to my accounts of the concepts of "reflexivity," "sociality," and "a course of activity," each of which is crucial to my understanding of what is at stake in any sociologically oriented discussion of historiography.

Permissions

I am grateful to the following journals for permission to reprint the following previously published materials:

"History and History's Problem." Winter 1986/7. *Social Text* 16:136–61.

"Ideology and the Metaphysics of Content." Winter 1983/4. *Social Text* 8:55–84.

"Issues in the Historiography of Communism, Part One." Spring/Summer 1987. *Socialism and Democracy* 4:7–38.

"Issues in the Historiography of Communism, Part Two: Some Principles of Critical Analysis." Fall/Winter 1987. *Socialism and Democracy* 5:1–34.

"Left Futures" (with Randy Martin). Spring 1995. *Socialism and Democracy* 9.1:59–89.

"Socialism in Transition: Documents and Discussion, an Essay on Rethinking the Crisis of Socialism" (with Randy Martin). 1991. *Socialism and Democracy* 7.3:9–56.

"*Society Against the State:* The Fullness of the Primitive." Fall 1978. *October* 6:61–75.

1

Introduction

Communism, Society, and History

Most of the chapters in this book were originally written as essays in what was to be a monograph on the relevance of historiography to sociological theory and of sociological theory to the humanities. It presupposed a definition of sociology as the study of the social, or collective, aspect of human affairs, where that aspect was seen as necessarily connected to the study of political movements and other noninstitutional, or "informal," critical activity. Many were written in the immediate aftermath of the breakup of the Soviet Union and were concerned with how the events associated with the breakup were being discussed in the United States, especially by those committed to progressive values and those intellectuals who had become disappointed in what they thought of as the Left according to one of two hypotheses. The first says that Communist ideology and practice are distortions of progressive ideals and need to be purged if those ideals are to have a fair hearing. The second says that they are endemic to the Left, thereby providing a sufficient reason to repudiate or at least marginalize it at virtually any cost.[1] What Theodore Draper has referred to approvingly as "professional anticommunism" had its roots in either the history of the internal politics of "official communism," in which Draper had once been intensely involved, or the official politics of the Cold War.[2]

The first approach denied the legitimacy of "protest" in favor of "dissent" and insisted on an orientation to "social problems" within the limits of institutional politics rather than on a more generalized politics responsive to the contradictory structural features of society such as the relationship between socialized production and the privately controlled disposition of wealth. Resistance to institutional politics was thought of as irrational, an expression of youthful idealism, hypocritical or otherwise dishonest, or bordering on the fanatical.[3] The emphasis on institutional politics invoked such values as rationality and civility, thought to have a universal core of meaning regardless of how the words are momentarily defined. These were said to be uncontaminated by the Left ideologies that had promoted misleading and, given the progress of society under liberal democracy, potentially dangerous ideas such as exploitation, classes, and class struggle. The appeal of those ideologies was presumably based on a belief that was essentially utopian, namely that socialism is the rational completion of the capitalist revolution insofar as it is aimed at reinforcing the conditions of abundant production brought about by capital's historic socialization of labor.

What was thought to be utopian about this was the implication that it is necessary to transform the relations of production from an emphasis on the private exercise of power based on wealth to an emphasis on societal authority over those means of production that have to do with the reproduction of society. From this point of view, the Left was seen as unrealistic; at best, it expresses values that, while admirable, are distorted by attempts to short-circuit the natural historical process by which, alone, they are capable of realization under the conditions of democracy. Leftists were advised, in the name of reason, to work within the context of a two-party system in which ideologies had become increasingly irrelevant and that provides the basis of a stable, self-perpetuating, and intrinsically progressive, polity. To do this required eliminating any connection to their radical past. It seemed evident to the critics of the Left that progress in America depends on affirming its institutions, and that, by the end of the 1950s, the constitutional protection of dissent provided a reliable foundation from which to work rationally and effectively for social change.

While this position may have been defensible on its own grounds, it effectively proposed an abandonment of further inquiry, other than self-confirming accounts, into the possibility that a rational basis exists for the persistence of radicalism. Consequently, research turned toward psychological explanations that focused on attitudes, beliefs, and the family backgrounds of activists. An elaborate defense of this position by prominent scholars, including Seymour Martin Lipset, Daniel Bell, and Talcott Parsons, doubtless contributed to a drift to the Right among many radical intellectuals who lived through that period, over and above the revulsion with Stalinism. The latter might have accounted for a growing antipathy toward the Communist Party USA, and toward the Soviet Union as a model. But only a general analysis, coupled with fears not obviously connected with official communism, could have supported the rejection of radical politics as such.

I will discuss the analysis and its context in later sections of this chapter. For now, the drift toward the Right by some progressives can be seen in part as a reaction, first, to the militancy of the Civil Rights Movement, the apparent excesses of the Student Movement, radical elements of the feminist movement, and the generalization of anticolonial struggles; second, to the fact that these movements were far more ambitious than could be tolerated by gradualists; and third, to the continued existence of prominent, though relatively small Left parties. One result is what appeared to be a generational division but, I believe, is best understood as the re-emergence of an authentic political difference between those who resolve doubt in favor of institutional politics and those who resolve it in favor of what C. Wright Mills spoke of as "structural criticism." Thought of this way, the difference is familiar and virtually constant in the history of modern societies. What is more relevant to the concerns of this book, however, is the way in which the politics of this difference worked itself out at the end of the twentieth century and, in particular, its effects on the Left today and on current discussions of programs for a Left future.

The abandonment of inquiry in favor of self-confirming accounts of the Left also had bearing on deciding how the history of American society ought to be understood—e. g., as the history of democracy rather than the history of capitalism—and whether the emphasis should be on politics and the state or on exploitation (including slavery), conquest, the role of social movements in social reform, and the social ramifications of what Karl Polanyi referred to as the "price-making money market." It is obvious that neither emphasis excluded the other, and this was no less true in studies of labor published by International Publishers than those in the standard bibliography of American history; but it is the relative emphasis that counted in contributing to the general understanding of society during the Cold War.[4]

In either case, whether the relationship to communism was thought to be internal to the Left or a surface feature easily shed on behalf of reason and civility, the possibility of a Left future was said to depend on severing the connection and divorcing every socially progressive project from even traces of it.[5] I believe that two things were, above all, crucial to the disappointment with the Left, apart from the uncompromising one-dimensional reaction of the "professional anticommunists" and apart from objections to style. One is a misleading conception of communism, including its manifestations as a political party, a type of society, an ideology, and a type of state. The other is a misunderstanding of the Left—insofar as it is more accurate to see it as a heterogeneous manifestation of an irrepressible and irreducibly critical aspect of "societies in which the capitalist mode of production prevails." The first is understandable in the light of the well-known debasement of the post-war literature on communism, in particular, the complicity of its academic mainstream in the agencies of American foreign policy. The second is understandable in terms of the historiography of

American studies insofar as it emphasizes features of American society that would make the existence of a Left virtually unimaginable.[6]

The third and fourth chapters of this book focus on certain prominent manifestations of the debate, from the 1960s to the 1990s, between established anticommunist scholars, most notably Theodore Draper, and a fairly representative sample of the new historians of the Left. By "new" I mean those post–Cold War professional historians committed to finding a theoretically sustainable basis for their study consistent with a holistic conception of society in contrast with the narrative histories written by most of their forebears and driven by a rather different agenda, one for which such a conception was irrelevant, unnecessary, or ideologically unacceptable. In this regard, their work represents a number of substantive reorientations. For one, they generally take the existence of a Left for granted as a feature of American history, which, for them, means not only that there is no simple and comprehensive answer to the question "why is there no socialism in the United States?" but that the premise of the question is ambiguous and possibly false (cf. Foner 2002, chapter 6). For another, their view of American society makes it difficult to deny a persistent Left tendency and, therefore, to ignore the historical dimension of its manifestations. Third, they draw on a view of social movements as more than instances of the "collective deviance" by which those movements were classified by most sociologists writing in the first three quarters of the twentieth century, and as no less rational than many of the institutional or official forms of action to which "collective behavior" (the inclusive category that included crowds, riots, revolutions, social movements, fads, etc.) was invidiously compared (see Brown and Goldin, 1973, for a review). Fourth, their work attempts to rectify errors implicit in accounts of Left political organizations such as the Communist and Socialist parties, which emphasize leadership to the virtual exclusion of base participation and popular support. Finally, and perhaps most important to understanding the social aspect of the movements to which organizations of that sort typically respond, is the detail with which many of the new historians delineate the diverse and overlapping contexts of participation and activism.

Taken together, these reorientations represent a departure from the mainstream interpretations of the history of communism, and they represent an approach to historical study in general, deliberate or not, that differs significantly from the approach of the orthodox historians. That is, in order to specify both their objects of study and their contexts, they incorporate principles of research, concepts as well as methods, from other disciplines and traditions, especially contemporary sociology and the new "social history" (cf. Lloyd 1986; also Revel and Hunt 1995). Among the most important ideas adopted from sociology are the post-functionalist concept of a social movement, a more expansive notion of context, and a greater respect for the complexity of participation in political action and its relation to everyday life.

However, even without the influence of other disciplines, it was likely that a turn would be taken if only because of the ideological limitations of the mainstream of the literature at a time, the 1960s and its immediate aftermath, when it was considered necessary in all the human sciences—i.e., the disciplines for which a historiographical interest is essential to the intelligibility of their subject matter—to examine the impact of official policies and propaganda on what is financed, published, and generally brought into public awareness.[7] But there is also little question that the very idea of history was beginning to change as the field moved closer to the social sciences and to those disciplines within the humanities, including literary studies, that were particularly concerned with problems of meaning, interpretation, representation, textualization, context, and the idea of coherence, as well as with the constitutive role of nonprofessional discourses in all of the human sciences and the implication of that on the discussion of historical truth.[8]

Parenthetically, to the extent to which it was demanded of the Left that it disavow its past, a principle was introduced that would not have been accepted as reasonable for understanding and assessing other instances of human affairs, just as the view of Communist or Socialist societies presented during the Cold War was, with few exceptions, incompatible with the idea of a society.[9] For example, if they are to be about societal formations, theories of democracy cannot avoid coming to terms with the French Revolution, including the Terror, as well as with the vexing idea of a "state of exception,"[10] not to mention the constitution and limitations of democracy under the shadows of capitalism, slavery, and imperialism.

I believe that my analysis of the debates at the time these chapters were written, including the two chapters I co-authored with Randy Martin on the "collapse of communism," is basically correct, or at least reasonable, in identifying the frame of reference within which they took place. What makes them relevant today is that the same frame of reference and much of the substance of those debates continue to influence present discussions about the Left and about how a progressive politics, Left or not, might be re-imagined. In those chapters, the analysis bears specifically on the problem posed by anticommunism for how we think of Left ideas, values, and politics, with negative consequences that have proven difficult to overcome. This is why I believe that it is worth re-engaging those discourses. They accompanied what appeared to be not only the end of an era but an end to something that had once been thought of as a model for exploring possible solutions in other contexts to the political, economic, and human problems associated with capitalist modernity. Recent events in the Americas suggest that the judgment that the prospect of socialism had been foreclosed by the breakup of the Soviet Union may have been premature in its general conclusion; but it had the positive effect of opening the question of the Left's future once again. In particular, it reaffirmed the need of the contemporary Left to come to terms with the complexities of its past, including what had been excluded by those versions of the Left in their struggles for hegemony and what was regressive as well as progressive about them (cf. Butler, Laclau, and Zizek 2000, especially pp. 90–181).

As it turned out, however, the discussion of the Left past and its relationship to the possibility of conceiving of a future was dropped too soon,
at least among many of those writing about possible Left futures.[11] This was
partly in reaction to the 1980 U.S. election and the growing realization that
a strong Right was gaining popular support and effective power within national institutions and the media. But it was also due to the fact the controversy had proven impossible to manage even among progressives suspicious
of institutional politics, or convinced that working within those limitations
would be futile, and due to a growing recognition that it was necessary to
rethink the relations of class, race, and gender, which had become crucial to
the self-identification of progressive politics in the aftermath of the 1960s.
Finally, it also had to do with the crystallization of an altogether negative
public image of the Left and its putative past by the end of the Cold War,
something I discuss later as one of the more enduring of the many baleful
legacies of that period. On the other hand, a growing number of historians
began to re-examine the history of communism to the extent to which that
project is no longer confined to radical journals or conducted according to
methods any longer identifiable as parochial.[12]

In summary, it is understandable that post–Cold War discussions among
progressives about the future of the Left began to separate it from its past.
However, this had the effect of making the present Left seem altogether indeterminate, as if waiting in a kind of hopeful innocence for an integrative
idea with less controversial pedigrees than "socialism" and "Marxism," possibly a new party or a program aimed at promoting "radical democracy." At
the same time, there remains a growing literature aimed at confirming anticommunism and, by inferences often explicitly made, denigrating the Left in
general. The desire to separate the Left from its past poses a dilemma for
those who are currently advocating a yet newer Left than the new Lefts of
before. The Left can have a future only if it has a present that is somehow related to a memorable past. If it has such a past, it must repudiate or ignore it
for the sake of its own progress. Otherwise, something different from a Left
needs to be constructed and the idea of social progress redefined accordingly.
But, then, there is no imagining a future for what we might have thought was
under discussion, and what was under discussion was not just a particular
Left but the indispensable critical notion of social progress. To undo the Left
is, in that sense, to empty the expression "social progress" of all political
meaning, which, I take it, was the aim of official anticommunism from the
outset.[13]

The discussion needs to be joined again in regard to two interests, which
are shared by professional history and the other human sciences, including
politics. One involves deciding what a Left might be if it is to be something
that can be thought of as having a possible future. My argument will be that
this requires understanding the Left as a constant manifestation of something
immanent to society. The other interest involves inquiring into the difference
that rethinking the historiography of communism might make to our under-

standing of the history of American society, especially to our understanding of how to think of America as a society.

The present incarnation of this book is addressed to the human sciences as a whole rather than to any particular discipline, and to those interested in re-examining the idea of a Left from the standpoint of the relationship between representations of its past and possible futures. In this introduction, I mention and briefly discuss some of the most important suppositions, ideas, and analytical principles on which I have relied, and summarize some of the main themes connecting the different chapters.

On the one hand, the book as a whole is intended to be consistent with a holistic view of the disciplines of the human sciences according to two related ideas. The first is on the order of a *heuristic*, by which I mean an established practical rule for some activity (i.e., "normal" practice) for which there is no accepted theoretical justification. It says that an understanding of history, historicity, as an immanent feature of sociality is logically prior to deciding how to describe and account for certain apparently crucial features of historical explanation. These are exemplified by the following partial list of problematics, given that we are, for the moment, working with a conventional view of history as an account of events and successions of events in time: (1) how to make plausible an account of the temporal succession or structural determination of states of affairs; (2) how to express an evolutionary movement of societal articulation or any other version of social change over time, if "time" is defined in a nonabsolute and nonlinear way according to the internal temporality of the ostensible social entity and the temporal multiplicity of its environment; (3) how to determine what constitutes an event and what field of difference is thereby reorganized; (4) how to choose a perspective compatible with a philosophically consistent account of historiographical principles and then to test its adequacy to its subject matter; (5) how to distinguish between, on the one hand, "sources" and "facts" and, on the other, what appear to be one or the other but are neither; and (6) how to reconcile the professional obligation to exhaust sources without yielding to the conventional pragmatics of selection and organization and the interpretive biases that accumulate as any field takes on the aspect of a "normal science."

The second idea is on the order of a theoretical claim, or a philosophical claim with theoretical entailments. It says that the human sciences share a common object, which is *the distinctively human aspect of human affairs*, and therefore a commitment to bring accounts into line with the idea that there is a distinctively human aspect. That aspect is conceived of simultaneously as social and critical, and therefore as a course of activity rather than a state of affairs, though for certain rhetorical purposes it can be expressed as such. Apart from that qualification, the idea of a course of activity implies self-transformation and an essential reflexivity (roughly, the irrepressible display of momentarily unexplicatable socially pragmatic grounds).[14]

This establishes a principle of objectivity radically different from the objectivity studied by the non-human sciences. It thereby provides a basis for a general test of the validity of assertions, given the unavoidable tension between reference and representation that makes virtually all claims about human affairs reasonably subject to review. It also entails a general understanding of what would otherwise appear to be distinct products (e.g., meanings, values, things, relations, states of affairs) as what Harold Garfinkel refers to as "ongoing accomplishments" (1967). In regard to the first idea, several of the following chapters discuss some consequences either of ignoring the immanence of history to human affairs or of writing in a way that treats history as movement along a temporal dimension on which societies can be identified as particulars, allowing for the possibility of describing social progress as linear (or as a variant of the same, "multilinear") and for establishing typologies, analogies, and proximities among different societies, thereby taking historical textualization to involve, fundamentally, writing narratives of events (and describing them in a way that lends itself to narration).[15]

On the other hand, I do not purport to offer an analysis of the political Left, a vision of its possible futures, or an account of its past, though various chapters say something about each of these topics. Rather, the book is intended to raise questions about the ways in which these topics have been and are being discussed. These are concerned with what I will occasionally refer to as "latent constraints" on sociopolitical thought and discourse. Michel Foucault has shown that certain of these can, with some difficulty, be made explicit. To that extent, they become manifest in ways that I believe are essential to a self-conscious Left capable of projecting itself as such into a possible future.[16] Nevertheless, the distinction between latency and explicitness is not intended to be theoretical, since, as I will suggest, "latency" refers to an unself-conscious way of making something apparent (doing it in the course of an activity), and "explicitness" is identified with that activity's ostensible product. It is the distinction between a course of activity and its ostensible product that is theoretical, as is the term "ostensible." The force of these questions, what makes them particularly disturbing, is clarified by my critique of the distinction between the idea of a nation (an "imagined community" that operates as a totality under the principles of subjectivation and power) and the idea of a society (an imaginable community of strangers that operates inclusively, as an aspiring totality, under the principles of interdependence and "law," or "authority"). Unless otherwise indicated, I use the expression "the Left" to refer to manifestations of the intrinsically critical aspect of society, and the expression "the political Left" to refer to a specific manifestation of that aspect.

The literature of anticommunism has tended to typify virtually all Left formations either as expressions of immaturity or as subordinate to "communism" as that was imagined under the simplifying logic of the Cold War. That logic is most obvious in Theodore Draper's writing (1960, 1981), less so in the work of John Patrick Diggins (1991). But the difference between them is as much one of manner than substance, since both provide a great deal of information that any account needs to take into consideration: Diggins tends to patronize while Draper is always on the attack. The alternative to this literature is not procommunism, as Draper seems to believe. It is primarily, with some notable exceptions, interested in asking different questions: For example, in what way does the history of American society require the systematic inclusion of the conditions of possibility for a Left? How should social movements be represented in historical accounts? In regard to the first, attention is given to how those conditions are established. In regard to the second, the focus is on how those conditions are made manifest. The internality of the relationship between movement and society is one reason why the alternative to anticommunist historiography is so often self-consciously theoretical or sociological. The debate between the two positions, one specific in its focus, the other inclusive, is discussed throughout this book, especially in Chapters Three and Four and, from a different point of view, in Chapters Seven and Eight (with Randy Martin). But the debate itself is not my main topic. Rather, I am interested in what habits of thought are revealed by it so far as concerns our understanding of the relationship between communism and American society.

From another point of view, this book is about the persistence of anticommunism when the time of communism seems to have ended. I am not as much interested in how this might be explained, though I venture something of an explanation in this chapter, as I am in its effects on other areas of thought, in particular theory, the philosophy of the human sciences, prevailing discourses on and various ideas of a Left, and the subsidiary idea of Left politics. I am especially concerned with how the generalization of anticommunism—the encompassing abstraction it has become—has reinforced a historiography formulated against or indifferent to what I believe is a governing principle of the human sciences: That an account of human affairs is valid only if it refers to those affairs, or provides an opportunity to refer to them, according to their necessarily reflexive features of criticism and sociality. By referring to these features as necessary, I mean that they constitute what can be said about the distinctively human aspect of life, given the questions about human affairs that we cannot presently avoid and that currently organize the curriculum in the humanities, philosophy, the arts, and the social sciences. In this sense, "necessity" means "essential to the very possibility of conceiving of human affairs as distinctively human." To deny this is, effectively, to affirm that our knowledge of human affairs is sufficient to justify beliefs about them when it derives from one or another variant of causal analysis or is plausible solely as a matter of the structure of the specific narrative in which they are featured.

The distinction between the two types of sciences, human and nonhuman (with their very different domains of objectivity), is a familiar one, though it is honored in the social sciences more in principle than in practice. What is more important for present purposes is to note that a failure to honor it in practice leaves one unable to appreciate how problematic it is to impose an analysis of facts about "nation" on an account of "society," if only because the first projects a sense of determination and the second a sense of interdependence, in which case "units" are conceived of as what Bruno Latour refers to as active "mediators" in contrast with "intermediaries" (2005). This tendency must be rejected no matter how convenient it may be, not only because the conflation is illogical, but because it precludes a historiography responsive as a whole to what is distinctively human about human affairs. Nor can the emphasis on nation be taken heuristically, as is almost always done in comparative studies, because no argument has been made, and I suspect none can be made, which explains how that can provide a justifiable approximation of society. The substitution of nation for society avoids the very object that invites, and demands, historical study in the first place; to avoid this object is to forego the overarching purpose of writing history.[17]

But that criticism, though just, may be too general to clarify what is at stake. The pressing problem is that emphasizing "nation" introduces a bias that infects the selection of materials in every particular case and directs attention elsewhere than to what can be called "society," to a distinctly articulated polity and the sorts of events and series that might reasonably be expected to accompany the spectacular coherence of a nation and its celebratory performances of agency. Jean-Jacques Rousseau reminds us that when nations are at issue, the object of study is the play of states, indifferent to their societal aspect according to criteria of expediency that dictate the special type of rationality that governs celebratory agencies of power. In that case, the best that can be expected, so far as collective action is concerned, is that people are transformed from members (interdependent with all other members) to functionaries (dependent on hierarchy to the minimization, if not exclusion, of sociality).

I am not saying that histories written from that point of view provide nothing of value to the study of society; quite the reverse. Facts about nation are, more often than not, parametric to understanding society, in the sense that they are most often fixed by force. How those parameters appear in that ongoing life is certainly part of an adequate account of its history. This is so if history comes to terms with the mix of accommodation and resistance that, by the nature of our most incorrigible concepts, testifies to a distinctive dynamics of societal change based on a different kind of "externality" from that often attributed to "conditions" of power, climate, and geography. But references to such parameters can only be worked out on the axiomatic priority of society.

Before they are thought of as parametric, and therefore capable of being understood as such, national data constitute a record of something distinctly nonsocietal. They only appear formally parametric when understood as part of the course of power's reckoning with society. The relation between the two must be taken into account in determining the limits of the expression and realization of society as an ongoing accomplishment, but the language for describing (or approximating) society cannot be preserved in the language used to register national facts.[18] Historical accounts regularly refer to specific data, chronologies, and hypotheses that cannot be ignored and that must be understood and appreciated in their own terms for the sake of the continued enlargement of the human archive. But, to the extent to which these cannot be separated from standard inferential and interpretive procedures, it is reasonable to propose that the procedures should be examined critically for what they exclude (e.g., about society) before drawing the sorts of general conclusion that we are accustomed to drawing from historical studies.

In arguing against what I see as an elision of the critical aspect of society by marginalizing or ignoring its most important manifestations, I have in mind its possible effects on our understanding of the meaning and significance of "recorded" events (including whether or not they are properly referred to as "events"), the collective constitution of agency and not merely conditions of mobilization (and by derivation, intentionality), and the character of a historically conscious explanation conceived of as an account of society. In summary, I understand both criticism and sociality to be necessary features of the ongoing courses of activity from which we come to form the idea of a society in contrast with the very different idea of a nation, rather than as types of possible action or properties that distinguish some things people do from others. When stated this way, it is clear that the consequences of the elision of the critical aspect are profound, or so I argue in the next section on the logic of anticommunism.

My working hypothesis is that recognition of the critical aspect of society is presently compromised by a context of signification, the governing principles of which I describe as an abstraction and generalization of anticommunism.[19] The first takes the form of a specialized logic, and the second of a field of increasingly inclusive, fixed, and polarizing designators. Dependence on this context makes it difficult to incorporate internally critical manifestations of society in historical accounts. As a result, the latter are often tendentious to a weak notion of society in which criticism appears, first, as an event that might or might not occur and, second, as an exception to normalcy. It also makes it difficult to clarify the grounds of two important historiographical interests. The first is an interest in writing to the possibility of changes in the scope, concentration, and ramifications of critical activity. The second has to do with how a limited set of possible critical turns is conceivable at a given moment within the ongoing activities that constitute society.

The first can be illustrated by a passage in *The Communist Manifesto* that describes the contradiction between the "forces of production" and the "relations of production." The "forces of production" refers to the social organization of abundant production, and the "relations of production" refers to a relationship of "ownership" to "labor" described as exploitation. This is according to capital's account of itself as deriving the decisive part of its wealth, the basis of profit, from labor (in the form of surplus value) as the most variable factor in and most expensive cost of production. This is a contradiction because there are no means consistent with the realization of capitalist wealth that allow for the progress of both without each disrupting the other, and there are no capital-friendly policies that can overcome this dilemma other than a self-defeating emphasis on one at the expense of the other. It manifests itself as an ongoing crisis, and therefore a constant tension, in which only two highly general but determinative consequences can be imagined under the conditions of the reproduction of the capitalist mode of production stipulated by the defense of capital. Both are manifest in each and every instance of human affairs subject to capitalist production. That is, they are inclusive and definite. Either the political economy of industrial/postindustrial capitalism moves toward reinforcing the social dimension of production (the infrastructure of "cooperation" and its general form, sociality), in which case it undermines the conditions of exploitation and competition, or it moves toward reinforcing the domination of "the society of the producers" by nonsocietal agencies in control of the means of production (which are always the only fully realizable form of wealth).

It might be said that the move in one direction or another is a function of politics. But that would be a leap not justified by the analysis drawn from capital's point of view. If it is not so justified, then the question is open as to what might constitute politics from that point of view, and what sort of analysis might provide for its identification. This has to be answered before one can justify a political sociology or a history of politics. Even if one were to succeed in identifying what is distinctively political in or about society, one would have to identify the source of its efficacy, and that requires theory. But from the point of view of the immanent critique of capital, the precise direction of change cannot be the object of a prediction, nor can the means by which a concrete change of any sort is likely to take place be such an object of prediction—though more or less reasonable expectations are possible, depending on circumstances that fall outside of the purview of theory and normal practice and depending on what is meant by "reasonable."[20]

What is powerful about this part of the Marxian critique is its demonstration that, according to the logic of capital's defense of its mode of production, what we now call "economics," only two general possibilities (for policy and programmatic politics) can be conceived of, and that they constitute in this respect a disjunctive relation internal to the mode of production. The first is the maintenance of society. From capital's own account of its capacity to reproduce itself by realizing its distinctive form of wealth, the account that Marx explicates in *Capital*, this requires continued social progress. That is, it requires a continual socialization of labor on an ever-increasing scale. The immediate reason is that monetarily indexed assets expand under conditions of socialized labor (cooperation under the condition of interdependence) only if the latter progressively expands, and output relative to labor cost thereby increases in an accelerating curve. In other words, socialization intensifies production on a continually expanding scale. Since the overall cost of socialization itself cannot be borne by capital, and the only available form of wealth is under capitalist control, the connection between productivity (based on cooperation) and profit (based largely on the cost of labor) cannot reproduce the conditions under which the surplus value produced is realized in the form of re-investable profit. This is what Marx and Engels refer to as the contradiction between the forces and relations of production. By the logic of capitalist production, and not by virtue of a separate theory, it constitutes an absolute limit of capitalist reproduction that is always manifest. But it does not constitute a limit on abundant production *per se*. The more general and ultimately decisive point is that the progressive socialization of labor is not only a condition of the production of capitalist wealth, acknowledging it is a condition of recognizing that the substance of societal wealth cannot be measured in monetary terms but consists of means of production now understood as "forces of production," which are fully socialized as what Marx refers to as "the society of the producers."[21]

To reproduce the socialized labor that creates capitalist wealth turns out to be incompatible with the money-based principle of the private control of that wealth. It is, therefore, inconsistent with the very concept of capitalist wealth. This is because that concept envisions a separation of wealth, which becomes "fictitious capital" in the course of capital's constant speculative flight from the costs of socialization, from productive capacity itself. But this capacity constitutes the real wealth of society when the analysis of the mode of production is extended beyond its initial simplification as the production of directly useful goods (see the first chapter of Marx's *Capital*, Vol. I). It is what is constituted under the auspices of capital as the source of abundant production—in the face of the under-production presumably characteristic of precapitalist, presocialized modes of production, but, in fact, internal to capitalist production itself.[22] The separation of "wealth" from production guarantees that policies based on that separation can only be irrational both in regard to the progress of society and in regard to the maintenance of the capacity for abundant production. What is revolutionary about socialized labor is the very fact of its being collective. The practice of continuing to work cooperatively, as instructed, where no alternative for the "bearers of labor power" exists, is what Marx meant when he spoke of capital creating its own gravediggers. He did not mean that the "immiseration" engendered by capitalist exploitation is, in its personal effects on a sufficiently large aggregate of individuals, an effective cause of revolution. Even if it were to turn out to be true that the misery of the many is a sufficient condition of revolutionary thought and action, lacking such a distribution would in no sense undermine Marx's conclusion, which is based on his immanent critique of political economy, that capitalism ultimately revolutionizes itself. It does not follow that Marx himself would reject an appeal to "the condition of the people" in trying to understand the politics of popular protest and rebellion. In fact, he discusses that condition in detail throughout the first volume of *Capital*, most often in footnotes. It is just that the revolution of which he writes systematically is the totalizing transformation compelled by capitalist conditions of production—toward an autonomous society of the producers or toward the socially destructive domination of increasingly unproductive, or "fictitious," capital. To understand popular resistance, rebellion, and "revolution" in that sense of the term requires a different sort of theory from the immanent critique of the defense of the capitalist mode of production.[23]

On the other hand, as the second possibility indicates, the standard notion of revolution through the exercise of coercive power belongs to capital as its only reliable option, even though it too amounts to a radical change in the course of reproduction (from production to speculation). This involves imposing an increasingly generalized market on human affairs (the unlimited universalization of exchange, in which the demand for liquidity effectively replaces productive investment and in which the wage progressively declines in its capacity to assess and to satisfy needs). This is revolutionary so far as society is concerned. That is, it is incompatible with the cost of the social progress required if the real wealth of society, which is society itself as a productive force, is to be expanded.[24] This is the sense in which labor presents itself metaphorically as capital's "gravedigger." The point is that the private control of the means of production is not rational to the maintenance of the human forces in their hitherto most productive form—social production organized according to the pragmatic values of efficiency, effectiveness, and mutuality—as a society of producers that, in turn, must continue to advance its sociality in the fullest sense of the term if it is to realize itself as a historical society.

This is clearly not a prediction in the determinist sense of the term. It is a conclusion drawn on the basis of what a certain mode of production, understood in its own terms and therefore from the point of view of its proponents, constitutes as its own perpetual and historically incurable crisis. To the extent to which capitalist production is parametric to the society it constitutes as its collective labor force,[25] and it is insofar as what stands for wealth circulates in the form of "fictitious capital" (and therefore in opposition to production), there is no other choice but to imagine the two options without any rational middle—subject to other considerations that are bound to emerge in the course of expanding upon this imagination. What are "predictable" are the options. Nothing can be said about a specific direction, inevitable or likely. One can specify what would be rational, but only within the parameters set by capital, to the extent to which it is fair to say that its imperatives are hegemonic over those of society.

For society, for the society of cooperative production, the only rational direction is toward more of itself. The situated interests of capital's operatives are constrained by competition, from which it follows that no long-term interest for which there is a rational practice can be attributed to capital. Therefore, for capital, the only rational direction that is also practical is toward decreasing relative cost. The former presents no further logical contradiction for abundant production except for its incompatibility with the continued freedom of the capitalist market and the private accumulation and disposition of socially produced wealth. The latter represents the competitive, or "anarchic," aspect of capitalist investment that is the source of capital's inability to engineer and tolerate the sort of planning essential to the maintenance of society. Therefore, capital's solution can only be imposed by force or guile, and it only becomes legitimate by successfully eliminating alternatives. The solution paradoxically reproduces the contradiction between the regressive privatization of socially necessary resources and the constitution of capitalist wealth by socialized labor. There are no other rational options under the conditions set by the explication and defense of capital since there are no other conditions of capitalist self-realization imaginable within the logic of capitalist production but the exploitation of human labor and reliance on the "price-making money market," any more than the reproduction of society can be imagined through capitalist means alone.

This account of the Marxian critique is intended to illustrate how one might analyze "the possibility of changes in the scope, concentration, and ramifications of critical activity," where the idea of a society is distinguished from that of a nation. This was the first historiographical interest mentioned above, and the example shows how criticism can be conceived of as an immanent feature of society, an aspect, from within an immanent critique of a "theory" (e.g., the defense of capitalist production and its operational principles), which seems to deny that very possibility but which nevertheless discloses it as internal to whatever (in that theory) makes society conceivable. The second historiographical interest can be summarized as a concern for how so significant a contradiction might become visible at a given time and then be brought to the notice of those available for mobilization and possible action.

It might be claimed in this regard that the disciplinary field of politics has partly to do with clarifying contradictions by identifying the acute crises they engender and drawing principled and communicable conclusions from the result. In that case, the political appears as a vehicle for conveying the results of theorizing the mode of production to the concrete sites at which the crises are most immediately experienced. It is tempting, then, to say that this transfer of ideas by means of political action is how politics makes manifest the critical aspect of society, though it is difficult in that case to show why the latter is an "aspect."

However, this poses an immediate problem. The metaphor of a "vehicle" does not easily support the crucial idea that a critical subpolity is internally related to society and therefore already in motion before becoming articulated, say, as a specific instance of intentionality with its own direction, range, tenor, and scope. The metaphor leaves one with a sense of something (e.g., politics) that carries the result of something radically different from it (e.g., theorizing) to some receptacle different from both (e.g., a public prior to or independent of politics). Apart from the problem of definition posed by conceiving of these three as externally related, it must also be admitted that a political project designed only to influence or mobilize people is, for the moment of the attempt to exercise that power, not internal to society (and society is not described such that it might be imagined as open to those effects). The attempt to act on others no longer (at the moment of the attempt) expresses the irrepressibility of the sort of criticism that gives noninstitutional politics its "organic" connection to society. A practical interpretation of this essentially theoretical point suggests that this may be one cause of the difficulty self-explicating political groups have in recruiting large numbers of participants when they define themselves or come to be defined as a way of exercising influence on people or mobilizing others to act in one way or another. This, of course, does not mean that such efforts are doomed or worthless, or even to be regarded with suspicion, only that they pose problems for the historian that cannot easily be resolved if one starts with the premise that the topic of politics can be isolated and given substance before being identified within society itself.[26] On the other hand, the more familiar tendency is to interpret contradictions as *generating* conditions of acute crises. To be acute is to be noticeable, to be a matter of experience. To that extent, such crises are available as topics of public discourse, subject to its vicissitudes and special vulnerabilities to hegemonic projects.

In either case, historiography often lights on the history of politics, but identifies "politics," *post facto*, as a causal element in changes, the direction and character of which are construed *initially* as subject to mediations that, by the nature of the case, cannot be anticipated theoretically, from which it follows that they are essentially unpredictable. That is, politics can be presented as having been predictable only after the fact, and it is necessary to attribute properties to political activities that would have been theoretically unlikely before the fact (e.g., specific and unqualified dispositions, and rationality in the sense of being based on justified beliefs and clear and ordered desires, decisiveness, and originality).[27] To construe them as having been predictable at the time, therefore subject to better or worse decisions or governed by what might appear to have been determinative predicaments or emotions, it is necessary to rely on concepts of politics, agency, mobilization, and the like formed independently of what is required by considering them under the aspect of their being internal to society. This is evident in the common assumption that authentic contradictions reside in the depths of society while acute crises are occasional and contingent and, therefore, possibly causal in a way that deep and, therefore, generalized contradictions cannot be. It is difficult to imagine how one might think of society as an ongoing affair in which criticism is an immanent feature and, at the same time, attribute to it a distinction between depth and surface.[28] Even if one were to rely on that distinction, it would be no easier to imagine how the independent causal efficacy attributable to surface events could yield actions that are conceivable as rational, decisive, effective, communicable, and originary—qualities associated with an idealization of politics abstracted from society.

Another problem with this sort of retrospection is that the idea of "depth" effectively displaces the critical aspect of society. Politics appears as an eruption, a sudden, possibly coherent, and momentarily original reaction to a relatively independent event (the *acute* crisis, acuteness). By contrast, Marx attempts to show, in *Capital*, that there is no point at which capitalist production can be described without either glossing over its contradictory counter-reproductive aspects or admitting them and, therefore, the consequences mentioned above. If there is a political meaning to this, it is that "politics" names the critical condition of being in a society in which the capitalist mode of production prevails before it indicates a specific state of affairs or a social formation, or constitutes a particular line of action. This is not to say that a politics that can be designated is historically or sociologically irrelevant, only that it should be understood at the outset, most generally and as a matter of practice, as expressing a critical aspect of society that always displays itself in one way or another, and does so in everything that can be taken as an instance of human affairs. In that case, the singularity stipulated by a name is significant only in regard to a momentarily localized context in which courses of activity intersect (or are mixed) in particularizing ways that are both mutually exclusive and, at the same time, constitute relations of necessity.

This does not naturally extend beyond that context, which is why it is indispensable, though difficult, to distinguish between two sorts of politics. One involves what Bruno Latour refers to as "reassembling the social," i.e., asserting a norm, from the myriad ongoing activities to which such reassembling (which is always assertive) is almost always an exceptional act, an activity in its own right and in regard to its own projected circumstances (2005). As I read Latour, this means asserting a momentarily totalizing interpretation of what has been going on and submitting it for further action to the putative parties to those activities, as a possible constituency. For obvious reasons, this sort of politics typically transpires locally and is rarely intelligible beyond that context (its ongoing courses of activity). Because it is so confined, any generalization of a "reassembled social" requires a rather different sort of politics, one that is directly oriented toward mobilizing people in a way that is either indifferent to specific, local, situations or points to a more generally shared interest, condition, or desire.[29] Consequently, it tends to idealize its themes or to abstract itself by appropriate representations from normally ascertainable conditions of action. It does this by way of asserting the relevance or necessity of the locally intelligible assembled social to the virtual extra-local constituency it aims to make actual. This is often associated with the idea of a party or a social movement; but for Latour, the idea of politics need go no further than the moment at which the reassembled social is presented to the others whose observed activities are presumed by the reassemblers to have been taken into account. For this concept to be relevant to our understanding of politics, it is not enough to stop at the point of the accomplished reassembly. The process of reassembling as well as its aftermath prior to its acceptance or rejection by the others need also to be considered; and that brings organization into the picture in a somewhat different way.

One might define a political party sociologically as a collectivity composed of volunteers that operates in a context in which the difficulty of distinguishing between power and authority makes it unreasonable to discount power in favor of system imperatives. In that respect, parties are oriented primarily by the facts of power, and to that extent they are ambiguously situated within their society. It may not be too misleading to say that such politics are to the state as the underground economy is to the economy—if we understand so-called "parties in power," with few exceptions, not to be parties in this sense. A party defined in this way presumably operates through processes of deliberation and discipline, centralized or not, often but not always according to explicit values and corresponding forms of expression. Its effectiveness depends on combining analysis and program with a recognizable organizational resource. The latter, if well-formed in the sense of standing for agency, provides reliable practical support for collectively valid decisions about the possible utility and feasibility of one line of action over others and about whether or not competition among different options should be discouraged (cf. Butler et al. 2000). The social aspect of the party can be thought of as reflexive to the special relationship it constitutes, in the course of its activities, between participation (informal) and organization (formal); to that extent, loyalty is a prime virtue for *members*—and deference a virtue for *associates*. Loyalty is likely to be accompanied by the shared pleasure that individuals experience in regard to their participation in the collective exercise of practical reason—an exercise that conjoins committed discourse, the working through of differences, and shared reflection on the ongoing accomplishments of the collective. Left self-criticism typically focuses on what appears to be a failure of one or more of these characteristics; and, because it is always difficult to coordinate the internal exigencies of organization with the external (contextual) conditions of effectiveness, especially where power is an issue, such criticism inevitably accompanies party formation and development.

Social movements are not typically described as formations, in organizational terms, but as unauthorized processes always awaiting formation, perhaps in the sense of being available for "reassembling." In this regard, they are thought of not as instances of agency but as conditions under which collective agency is a prospect that is always virtual and never realized. Therefore, participation is likely to be limited and, in any case, never realized as membership in the formal sense of the term. The "identity" often associated with participation in social movements, as in Amy Gutmann's references to "identity politics" (2003), typically registers itself momentarily as an appropriated ideal type rather than a *praxis*, though there is undoubtedly a politics associated with the appropriation so that the identity of the participant changes in the course of the movement's activity such that *praxis* cannot be excluded from the concept.

The concept of a social movement found in late twentieth-century sociology is essentially reactive and difficult to separate from the functionalist idea of a social system to which it is the logical other—as in the familiar distinction between institutional and noninstitutional politics. By the same logic, it can be argued that the very concept of a social system, as a "structure of action," includes the prospect of extra-rational forms of collective deviance to the extent to which the conditions of action that comprise the basic units of the system vary in their degree of integration—as the theory says they always do. A relatively conservative distinction is often made between social movements that are "norm-oriented," in regard to an apparent failure of system-based norms, and those that are "value-oriented," in regard to a sudden and general decline of functionality or to an apparent crisis of legitimacy (Smelser 1963). The first is oriented toward changing an already existing practice and the second toward asserting an established system value within which the rationality of specific practices might be determined and in regard to which the application of any such practices might be judged. Both are said to concentrate a popular disposition to overgeneralize in reaction to the anxiety associated with "system strain."

I refer to this distinction as conservative because it defines different types of "collective behavior" (including social movements) in a way that precludes their being thought of as political, that term being reserved for institutional procedures that establish and allocate the offices in which the "rational-legal" authority to act for the whole is vested. In passing, recent theories conceive of social movements either as more rational and focused or as expressions of "civil society" though still fundamentally reactive. This undoubtedly addresses some of the problems posed by the earlier functionalist model, but at the cost of reconciling the political idea of a social movement with an idea of society, and, more importantly, at the cost of excluding from the designation what would otherwise appear to be instances of politics and of invalidating the idea of a generalized politics along the lines discussed above.

The more generalized politics of mobilization and effectuality share at least one characteristic with the local politics of "reassembling the social," which yields the following more inclusive definition. Manifest politics can be thought of, most generally, as an oriented practice that projects (or in some other way realizes) a context in which power apparently cannot be ignored, and orientation varies in regard to that fact. It takes form, whether as a movement or a party, as a self-intensifying activity reflexive to a play of power immediately perceived as incompatible with the imperatives of society. Absent such a definition, the political appears only as particular phenomena. Each instance takes form as a momentary aggregation of individual states of mind (the possibility of actionable consensus) and as uneasily connected focused performances that anticipate or react to particular problems or predicaments, rationally or not, having to do with momentary dispositions or distributions of power. These take place within the causal, intentional, or structural limits of their most immediate situations.

For local politics, power is subordinate to issues, and action is more tactical than strategic, judged by immediate effects rather than by success in shifting relative position. For politics understood as beyond specific locale, issues are subordinate to power and, therefore, to the problems posed by power for the very possibility of society. From the local point of view, politics is nothing more than reactions to power that originate within individuals according to their particular interests, which may or may not coincide or overlap. This may be consistent with the idea that the availability of commitments based on such a situationally induced and thereby limited need for reaction can be understood as related to something about society. But that is not what the critical aspect of society requires. Rather, it requires an interpretation of a given manifestation of criticism that does not reduce it to an assembly of individuated cognitive or motivational dispositions. In this sense, criticism is, first of all, a social fact. The relationship between politics as local organization (assembly), individual commitment, and potentially specific influence, that is, typically designated politics, and politics as an expression of the social/critical aspect of society is beyond the purview of the sort of theorizing exemplified by Marx's *Capital*. But, then, it is also beyond the grasp of orthodox historiography to the extent to which the first sort of politics, which is identified in its strictly local form, is taken as generally definitive.

Parenthetically, it might be argued that any designated politics can be seen as merely a *residual* expression of the critical aspect of society and, in that sense, as relatively autonomous and contingent. In that case, its history can be written as an account of an emergent phenomenon. But even then, one must be careful not to extract it (as if an instance of human affairs can be extracted intelligibly from its essential conditions) or its conditions (as if they are separable from the ongoing character of society) from the logic of *society*, or to assume an explanation after the fact that could not have been imagined before it. The history of politics is often confused with the history of national institutions. When this happens, its forms are said to range from the normal to the deviant. Deviance is thought, in turn, to accompany any system of rules divorced from informal practice (therefore "institutional"), where socialization is, as Talcott Parsons put it in his general theory of deviance, "imperfect" and where practical conditions are said to vary across the possible sites of politics (1951, p. 39). The problem of order, which is conceived of as a national problem, is exacerbated, if not caused, by society itself. To the extent to which this sort of history relies on defining "institution" as value-justified rule-governed behavior—where the rules are said to form a coherent subsystem centered by the notion of a distinctive *telos* (e.g., "value for the inclusive system")—it easily slips, conceptually, to the side of nation in the flawed distinction between nation and society.[30]

Both historiographical interests, in change and in its aspect of agency, are undermined when the perspective of *nation* overwhelms that of *society*. That is, a description of politics apart from the deliberate exercise of power is valid only if it is consistent with the idea of a society. I have argued that a minimal conception of society has it always in a motion that is essentially reflexive, and that this is most generally described according to contradictions between the form (e.g., a course of activity) and its parameters (forces that tend to fix activity), and within each. These contradictions are not only conditions of reflexivity, but they also represent limitations of what can be conceived of as the durability of the form and the continuation, or reliability, of its corresponding context. The limitations are implicit in the discourse in which such relationships are described as (possibly) reproducible (or as supporting a continuous identity).

I have also argued, in effect, that political sociology is sociological to the extent to which it identifies political affairs as manifestations of the critical aspect of society, which means that certain things often referred to as "political" lie outside of that frame of reference insofar as they pertain to the idea of a nation in contrast with and opposition to the idea of a society. In this respect, political agency can be imputed only on the basis of the aspect of criticism. Each such imputation is reflexive to its relationship with the referent it purports to identify, specifically with the activity in which the particularization of the referent appears momentarily irresistible. The fact that both imputation and referent are *of* society implies that any such identification is ostensible and momentary, passing even as it is enunciated. It follows from these conceptions of "society" and "politics" that it is possible to decide what should or should not be considered political only on the logically prior condition of an account of society in which, first, political activity is already located within courses of activity underway, and therefore cannot be said to have been initiated as such or to have initiated itself, and, second, such activity is shown to manifest the immanence of criticism and sociality.

Today, there is, a great deal of historical research consistent with these criteria. Prominent examples that are particularly relevant to the theses of this book are Edward P. Thompson's study of the English working class (1963); the work of the "people's historians," e.g., Peter Burke (1978, 1981) and Raphael Samuel (1981); histories of unauthorized collective behavior, e.g., George Rude (1964) and Eric Hobsbawm (1984); and historical studies of popular culture, e.g., Michael Denning's account of the "popular front (1996)."[31] The field of cultural studies has developed its own historiographical principles to some extent along these lines, as is indicated by the influence of the "new historicists," notably Stephen Greenblatt (1991; cf. Veeser 1989). Again, the problem arises when the topic supersedes its content in a way that belies the essential reflexivity of the content conceived of as a course of activity—e.g., when a sociologist or historian sets out to study something like "the Left" before coming to terms with the idea of society necessary if a Left is to be conceivable as a possibility within society as well as a possibility for it. In the next few pages, I will briefly comment on the relevance of these considerations to several prominent studies of this history of the Left, following which I will discuss the generalization of anti-communism and its effects on historiography and political discourse.

John Patrick Diggins's *The Rise and Fall of the American Left* (1991) provides a not always unsympathetic history of the Left that seems at first to be consistent with a notion of society. However, it appears to exclude the possibility of *immanent* criticism, though not the contingent possibility of critical action, and, on my reading, it is unmanageably ambiguous as to the relationship between society and nation. In that respect, his conception of society is too weak to support any view of the Left but one that elevates its ostensibly reactive aspect above what he takes to be its positive, value-oriented aspect. He sees the latter as a foundational interest in freedom, and, correspondingly, characterizes the post-1960s Left "episode" as having be-trayed that interest (see chapter 9 of his book in contrast with his first chap-ter, "The Left as a Theoretical Problem"). The reactive aspect is given its priority by Diggins's characterizations of abstractly demarcated episodes in terms of generational differences and their expected corresponding tensions. Like the idea of a "historical episode," neither the differences nor the ten-sions is conceptualized and substantiated accordingly.[32] It is in the light of what these expressions mystify that he is able to characterize his own study as an account of "episodes," such that "the interim period between the death of one Left and the birth of another has been discussed to highlight genera-tional tensions" (1991, p. 15). It goes almost without saying that the ideas of an "interim period" and "the death" and "birth" of Lefts are problematic, at the least because they are derived from a prior commitment to the ideas of "episode" and "generation" that predetermine his narrative and the lessons he draws from it.

The specter of society nevertheless makes itself known in Diggins's working assumption, with which I agree, that specific organized and desig-nated politics may reflect social movements already underway:

> The American Left was born in the United States. Contrary to popu-lar belief, it was not the product of foreign powers and alien ideolo-gies. Although each Left generation would have its rendezvous with European Marxism, Marxist ideas were usually embraced to support a radical movement that had already come into being. (p. 17)

However, Diggins's account of the indigenous aspect of this movement is consistent with his emphasis on ideas[33] and generations and a corresponding de-emphasis on conditions of criticism of the sort discussed above. Thus, he writes that the Left, "sprouting from native soil," "often erupted in a fury of radical innocence and wounded idealism so peculiar to American intellectual history" (p. 17). This image, with its insinuation in all respects of irrationality, suddenness, and extremism is part of the rhetorical paradigm constituted by organizing a historical interpretation of what is supposed to be an instance of human affairs on the basis of precisely what cannot yield a sense of what it is to be such an instance—namely the unqualified ideas of particularity, episode, generation, and generational tension.

Over and above what this paradigm dictates, it is possible to see how Diggins might, nevertheless, justify his interpretation of successive Lefts as if it had not been implicit in its most general presuppositions. Like many other such histories, including some by authors to the Left of Diggins, his has its own intellectual agenda based on a view of American society as emerging under the impact of romanticism. Corresponding to that is what appears to be an expressivist view of unauthorized politics, coupled with a view of society as determined largely by indigenous cultural forces, incompatible with much of the newer theoretical work in the human sciences. He is not friendly to that work, which he often categorizes in ways that both minimize and distort what is complex and important about it (cf. pp. 21–22 and chapter 9). He therefore fails to see one normative implication of it that might have contributed to his own account, especially to his stated desire to understand the Left as something "born to seek and to struggle" (p. 23). That is a willingness at least to rethink the conflation of nation (and its disembodied ideational system and implication of power) and society (and the courses of activity in which participatory membership is constituted), an error to which he falls victim, and to rethink the corresponding tendency to particularize politics by characterizations that allow for just such a premature objectification—e.g., in terms of putative ideals. His account of the history of the American Left, that it "was born from the idea of freedom, an idea that implies the power of ideals to be actualized" (p. 383), concludes with the claim that the "fall" of its most recent incarnation is a consequence of its having traded its founding interest in freedom for an overly ambitious and self-defeating critique of Enlightenment reason (chapter 9).

A further point needs to be made about the perspective of generational differences. An emphasis on generations is nearly always "dramatically ironical," and, to some extent, self-serving insofar as it situates itself beyond the foibles of those bound to predicaments not of their society but of their kind.[34] And whatever that trope is reflexive to, it is unaccountably beyond the logic of generations itself. A generational account can only justify itself as an exception to a more inclusive but unstated historiographical principle, or if the writing of history is somehow exceptional to the generational determination—or, in the case of Diggins, if the Left is an exception to the rationality of which historical consciousness is presumably a feature.

The idea of Left exceptionalism is not unrelated to the idea of American exceptionalism on which Diggins's account depends and that can be seen as its subtext. In that respect, given what is necessarily assumed, I would place him among the "orthodox historians" of communism, from Draper to Klehr (cf. Brown 1993). Parenthetically, it must be admitted that this typification of orthodoxy also has the obvious weakness of all such simplifying categories, including those by generation. The reason I use it here is not because I believe that it is relevant to writing a history of the "history of communism," but because it is a distinction imposed on the literature by the rhetoric of the debates discussed in Chapters Three and Four, particularly evident in Theodore Draper's insistent hostility to the work of other historians whose attempts to replace the anticommunist agenda by a more theoretically conscious methodology he consistently rejects on the apparent grounds that the complexity and qualifications of the interpretive result of their research violate the truth of anticommunism.

Nevertheless, it is possible, roughly, to distinguish between works that emphasize nation over society and those that do not; and my reference to "orthodoxy" is intended to bring that to mind, rather than to focus on the specific point of view those historians have about the meaning of the Communist experience. On the other hand, I will try to show that the emphasis on nation and a corresponding *concept* of power (no less than an emphasis on ideas divorced from practices) is particularly susceptible to the abstraction of anticommunism as a logic that burdens political discourse to this very day. In this respect, I will refer to it as disposed toward intellectually and morally conservative interpretations based on choices of principles of organization within several sets of options.

The first option is, as indicated, a preference for an emphasis on nation rather than society, except in the weakest sense of the term. The second is a reductive emphasis on particularized intentionality over collectivity, with the consequent loss of a concept of the collective and a separation of the idea of culture from the more fundamental idea of society. The third is an understanding of rationality based on the quantificational logic of exchange in contrast with what Alfred Schutz referred to as "social rationality" (the rationality of sociality as such) and the logic of difference (and value) that corresponds to that idea (1967). The fourth is a reductive view of agency as essentially individual and sufficiently explained by reference to individuals beyond the practices within which they are individuated. There are also several metaconceptual decisions that are crucial to evaluating the difference between the two types of approach to the history of communism. One rejects the possibility of basic contradictions at the heart of the relationship between society and its national parameters (including especially its mode of production/reproduction), and the other rejects class as a basic socioeconomic category. There are, of course, accommodations to the demands of each unorthodox alternative, but, together, the choices comprise significant features of a conservative frame of reference.

There are two effects of this that are germane to my later discussion of the debates. One is a refusal to give any significant benefit of the doubt to what C. Wright Mills thought of as "structural criticism." The fact that Diggins not only values criticism aimed at overcoming restraints on freedom but also uses this as a test of the contemporary Left is not an exception. His concept of freedom (as a simple and sovereign ideal) is far too abstract and unqualified to distinguish among political tendencies and too general to use in understanding the difference between Right and Left (presumably the priority given authority or freedom, as if the two can be defined independently). In any case, it is a value that is not easily historicized in relation to those features of society that might be contradictory in the sense discussed above. This, I take it, is what tempts the ironist to condescend and patronize, and to identify Left movements as essentially generational rather than rational, and therefore deviant so far as the privileged order of the nation is concerned.

The other effects are a tendency to give greater weight to the testimony of those who separated themselves from the Left than to the testimony of those who remained committed to it, and a shift from an emphasis on the social movement to an emphasis on possible results, such as on policies, on popular attitudes, or on the outcome of elections, and a corresponding emphasis on formal organization at the expense of participation. This is as visible in Diggins's writing as in Draper's. In regard to the testimony of those who reject their pasts, Draper's irrationalist account of the attraction of communism, from a point of view determined by his own rejection of it, makes it impossible to imagine how anyone as intelligent as Draper could have become involved in the first place. This inability to imagine oneself biographically, to lose empathy with what one had been, is part of what leaving the Communist Party meant at a certain time. Such a conversion experience is not likely to provide the testimonial reliability necessary to contribute to understanding the Communist movement and its appeal to so many during and beyond the 1950s, even in the face of internal and external criticism. The possibility of a rational decision to remain involved should be part of any account that attempts to prove that the movement was a failure no less than one that attempts to situate it in American life or oppose it by an appeal to progressive possibilities within institutional politics. This is largely lacking in the orthodox histories, and it is in this regard that they contribute to the more general tendency to marginalize the Left, Communist and non-Communist, in nationalistic accounts of American society and, in doing so, beg the question of what it is about that society which is immanently critical such that the social movements presumably reflected in political organizations might be made intelligible as such.

An elision of the Left, either by marginalization or omission, or by an account that refers to causes conceived of as logically independent of the dynamics of society, tends to confirm a view of society as an institutional order or functionally integrated system, as not immanently critical though liable to occasional bouts of deviance, including collective protests, fads, rebellions, internal strife, social unrest, and the like. I have discussed why I believe that such a view is self-defeating. It places the Left outside of society even as it purports to recognize the influence of the social on its various manifestations. What it places the Left outside of is not society as such but a particular conception of it derived from the idea of a nation, in the light of which "society" remains fatally untheorized. The view I am defending requires situating the Left, and politics in general, within the critical disposition of society conceived of as already in motion and subject to the irreducible and irrepressible tensions of its contradictory aspects.

This affords an understanding quite different from the ironical accounts of the orthodox historians.[35] Above all, it attempts to identify the Left as a manifestation of society. It attempts to show what it is about society that is immanently critical, and what it is about certain societies, those "in which the capitalist mode of production prevails," which manifests that critical aspect, suggesting a more comprehensive notion of the Left than is found in the standard topical accounts. I will be arguing that the orthodox frame of reference effectively elides the Left, as do most popular accounts of American history (taken as histories of a society), where both the political Left and the critical disposition of the body politic that it manifests simply do not figure in a comprehensible way.

At this point, I want to consider the context of the elision, in whatever form it appears, as one that depends on a highly generalized continuation of the logic of the Cold War "by other means." As such, it takes shape in a way that is relatively rare to the latent aspects of discourse, namely as a self-consciously imperative coherence of meaning and feeling. Its constitutive categories are binaries, representing polar opposites, and they accumulate in the associative form of a paradigm[36] predicated on yet more general dimensions. By way of treating what appear to be *exemplary* as *emblematic*, the accumulation is correspondingly moralized. Each specific instance picked out at the points at which the categories intersect appears to be identical with its universal principle. That is to say, it appears to represent in all respects what it is taken to be an instance of. This makes the dimensions, which describe variations within the paradigm, relevant to virtually all subject matters having to do with the social aspect of human affairs, and relevant in a way that insistently promotes an image of actions as particulars and, at the same time, idealizes interpretation by eliding its own obligation to self-criticism.

The logic of the Cold War is with us today, as much as it was two decades ago, even though the content to which that logic most directly applies is no longer exclusively substantiated by reference to Communist parties or governments. To some extent this is a result of a generalization of anticommunism, no less than the familiar background of chauvinism for which grounds do not have to be given, in the light of which communism comes to exemplify the more inclusive category of "totalitarianism." The latter is ultimately identified, in turn, as a subcategory of the suprahistorical discursive category of "statism" (domination beyond hegemony) that signifies total control without any prospect of democratic constraint. The corresponding idea of democracy is the myth of pure communication among equals, free of anything but popular impulse, a movement of dialogue that, in the name of civility, must never go beyond itself. This generalization is, of course, only one way in which the elision occurs. I focus on it because it is currently incorporated in the post-Soviet American literature on "civil society," and, by virtue of that, has had considerable influence in the social sciences and humanities (cf. Cohen and Arato 1992).

Whoever cannot participate in that overarching evaluation of this dialogical indefiniteness, whoever cannot abide dialogue that feeds on itself, is excluded from the very concept. In this way, the idea of resistance is removed from the context of its referents. Resistence thereby becomes essentially unintelligible—the one exception being, as Stuart Hampshire reminds us, reactionary "resistance" to organized politics altogether (cf. Hampshire 2000).[37] There is, however, another exception typically granted by some Left intellectuals to "new social movements," familiarly identified as "identity politics" but more generally described as anticipations of democracy. While these fall within the definition of Left politics, their theoretical status is ambiguous. For one thing, this form of resistance is often defined negatively and to that extent is vulnerable to reactionary appropriation. The risk is greater when the various movements are identified with a particular form regardless of differences in content or apparent purpose. The form most often taken to identify their newness is the negation of politics as previously understood. On the one hand, they are thought of as informal expressions of desire relatively free of the burdens of power. On the other hand, this transfers most of what remains of identifiable political content to the involutional expressivity of "civil society" (see, for a version of the first part of this, Mouffe and Laclau, 1985; for the second part, see Cohen and Arato 1992). That portion of the original content that had been developed organizationally and, as it were, historically now appears to be nothing more than an ideological expression of unyielding organizational imperatives (e.g., of party or state).

This vision of a society without politics (except for what is reluctantly adopted or somehow deemed occasionally necessary) equates "democracy" with the idea of "hegemony without internal qualification," which is to say without relevance to any imaginable movement of history. Civil society is effectively *released* rather than constituted. It does not and need not realize itself substantively, except in reaction to what it is not. This presumably occurs in several steps, first by the generalization of the "Law Merchant" in regard to specific rights connected to property and exchange, and then by the constitutional process of institutionalizing democracy. That is its only history; and it is historical only if "history" invokes nothing that can be thought of in terms of contradiction, difference, opposition, and struggle. Civil society exists for itself and is relevant only to itself: It stands, then, as the only model of society worthy of respect—and the capitalist mode of production need be mentioned only for the distortions its own possible excesses may or may not introduce in the republic of dialogue without end.

This brings into theoretical play another altogether idealized opposition, that of civil society and the state. The former is defined precisely as the antithesis of the latter, which is then taken to represent the general disposition of *statism*—with the corresponding equation of (1) the bureaucratically rational *aspect* of organizational self-realization and (2) a totalistic realization of the Weberian "iron cage" independent of any other aspect of reproduction. Weber's expression, which was not intended as a concept, is only intelligible as a critical notion designed to sustain, as in memory, what is already known: The success of "formal organization" (specialization, impersonality, hierarchy, jurisdiction, rules, and accountability) depends on its capacity to sustain "informal organization." This means that productive order not only stems from hierarchy but from courses of activity at the base. The presumably static aspect of organization is inconceivable without the social activity usually described as interpersonal interaction. The "iron cage" metaphor shows the irrationality of conceiving of social order as such only in terms of a relationship between a single value (and a corresponding emphasis on efficiency in its pursuit) and an organizational form (e.g., bureaucracy). Parenthetically, this is why Parsons's claim that Weber asserted a historical "law" of increasing rationality is mistaken.

It follows that interaction, informal sociality, can be thought of as the ongoing activity of recovering the sense of intentionality (which maintains, for its parties, not only the prospect of mutual surprise but the prospect of mutual response) as a feature of even those "total institutions" that appear to have eliminated all instances and traces of it. From this point of view, "formal organization" does refer to a *lack*, but it is one within the formal itself and not *for* "members" or "functionaries." One reason is that the very concept of an organization necessarily includes realization and, therefore, activity. What is called "informality" (and appears as interaction) is a necessary accompaniment to realization, and it presumably expresses this lack, as is indicated in research on the incessant display of sociality under even the most rigidly controlling of circumstances, and in research that reveals the generativity of what is otherwise referred to as "deviance." What is called "deviance" can be said to appear, as Emile Durkheim (1982) reminds us, at the very moment at which rules are instantiated (e.g., in studies of "red tape," of exaggerated adherence to rules, and of pressures toward individuation in stressed contexts such as "panic"). Thus, it is inconceivable that rational organization, in Weber's sense, could lead to the iron cage without an imposition of the nonrational element of force, unless one conceives of organization minus the logically necessary aspect of realization. Consequently, the idealization of civil society as a counter to that possibility does little more than create a myth against a myth, curiously, a negation against (but not of) a negation—an external relation of mutual denial that has no dialectical significance for either. The question is, how does a myth of that sort come to play so prominent a role in current political discourse and in the disciplines of the human sciences themselves? In what sense is it indicative of a generalization of anticommunism or, at least, of whatever anticommunism is an instance of?

The use of the expression "iron cage" gives weight to a particular extratheoretical desire, one that is more than understandable in the light of the past three quarters of a century: to be able to criticize any line of activity that, extended in the direction of its putative "ideal type," appears to foreshadow an unacceptable probability of total and unremitting control. The classical example would be a society in which goal-oriented social actions of scale are coordinated impersonally through the exercise of jurisdiction by the incumbents of "offices," so that the coherence of formal cooperation replaces the uncertainty of informal interaction and, to that extent, appears as a rational solution to the instrumental problem of maximizing, at one and the same time, efficiency and effectiveness.

Decision-making is far more complex in actual practice. Diverse interests are unavoidable, if only because populations change, the socialization of members cannot be uniform, and every historical society constitutes divisions among people, which then appear as differences of interest. Organizational facts invariably take these more general facts into account. It is, of course, possible for interests to overlap, though it is difficult to imagine how the degree (or reality) of overlap could be assessed for its sufficiency to a reasonable expectation of a just social order; and who would be neutral enough to assess it? In many cases, it is not clear that even overlapping interests can be reconciled in such a way that the different parties can respond to the areas of overlap; indeed, it is not even clear that it would be rational for them to do so, especially under conditions of limited and suspect information about the other parties and the beliefs of those parties about the conditions under which they are enjoined to act. Such facts may require modifications of goals initially thought of as strictly organizational such that efficiency itself is put into question.

Even if it were possible in a given case to reconcile different interests with an overall value or set of goals, situations are bound to arise that require modifications of previous procedures or other sorts of innovation, and such operational innovations are almost certain to be controversial. Moreover, to the extent to which the diversity of interests and the need for innovation effectively lead to a reinstatement of "informal organization," as most organization theorists believe is necessary if the collective is to retain its identity and endure, then the tendency toward formalism remains just that, a tendency. It is a disposition that can never effectively realize itself. Thus, what I called "the classical example" is not an example of a society (or organization) so much as a pre-ideal "ideal type," a postoperational abstraction that precedes the formation of the methodologically adequate pure idea. The pure, methodologically adequate, ideal type is summarized as bureaucratic rationalization organized according to a particular classificatory and calculating version of reason. Given the desire to avoid the "iron cage," the type might be projected onto what appears, in retrospect and metonymically, to exemplify it.

This line of theorizing moves from an apparent reality to theoretically projected normative implications of the real as an ideal in itself and then, by a metonymic concentration of meaning, to a purified ideal type that replaces the instance. It is easy to see how it can provide a basis for drawing essentially moralistic conclusions. In regard to the above example, it might support a judgment against planned economies, restrictions on the free market, modernization (i.e., diversity, complexity, and scale), and politics organized in part according to the subvalues of efficiency, effectiveness, and durability. Indeed, all of these have been subjected to just that sort of critique—in the extreme case, as potentially fascistic.[38] In that light, any or all might appear to be totalistic in principle, not merely totalizing in the Sartrean sense of being progressively inclusive.

It is tempting to see this chain of reasoning as an instance of what Neil Smelser once referred to, in regard to crowd formation, as a "hysterical belief" (1963). It is too encompassing in the capacity it attributes to its object, too generalized for the reality it is intended to make comprehensible, insufficiently historical and overly categorical in its failure to consider the prospects of change immanent to even the imaginably most formal of arrangements, and presumptuous in its one-sided attribution of an unacceptable state of affairs (the iron cage) to the putative efficacy of a "type" of organization that can only be conceived of in the first place as functioning within a context of mediations it cannot control. It is also committed, metonymically, to a reductive view of the fate of organizations (and ideologies) in terms of the worst of "worst case scenarios"; and it fails to reckon with the unanticipated cognitive, political, and moral costs of relying on the opposition of one myth to another regardless of what is conceivable about their possible realizations.

Finally, apart from these criticisms, it is impossible to think of an activity or project for which there is no conceivable possibility of an unacceptable end state (temporary though its existence would be) even if one cannot establish an implication or rational probability of so unlikely an aftermath.[39] The principle of this line of reasoning would potentially discredit any and every line of action, which is why its deployment is almost always selective according to agendas and their social supports unaccountably considered immune to the analysis itself. To reject all political involvement but that which bears no risk of a logically possible "normatively negative" extreme is to reject all involvement whatsoever, since nothing can guarantee that a worst case possibility—or, for that matter, any imaginable possibility—will not become increasingly probable, though it is difficult to imagine how and from what point of view such an increase might be assessed.

In this regard, it is crucial to remember an elementary principle of sociohistorical analysis, that the path from a stated political program (or an existing "state of affairs" idealized by a cross-sectional analysis) to a final consequence cannot be conceptualized as linear since, from the moment it is put into motion, there are countless and accumulating mediations, events, and conditions of reflection impossible to anticipate.[40] It does not follow that projections of linearity are not relevant to certain purposes and justifiable under certain conditions; e.g., the assessment of possible physical dangers, the immediate threat of invasion, etc. Even then, however, judgment must be tempered by the realization that linearity is inconsistent with what must be acknowledged in general about possible courses of social change. When change is represented otherwise, as linear, the representation typically expresses a point of view from which a worst case scenario is all that counts, which is to say that once such a scenario is imagined, the putative future is virtually at hand. In that case, it is unlikely that the analysis and the policy it is designed to support could be rationally communicated. This is why a politics of anticipation (e.g., the politics associated with the defense of the theory of "civil society") that explicates itself along a dimension of successive approximations of a final state of affairs can only present itself as conclusions for which reasons (and their inevitable complexity) become less important than dramatizations of the mere possibility that "where there is smoke there is bound to be fire, and where one imagines fire, what might not have appeared to be smoke is."

When proponents of a politics of "civil society" speak of "statism" as an ultimate normative implication of socialism or communism, not to mention fascism (like the "iron cage" as an ultimate implication of organizational rationality), they are not only simplifying what those terms can mean, they are arguing from the idealist's premise that if the thought exists reality will follow, from the arch-positivist's premise that if you've seen some you've seen them all, and from the antirationalist's premise that certain formations and ideologies are bound to develop in a linear fashion consistent with the *telos* of their ideal type. But this is not simply the province of the Right or of conservatism; Many on the Left are vulnerable to this way of thinking as well.

It was evident among some Left intellectuals during the late 1980s and 1990s, in an overly optimistic attitude toward the solidarity movement in Poland (as a popular workers' movement against totalitarianism) and in a failure to criticize the radical desocialization of economies in the former Soviet bloc and beyond. I am not arguing that no humanitarian reasons could be given for supporting Solidarity and endorsing an end to the version of social economy that existed under the Communists. I am suggesting that there was an uncharacteristic leap of faith by many whose experience should have made them more wary of such enthusiasms, especially to the extent to which they were predicated on a stereotypical characterization of the relationship between state and society in the Communist nations and on a failure to appreciate the significance of the radical differences within the movement and the various reasons given by those in Poland who disapproved of both the existing government and Solidarity. Rather, socially progressive attitudes toward Solidarity, no less than toward the re-organization of those political economies, would have been better served by subjecting both to the same principles of critical analysis ordinarily required of any account of societal change, actual or projected. The widespread disappointment with what occurred after the "break-up of socialism" should be taken as a cautionary reminder that the evaluation of such change requires remembering what is conceptually indispensable to understanding it.[41]

Even if one wishes to keep open the option of evaluating certain forms by a criterion that says that the end of their development is implicit at the outset, thereby supporting action based on the judgment, it is not at all clear how that can be made theoretically defensible. So far, despite many attempts to do so, no analysis of social formations demonstrates anything close to such a line of development, though Draper's interpretation of the history of American communism certainly exemplifies the aspiration. At any rate, with few exceptions, historians now agree in principle, though not necessarily in practice, that historical change rarely, if ever, occurs along a linear path.[42] Even if a given case were to have followed a linear path of development, it is difficult to imagine how one writing its history could know that as a fact. To the extent to which a narrative imposes linearity on its material regardless of what it otherwise introduces by way of, say, overdetermination and structural breaks, it suggests that the beginning is already an intimation of an end that can only be known after the fact. In other words, the determination of an intimated end is subject to judgments that cannot be reconciled with a nonarbitrary version of history.

When the beginning is written in a political history as if its end is implicit and the facts do not themselves lead the historian to an unequivocal identification of that end, the temptations exist to preserve the initial sense of direction by identifying conditions that either mitigate against its fulfillment, which is to say the self-realization of the subject matter, or to contribute to the equivocal character of the end as finally written. I have argued that Diggins's overall characterization of Left history as the betrayal of a dream is an instance of this way of writing history, and have listed, mostly in footnotes, texts that exemplify rather different approaches. There are, of course, other temptations some of which are discussed in the following chapters. And there are many variants of linear and narrative accounts that do not suffer from the same problems as those that arise in some of the literature on "civil society" and in regard to the historiography of the Left, which is the literature that is mainly at issue in this book.

Similarly, it would be false to conclude that the path of social change is multilinear, though that brings historical interpretation closer to Novick's notion of "overdetermination" (1988). Regardless of what one thinks about narrativity and historical objectivity, and the problem of preserving the sense of temporality, there seems no reason to dispute the claim that one of the most important tasks of the professional historian is the development of a factual base for historical interpretation such that (1) every interpretation is always subject to the sort of criticism that demands that the historian have exhausted existing sources and anticipated possible sources, and (2) the factual base itself is always subject to review for the constitution of the categories of difference, the assignment of properties, and the analogies by which the elements selected for interpretation are declared factual and then related to one another, and by which those construed elements are made more or less coherent as a referential field (White 1973; Novick 1988).

This elaborate and ultimately self-defeating logic inherited in part from the Cold War, though in evidence in the business press and in official reports on labor and immigration since the end of the nineteenth century as well, becomes, through the movement of its own thought, a positive ontology of form and an idealist theory of normative entailment. It is ontological insofar as its categories are treated as real and the possibility of mediated change is effectively denied. It is normatively idealist insofar as it draws upon an ahistorical conception of communism as totalitarian and ultimately statist. The inclusive category *statist* now appears as a purified abstraction, the idea of a directly projected final state entailed by both the party form and the governmental form. This is easily generalized to apply to the critique of capital (and the corresponding critique of the ahistorical, property-based, regulatory aspects of civil society). This recourse to a theory in which a given historically relevant formation or event is held bound to realize a totalistic, or absolutistic, disposition without qualification and without the possibility of mediation can be accepted only if most of what is otherwise believable about society is false; and the theory not only does not address that possibility but relies in almost all respects on the very sociology its own applications belie. Yet, it is still necessary to come to terms with the historiographical principles that follow from such a position, which I see as one version of the logical end game of the Cold War.

From the point of view of that extension of anticommunism to a theory of a self-generalizing trend toward total control, and the self-serving distinction between totalitarianism and authoritarianism, it is not only possible but necessary to classify social movements as either tending in one absolute direction or the other, toward statism or toward democracy, regardless of the absence of a theory that can account for such a binary. Thus, the "old social movements," organized in some but not all respects by unions and parties, appear to embody one expected normative outcome, namely absolutism. In contrast, the idea of horizontal sociality (as a putative variant of or basis for "radical democracy") attributed to the "new social movements" is too fluid to use to identify the coherence presumably indicated by preserving the expression "social movements." Moreover, quantifying "social movement" by relying on a severely truncated temporal dimension makes "oldness" and "newness" either virtually unintelligible or significant only in regard to their rhetorical or ideological force. Since the rhetorical aspect is, by this account, the positive feature of this discourse, it is worth considering what it accomplishes. It is momentarily able to avoid the worst case scenario—statism—from the outset, and therefore the danger of an interminable "state of exception," which qualifies and challenges all notions of democracy. Again, it is able to do this only by sacrificing the intelligibility of the expression "social movement." Alternatively, the "new" movements are conceptualized according to an ideal type in radical opposition to the Weberian model of the "corporate group" in their manner of integration, which is to say to anything that suggests leadership, ideology, or stability. In this respect, questions are begged that ultimately cannot be begged, having to do with mobilization and efficacy. The reason that they cannot be begged is that they are imposed by a context in which power of the sort substantiated by the formal operations of the nation admittedly cannot be ignored (cf. Aronowitz 1996; but see his later, 2006, book for an apparently less negative view of vertical organization; cf. also Zizek 2001).

This is not to say that thinking of civil society in the context of a theory intended to validate one sort of politics over another does not allow for any organizational stability whatsoever, or that the notion of the new social movement does not express an intuition that may be valid. But it seems worth looking at the claims and not, for the moment, the purposes that might be served by making them. If we take the theory that connects civil society to new social movements seriously as it is most prominently presented (cf. Mouffe and Laclau, 1985, and Cohen and Arato, 1992, for somewhat different versions), the line between what would be politically and socially acceptable and what would not can only be discerned after the fact and, therefore, without a clear enough sense of what might have given rise to the unacceptable form (or give rise to it in the future)—a sense that the proponents of the position are most eager to convey. In other words, asserting such a line is already an instance of the politics the theory is supposed to disavow. However, the important question is not merely epistemological. It is how a requisite degree of integration is to be explained without reintroducing the rejected form and without accepting the risk of misjudging possible outcomes, as is required by the strategy of confronting "the worst case scenario."

I suppose that the hidden positive basis of horizontal integration (social versus formal) might be something like a "natural hierarchy of merit," or legitimately dominant ideas that, having survived the "marketplace of free dialogue," have demonstrated their relative superiority. The main trouble with this is that once established, the crucial principle of dialogue is no longer sufficient to account for civility in the maintenance of the dominant ideas, and this introduces precisely the possibility of the power to exclude, which the theory of civil society was supposed to warn us against. It is hard to imagine any other basis for going from the idea of a "new social movement" to the possibility of its being a "movement," though further thought might yield alternatives. The recent history of Eastern and Central Europe has not yet provided enough evidence for continued optimism along these lines, so the alternatives will, again, have to be produced, as it were, theoretically.

In any case, it seems impossible to imagine a role for history in such a conception, if by "history" is meant the working out of difference and if difference refers to momentarily incompatible courses of activity (cf. Brown and Goldin 1973; Butler et al. 2000) founded on constitutive oppositions that accompany a transformation of the relation between form and content from one set of generalizing conditions to another—i.e., from a subsistence economy that is underproductive relative to increases in demand and the generalization of trade, to a socially organized market economy that is over-productive relative to the possibility of realizing value and, thereby, unable to guarantee its own reproduction (the continuation of abundant produc-tion). A disclosure of this requires the sort of immanent critique represented by Marx's *Capital*, which the countervailing position is bound to ignore or actively to marginalize or reject out of hand. It is worth noting in this regard that there are no other comprehensive critiques of the mode of production as such that deal with the problem of reproducing the relations of produc-tion under capitalist conditions. However, there are some quasi-theories that are designed to show how markets can work for the good of all, how inequalities are either good for the progress of society or unavoidable, or are capable of a satisfactory degree of amelioration by minor changes in rules of distribution or methods of determining need; or how reforms aimed at mit-igating the relationship between wealth and power might be devised within the contexts of the market and what that requires, namely the private ex-ploitation of social labor. Occasionally included is the hypothesis that the irrepressibility of "civil society" makes it more than likely that reforms will progressively develop in a democratic direction (and, presumably, that this progress can be maintained by the self-same agency and no others incom-patible with it). Absent an alternative, then, it is not so much sink or swim with Marx as it is necessary to try and understand what it is he was doing in that text. Without going into detail, I believe that he was not developing a positive theory, of the sort David Laibman (2007), G. A. Cohen (1978), and others have attributed to him, but was engaged in the sort of immanent cri-tique in which everything flows, as Raymond Williams pointed out (1977), from capital itself.

The contradictions that emerge in the course of Marx's analysis are not so much "laws of capital" as they are a succession of exigently and partially solved problems that appear in the course of the attempt to defend capital and justify policies made in its name—to which Marx presumably gives ad-equate voice. The unsolved parts accumulate until the paradox they repre-sent becomes impossible, in good faith, to ignore. The result is not a positive theory of how capital works or how societies in which capitalist production prevails operate, though there is a great deal of commentary on both. It is a demonstration that, on the grounds given, no policy made in the name of capital can show itself to be rational relative to the two overriding legitimizing values, *the common good* and *the continuation of capitalist production as such*. It also substantiates the principle that a critique ends, and then only momentarily, when what was left out of its object reappears with a sense of unavoidable urgency (e.g., production, otherness, etc.). It is in this light that the generalization of anticommunism can be seen as evading three obligations: the obligation of theory to begin with an immanent reading; the historiographical obligation to demonstrate, in regard to constitutive contradictions, the historical limitations of a given, identified, form; and the political/conceptual obligation to identify what has been left out that might have to do with a continuation of the mode of production (cf. Spivak 1987, 1988, and 1999).

Parenthetically, there is also a default hypothesis available when those arguments either fail or seem uncertain. It says that, whatever the difficulties imposed on society by markets, or whatever problems are introduced by unregulated markets and accelerating antisocietal accumulations of wealth, the alternatives are problematic in enough respects to reject them altogether. But to evaluate the so-called alternatives, given the state of the evidence and the prospect of adequate evidence when mechanisms of planning cannot easily be separated from even the most established capitalism is unproductively tautological to the extent to which the judgment is implicit in the theory. In any case, the good alternatives to or qualifications of unregulated markets are said to arise within civil society as the most general aim of the new social movements, in contrast with old forms, parties, unions, etc., which are thought to be unable to resist their characteristic disposition to absolutism. Without going further into this, it seems that the conceivable distance between what are called new social movements and the possibility they presumably stand for is greater than that between the old Left political formations and their more limited aim, which is to establish policies conducive to the reproduction of the society of the producers. It is only when one envisions emancipation as such that the first distance is irrelevant, since its idealization of radical democracy becomes the standard against which the adequacy of any instance of politics is evaluated. When an ideal is historically justified as immanent rather than a goal to be achieved, as in the emphasis on the completion of the capitalist revolution by the progress of the society of the producers, the standard always points to the relationship between the forces and relations of production, and no further.

What makes the distinction between the two types of social movement compelling is not its clarity, since it has proven difficult if not impossible to specify a "new" social movement that does not display at least some of the "old" ordering principles and vice versa. As discussed above, this failure of plausible interpretation makes the line between the two impossible to discern, and therefore makes it likely that any attempted application of the distinction will be either mystifying or, contrary to the principle of dialogue, reactionary. What is important to the present discussion is the way in which the logic of the Cold War becomes available for more general applications and remains implicated in a way of writing history that elides the critical aspect of society by marginalizing its most obvious manifestations, and how this bears on evaluating developments in the historiographical practices of other disciplines of the human sciences. But the influence of that logic goes far beyond the disciplines, not only to those centers of public discourse still committed to the idea of American exceptionalism but to the Left itself, at least since the election of Ronald Reagan in 1980.[43]

 - One effect on socially progressive politics is discussed in Chapters Three and Four, and, in regard to yet another set of problems, in Chapters Seven and Eight, which were written with Randy Martin. It is that the political life of the Left has remained contentious and its debates interminable in regard to how its past should be understood and what political expressions should be excluded. There is less disagreement about the proper diagnosis, despite uncertainty about what it means: The Left is said to be fragmented, its cure a new principle of unity (excluding what presumably needs to be excluded and assuming that Left mobilization is primarily responsive to well-formed ideological appeals). In regard to diagnosis, Stanley Aronowitz is among those who use the term "fragmented" in a way that is useful in reminding us of the lack of integration on the Left but, I believe, is misleading, if only because such a lack is endemic to criticism or any attempt to cure it (e.g., in terms of one universal or another) can, as Zizek and Butler have pointed out, only appear to be yet another instance of fragmentation (cf. Aronowitz 1996, 2006; and Butler et al. 2000). At the same time, it has become virtually impossible to imagine a political vision or program that could be inclusive, retain Left values, develop a continuing public presence, and, at the same time, be effective, without becoming an instance of the type of politics the theory of civil society concludes is either obsolete or normatively unsuitable. It is the exclusion implicit in the diagnosis, and its failure to incorporate difference in the conception of a possible unity, that I believe weakens Left discourse today and threatens to leave it burdened by the residual logic of the Cold War. This is not because such a judgment in favor of a new "new Left" oriented to "civil society" cannot be justified by any conceivable version of the idea. It is, in addition to the criticisms of the most notable versions discussed above, because it is based on a decision about a complex experience whose history has been addressed largely from the point of view of an exclusionary agenda of challengeable origin, and compromised by an attempt either to ignore the effects of the Cold War on the Left itself, or to act in a way intended to minimize them by endorsing an anti-organizational ideal of dialogue the possibility and the grounds of which are not intelligible as things stand.

Even the most dedicated and reasoned case against communism in general, whether or not it includes the political Left or moderates debates within the Left, relies on tendentious examples, arguments from the perspectives of different ways of anticipating possible futures, experiences that cannot easily be generalized, facts that pertain to part of what is then judged as a whole, or undecidable arguments about "actually existing communism" that compare it to an ideal. Of course, most arguments in politics rely on such shortcuts, are tendentious to conclusions already determined, and seem, often unself-critically, either to make too much of too little or to make too little of too much—without reflecting on the internal relation of the "too little" and the "too much" and the problem it poses for how to think about the history of politics.

ˈ   This by itself does not disqualify a discourse on civil society. But it does allow us to reconsider the judgments on which that discourse depends, to the extent to which conditions allow us momentarily to imagine that those judgments are rational and have no interested politics of their own. One reason to reconsider that discourse is that a judgment (exclusionary) aimed at the past of a present yet to be defined, and with the hope of an otherwise unprecedented future, posits a break in continuity that should not be taken for granted even if it could be made comprehensible. That is, there is nothing about the ostensible present form—i.e., the Left presumably divorced from its past—on which to base the connection between it and a possible future; and that connection is necessary if we are to be persuaded that there is something to be conserved, a Left to be reproduced and not merely reiterated. My purpose is not to refute such judgments so much as to dispute the generalizations on which certain of them depend when they are said to speak to the possibility of a new Left, and to do this in order to begin a discussion of the logical conditions of considering a future for the political Left that is compatible with what is immanent to society. Once a judgment—e.g., about what politics must be excluded in advance, either historiographically or politically—is used in a way that totalizes the past as a condition of thinking about the future, it becomes impossible to speak of a Left future that is not simply a matter of being absorbed by the "institutional politics" of a society in which capitalist production (private accumulation and exploitation) prevails.

I believe that part of what we are seeing in at least some debates on the political Left is an exclusionary effect of the logic of interpretation that developed in the context of the Cold War as part of sanctioned public discourse on politics, culture, economy, and society. Entering that discourse submits one to that logic to a degree difficult at best to resist. It may not be too speculative to suggest that this is evidenced by the progressive weakening of the critical features of Left discourse and the apparently interminable aspect of the debates, no doubt as well under the limitations regressively imposed on society by a relentless, powerful, and reactionary Right. The accumulation of formal constraints on progressive reform by themselves make it difficult to imagine how even approximations of progressive goals might be achieved much less recognized as achievements.

To clarify the logic of political exclusion, the attempt to purify the Left by denying its possibility, it is necessary to move from a description of its increasing generalization to an account of how it might operate in discourse and in literatures that are either beholden to political discourse or are intended to influence it. My aim is to defend an understanding of theory as critical activity limited only by relations constituted by its object and therefore without independent limits. This is exemplified, as above, by Marx's critique of political economy, and an attitude of self-acceptance on the part of Leftists based on recognizing the dependence of the very idea of a Left on a past that is complex, divided, unsavory in many respects and genuinely progressive in others, and that has been interpreted by forces committed to a sense of national order incompatible with the idea of a society.

As the concrete referents of anticommunism disappear, the generalization of its logic operates as a kind of latency, always anticipating an object but indifferent to specific content: It is available for any particular crisis, any criticism of policy, and any negative response to that policy. It is all the more powerful when combined with pre-existing exclusionary ideologies, with nationalism, and with the longstanding discourse of the obligations of empire, and it is available to justify whatever invasions are undertaken in the name of the nation. As a logic of crisis, it easily becomes a collective rule of historical and sociological interpretation, what Emile Durkheim would have called a "social fact," difficult to resist. This "political unconscious" acquires modes of substantiation in the course of its practical realization that constrain discourse beneath a surface of voluntary participation. I have discussed some of them above. They include the use of abstract categories immune to criticism; reliance on a method of fixing belief that organizes selected material offensively, as in a "brief" for one side or another of a legal case; a tendency to derive normative consequences from conclusive and nonhypothetical assignments of rigid typenames and to take the results as sufficient for judgments of what are thereby named; and a way of dealing with the risks of possible errors according to the format of a worst-case scenario.

These modes are defined by their ways of determining similarity and difference—e.g., us and them—insofar as the context, now endlessly referred to as one of permanent danger and imminent threat, demands a Manichean view of the world in which evil is identified according to national imperatives, increasing militarization, and uncompromising reaction. This demand is necessarily positive and antireflective. Despite the fact that its proponents use the language of sports to give force to the rules by which they substantiate their decisions, they distinguish them radically from the morally indifferent rules and moves of a game. When empowered, reaction has little choice but to see itself as engaged in an arena of struggle with a great evil, and to give itself the biblical status of the heroism of the few who know the evil, yet desire to save civilization even at great cost of life—with barely a glance at what I have been calling "society." This way of thinking does not necessarily extend to other aspects of life where conflicts and crises are managed according to the exigencies of very different contexts. But the possibility of such an extension cannot be excluded. We have certainly seen intimations of it in the sectarianism that appears so threatening in American society at the beginning of the twenty-first century. Yet, in regard to the specialized context of the national state, where the grand and moralized politics of elections only seems to satisfy the interest of society, the generalized logic of the Cold War serves the interests of power over and above and against the interest in social progress, increasingly limiting our sense of the possibility not only of a Left future but of a future for society itself.

A final point needs to be made in regard to the question of judgment, one that is especially important when the issues are as controversial as some of those discussed in this book. It has to do with an implication of the idea that thought and practice can only be understood as socialized courses of activity. This is logically prior to their being considered for the degree to which they approximate a normative ideal (of analysis, rationality, consistency, coherence, usefulness, etc.), which, itself, may or may not have an additional justification.[44] The criteria for adjudicating arguments in the human sciences, for coming to judgment, are necessarily constituted within the ongoing activity—e.g., of arguing—and cannot be taken as settled prior to it. Indeed, there is no obvious subject position from which it could be so taken and no known method for guaranteeing (in knowledge and in practice) the existence of a prior settlement. Even the *semblance* of settlement in advance, which could only occur under different conditions from those developing in the further course of activity, would be inconsistent with the notion of a judgment as a conclusion of an activity, any ostensible end of which can only be momentary (and nothing but an *ostensible* end can be imagined).

This is an uncomfortable, logical truth for those who prefer the convenience, and privilege of self-affirmation, of never having to look back. Many of the most serious and self-critical discussions about the character of the Left, imaginable futures, the historiography of communism, the significance of the Cold War, and the like, are interminable precisely because the criteria for settling them are constantly shifting with the course of their becoming "settled." This is not a defect in need of a cure. Nor is it a result of the failure of participants to reflect adequately on what they are saying and to clarify it. It is the very character of judgment, and the course of its development as such, that makes a prior settled criterion logically impossible—unless one conceives of the "end" of an argument as essentially dictated by its ostensible beginning, with nothing more needed beyond that but to fill in the blanks and persuade one's opponent. The very idea of discussion as a course of activity implies that the criteria for settling issues are themselves unsettled in advance. Judgment is, then, an "ongoing accomplishment" before its statement becomes a topic within another such activity (cf. Garfinkel 1967).

Judgments are to be treated, then, as commitments no less than as attempts to reckon with difference, at least to the extent to which one takes their statements as seriously intended. To that extent, they can be thought of as indicating a far greater choice, no less reified for being moral, by the momentary judge: namely, to be the very sort of self-constituting moral being who might conclude just what he or she concluded, and to conclude it in connection with yet other possible conclusions. It follows that the existential criterion for a judgment, what it unavoidably says for or about the "judge," which by now is itself a precarious notion, is no doubt part of a yet different discourse, whether explicit or not; and the discourse presumably giving rise to the judgment is never complete but is incorporated in this further encompassing one.

Judgment always presupposes a process, an activity, in which what is settled is not merely the given inscribed "result"; nor could it be. It presupposes that the conditions of deciding which "result" momentarily to accept are themselves ongoing accomplishments rather than fixed from the outset. This is, I take it, a logical fact. It is only problematic if one refuses to consider the existential, moral problem, in which case the options seem to be absolute assertiveness or skepticism, neither of which is tenable. It is presupposed by what I have written so far, to the extent to which it is addressed to the human sciences, in particular to the historiographical considerations that pertain to those disciplines, and to politics. In critiquing an argument, in offering alternatives, and so forth, the aim is always to unsettle finality and to try and come to terms with what might be, for the moment, at stake in attempting to come to a final judgment. But, of course, "what is at stake" is not merely determinate in advance, though "that something *is* at stake" might be taken by the parties to a discourse as an organizing principle of their own. The "what" that might be at stake generally must be said to be constituted in the course of coming to terms with one or another question. How that question comes to arise as incorrigible and urgent is another question, though I believe it lends itself to the same considerations. Normally the questions with which one seems to be beginning are not taken up without precedent; rather, they arise in the course of an activity in which questions of one sort or another, including whichever come to appear most important to continued activity, are instantiated. Debates within and about the historiography of communism seem to be instances of how discourse comes to be constrained in antidiscursive ways such that questions about the criteria of judgments and the moral/theoretical significance of any explicit criteria are elided, just as, or so I have claimed, the elision of the political Left in accounts of American society (*qua* society) amounts to an elision of the critical aspect of a society that cannot be understood apart from that aspect.

2

History and History's Problem

Perhaps no discipline has been more significant in cultural studies than British social history in its present, one might almost say Thompsonian, aspect as "people's history." It is, in fact, that aspect which makes original its critique of earlier research that attempted to evaluate the development of "societies." Peter Burke, for example, has not only described the biases of this research, he has identified with greater precision than E. P. Thompson himself the site or domain of the correction of those biases and has attempted to provide concepts for the type of historiography appropriate to the insight.

However, none of the "people's historians" has been able to move beyond a research emphasis on "the people" to an adequate theoretical formulation and statement of methodology. If "the people" is more than a demographic category, what concept does it signify? Clearly, more is involved than adding one part of a population, that which has been neglected, to another, that which has provided the traditional information base. The post-Thompson cohort of "people's historians" has forced us to reconsider issues in the philosophy of history that had been thought virtually solved—witness the debate between Thompson and Anderson, once so prominent—but has not yet reconsidered the implications of its own work for the theoretical status and significance of key descriptive categories—institution, experience, process, structure, group, society—which have done so much intellectual mischief in the past. The new emphasis on sociology is, to be sure, an advance for historiography, but only if the categories of sociology are subjected to the serious critique implicit in what Burke refers to as "the discovery of the people." The problem is most easily explored by a close, methodological reading of specific studies because that is where we will find the new historiographical principles manifest, whether or not they are made explicit in new theoretical formulations.

This chapter examines a discrepancy in the work of Thompson between stated program and empirical analysis, not in order to criticize the latter but to discover the covert program upon which his analysis in fact depends and which, for a variety of reasons, he has not been able to make explicit. I will discuss one article, his short study of anonymous letters of abuse (1975), and try to show that his analysis and interpretation of the letters attempts to resolve what otherwise appear to be methodological contradictions. My conclusion is that his method is different from what he says it is and has said it should be, and that Thompson is engaged in an inquiry of greater historiographical and philosophical significance than he and those he has influenced seem to have recognized.

Thompson: Conclusions and Principles

Thompson begins "The Crime of Anonymity" with what appears to be the statement of a fact—not a summary of what is to follow or an introduction to a problem but a conclusion for which the ensuing presentation of "evidence" and "argument" seems little more than illustrative:

> The anonymous threatening letter is a characteristic form of social protest in any society which has crossed a certain threshold of literacy, in which forms of collective organized defense are weak, and in which individuals who can be identified as the organizers of protest are liable to immediate victimization. (p. 255)

What is this statement, so definite and plausible, the conclusion of? The level of abstraction suggests that it follows a close study of an enormous secondary literature leading inexorably to just this theoretical conclusion. Its presence in a relatively short article suggests, on the other hand, that it is the statement of a law that is confirmed by a close analysis of precisely the sort of data whose analysis can and will confirm such a law. Its definiteness suggests yet a third possibility, a statement of something sufficiently well established to serve as the program for analyzing some particular state of affairs. Finally, the use of certain terms—"characteristic," "any society," "in which," "can be"—indicates a statistical conclusion on the basis of which the data can be entered in the encyclopedia of such conclusions. Each possibility, however, raises problems: Thompson has not, so far as I know, prefaced this conclusion with any other work or body of works providing the requisite review of secondary analyses of appropriate factual material; his article is too short and entirely too concentrated to confirm a law; the statement may or may not be sufficiently well established to serve as a program for empirical analysis, but that cannot in any case be taken for granted; and no statistics are presented that fit the terms that seem to signify the content of the passage.

Suppose we take the passage at its word. "Characteristic" implies a numerical sampling controlled by probability, at least in principle. "Any society which has" implies an authentic population of societies that share canonical dimensions along which their variation can be measured, such as literacy. The conditions listed as qualifying the main relationship between the characteristic form of social protest and the unstated attribute of every society that invites protest presuppose an accumulation of correlations within each condition sufficient to justify the inferred, or apparently inferred, proposition.

No literature exists that has established or even provided good and unambiguous reasons for these assumptions. Indeed, the sort of abstract comparative analysis indicated by the passage seems to be excluded in principle by the intensive historiography of our most important historians, including Thompson. Literacy is not a factor that can be formulated, much less understood, independent of the concrete specification of the structures and processes by which it is presumably determined and measured. Societies are not elements of a population of countable and independent entities in the sense required by the implied statistical analysis. Interpretable correlations of the sort required by Thompson's qualifications of the main relationship are difficult, if not impossible, to imagine.

These are such obvious points that it cannot do to assume that Thompson has somehow missed or ignored them. If he has not, however, then the passage is either not seriously intended or it maintains an intention that needs to be reconstituted through an interpretation of the whole text. We must, in other words, deal with the fact that his initial pronouncement seems to state the result of a set of inductions that are altogether impossible: as an inductive proposition, it is extravagant and beyond hope of reliable demonstrations. Yet, it is also a fact that what he says is so entirely plausible that criticism seems petty or beside the point.

Above all, one must keep in mind that the statement of conclusion appears in his article not at the end but at the beginning, and it does not appear to be a conclusion guaranteed by evidence introduced in any other study he has done (though, as we shall see, it draws some of its force from what has been so elaborately pronounced in his other research).

How has Thompson been able to produce a conclusion that is at once curious and certain? By way of preview, there is throughout his essay a kind of Sherlock Holmesian argumentation, for which the reader is his Dr. Watson, aimed not at proving a hypothesis positively so much as demonstrating that if we reject it we must reject an absolutely unexceptionable view of the total social world. Otherwise, the quoted passage is merely an empirical-type proposition that can tolerate no more than illustration beyond its statement.

If so, then, why does he bother with so much detail, so many examples, so intensive an examination of the letters in the body of the article? Given a certain level of literacy, a lack of organization among the have-nots, and an uncompromising legal order can it seriously be doubted that the anonymous threatening letter is both a vehicle for and an index of an underground of social discontent? If more than this is unnecessary, why do we read further and expect further edification (and why, as we read, are we edified? and we are)—beyond, of course, the desire to renew our acquaintance with Thompson's remarkable literary virtues, his humanism, and his social historian's sensibility?

The reason is, I believe, that Thompson's use—not his treatment—of these materials reminds us of some things that we already knew yet must, if we are to theorize, constantly and actively re-know or re-collect—as ordinary memory must continually rehearse even the most familiar scenes if the *sense* of their familiarity, their usefulness, is to be sustained. Behind this proposal is the assumption that certain pre-formal aspects of knowledge (oddly for the moment analogous to Thompson's idea that behind apparent history is the reality of an underlife), relatively incorrigible as base to any immediate act of theorizing (what sociologists have come to call a "frame"), lose the integrity they need to serve as an intellectual base unless they are rehearsed in non-theoretical ways. If they are not, the activity of theorizing, including the display of conclusiveness, begins to lose its fluency and hence the force of commitment without which it would not be theorizing at all. This "base-superstructure" contradiction—the necessarily incorrigible and the necessarily critical—is the dynamic that explains such theoretical activities as Thompson's initial passage in "The Crime of Anonymity."

On the other hand, and problematically, there appears to be something demonstrated, and Thompson's treatment of his materials is part of that demonstration. Without the detail, the examples, the textual analyses of the letters, the exposition and commentary, his initial passage is merely a subsidiary proposition to an argument that cannot, in principle, be made. With them, the passage somehow achieves "explanatory affect" and, in addition, redeems precisely the intellectual activity apparently repudiated by its positive form.

What we already knew but need to recollect is the following: (1) In terms of content, people act for substantial reasons, respond to the conditions under which they live, and reflect upon the social relations constituted ⟨ in and challenged by their conduct, though none of these can be explicit in the words they use or in specific acts since otherwise those words and acts would lose their essential fluency. (2) In terms of methodology, a necessary feature of all reason, and the "explanatory affect" of social scientific formulations in particular, is the obligation to establish the possible expansion of concepts and formulae beyond discipline boundaries (as metaphor, analogy, image, or provisional abstraction) such that they are, in principle, adequate to a consciously multidiscursive, dialogically realized view of society as such, regardless of the fact that such expansion can neither be guaranteed nor justified by any procedure yet described by the philosophy of science. The sense of a discipline is always, even for practitioners, extra-disciplinary. The *pragnanz* of concepts and formulations is a necessary feature of their plausible use and therefore of their scientific status. But that *pragnanz* cannot be taken for granted. It must be artfully and methodically sustained by making entirely too much of entirely too little if anything is to be made of anything at all, and by moving within limits that encompass but do not define this, that, or the other discipline, paradigm, or theory. Clearly, this obligation can only be rationalized in a discursive practice that is the discipline's recognition of the obligation; and historiographical practice requires empirical points of entry, real occasions precisely on the order of what is recounted in Thompson's initial passage.

However, if the point of entry is treated as the problem, as a hypothesis to be tested by the analysis of data and nothing more, then it inevitably is followed by either silence or by an endless engagement with the detail imposed on such a discourse by the futile and deranging prospect of empirical *demonstration*. It is only when the empirical point of entry is seen as an occasion to do more than collate and summarize that argument can move theory to its value-practical ground and lead to some provisional certainty about agreement and disagreement. It is the rhetoric and poetics of historical prose that guarantee the plausibility of a formulation, not empirical test, no matter how thorough, logically secure, and otherwise rigorous. What these latter do is altogether something else, though something certainly related to the achievement of explanatory affect. Neither silence nor an endless engagement with detail makes us sensible, breeds a community of knowledge, or offers an approach to *a* or *the* truth. Both indicate a failure to theorize and therefore to make sense of the world within a subjectivity that is, after all, of the world.

Thompson makes no such mistake. His point of entry to his topic (cf. below) provides the kind of recollection that is essential to scientific method in historical and sociological study and necessary for any "history" that can be recognizably real for *us*, those who need "society" and "history" at the same time. The remainder of this chapter attempts to show that rhetoric and poetics also are necessary aspects of that same enterprise, not merely flourishes, style, or deceptions.

The rhetoric and poetics of theory are necessary aspects of the validity of every theoretical proposal that intends to sustain referential claims about human affairs. They cannot be treated as separate from such proposals and, indeed, need to be part of any evaluation of them from the standpoint of both their science and their philosophy. Every such proposal must be extended and must display the character of extensibility through whatever discursive means are available beyond the immediate empirics of its occasion and the internal formalisms and techniques of its discipline taken as relatively autonomous of and abstracted from the universe of disciplines. Without the display of extensibility, such proposals lack conviction in the sense of socially communicative significance: They fail to be of the order of the society about which they purport to theorize. Inasmuch as they do fail, they must be read symptomatically, as demanding the insertion of extensibility; they must be read as situating metaphors. It is interesting to note that much of the work in sociology and political science, and some in economics, is *written* as if it is a thoroughly formal exercise but is *read*, even by fellow practitioners of the discipline, as if it is a thoroughly metaphorical exercise laced with argument. To see this it is only necessary to turn the pages in the literature review section of most articles that appear in professional journals. It is as if there is a tacit agreement between authors and readers that authors may cover their tracks in one way, readers in another; the one may provide accountability by argument, the other may provide the ingredient of communicability.

It is, after all, the character of social communicability beyond formal inscription that is the historicity of historical study itself, which makes historical research readable and directs it from itself to the human affairs it is intended to illuminate. The use and not merely the application of a formulation is necessary to any demonstration of validity, and use is an exercise in literary work. It is not sufficient, in other words, to consider the validity of a formulation as something that can be evaluated according to explicit technical rules. Indeed, "validity" used in that limited way is a metaphor signifying in the ways metaphors do, the sociology of research in relation to which technical "validation" constitutes only one sort of account of the activity involved. The use of the formulation involves the concrete labors of nontechnical discourses, the deployment and revision of the tropes and images of those discourses as well as adjacent disciplines, if the formulation is to serve as a basis for further discussion and research. The demonstration of validity, a prominent topic in textbooks on method in psychology and sociology, is a discursive event and therefore displays (or must be made to display) the conviction of a subjectivity "greater" than that of the speaker of a particular utterance or the writer of a particular text. Thus, one purges rhetoric from science only at the expense of science itself. Moreover, a critique of a formulation as propagandistic, deceptive, stylized, biased, or ideological is itself rhetorical, advocating, in effect, a purity of discipline not only unattainable in practice but inconceivable if science (sociology, history, etc.) is to be a human endeavor. The paradigm view of "normal science," then, is fundamentally incorrect, or correct only on condition that certain constitutive features of science are purged. But then the question must be what is constituted by the purge, and we would have to answer that what is constituted is science as something other than a historical event and human process.

In fact, as we shall see, Thompson's initial statement is itself false only on condition that we reject a view of the social world as dynamic and as constituted in the joint actions of people (a position we would have to reject if we accepted a philosophy of science that treated the rhetoric and poetics of science as somehow extrinsic). What is at stake in his essay is not his treatment of the letters or his account of their circumstance; it is the legitimacy of his use of the letters to *indicate* something that must exist (and has existed) if it is possible to conceive of history as the un-idealized affair that is *the people as society* and *society as historical*.

Thompson's essay is, from a certain point of view, reminiscent of Freud's *Psychopathology of Everyday Life*. Like the latter, it deploys concepts that are conceptual only insofar as they are generally communicable, in other words, only to the extent that they carry an obligation of expanded use across boundaries that would otherwise stand as obstacles to knowing them as concepts and therefore knowing them in connection with the total object, which is at once their base of self-critique and the referent that can only be completed, in principle, in the expansivity of conceptualization. What is important about Freud's research is not the tics, stutters, and slips of the tongue, nor his claims about the laws of their interconnections and structural derivations. It is the display of an obligation to view human activities in terms of a foundational contradiction of energy and direction and a dialectic of subjectivity/objectivity. What is important about Thompson's account of anonymous letters is not the letters or their social structural derivation but the display of a determination to witness society as the work of human beings and as, through and through, historical.

To show this, I will review some alternative ways of understanding Thompson's account, discuss his own methodological qualifications, and defend the hypothesis that the plausibility of his conclusion lies in its being an implementation of a view of the world that has practical and conceptual priority to any empirical study and that can be criticized only through the conceptualizing skills of dialectical reason, a varied working through concepts and formulations along the dual lines of deconstructive and reconstructive critical intervention.

The circumstances Thompson cites at the beginning of "The Crime of Anonymity" are intended to establish the existence of underground social protest during a period of apparent calm in civil society. They are the same circumstances that sociologists of "collective behavior" cite to account for a sudden shift in popular emphasis from "institutional politics" to innovative and subversive forms: Given the existence of grievance, a lack of institutional and organizational means for expressing discontent, and a manifest terror of reprisal for engaging in any protest whatsoever, it is hardly surprising that at least a few people will experiment with alternatives consistent with the resources available for political expression—in Thompson's case anonymous letter writing.

But the assertion that the existence of such a complex structure of intention is substantiated, much less proven, by the letters is only one of many possible conclusions—including that the letters are casual acts of vandalism, the work of cranks, hoaxes, or even provocations by members of the dominant classes intended to justify harsh policies of social control. Thompson says nothing that compels us to select one possibility over the others. He simply makes the choice, and we accept it to the extent that we are already disposed to interpret these forms of invective and threat as the substance of reasoned aggressive intent.[1] Despite this, his assertion seems unmistakably valid, and valid in terms that could only be rejected by the most idealistically reactionary of conservatives. Why, and in what sense, is this so?

Perhaps its validity lies in its manifest compatibility with other information we have about affairs at the time the letters were published—e.g., class oppression and general popular unrest. It is reasonable to assume that a generalized oppression, on the order of a class relation, is likely to lead to acts, individual or collective, of violence and rebellion, and that the intentions of these acts will find expression one way or another, depending upon resources, costs, and benefits, and depending upon the availability of alternative forms of expression. If so, then Thompson's essay illustrates a point already established. The problem is that it is so well established that another illustration is scarcely needed. But if trivia is all there is in this essay, why does Thompson write with an irony that suggests so much more? Why does he choose such exotic and fragile material on which to base a claim already satisfactorily made? Why does the tone of his piece and the complexity of its voicing suggest a disclosure of something new? To defend Thompson's proposal as pronouncing what had already been established would require that we ignore the rhetorical features of the piece and our own pleasure in reading it.

Doubtless, the cases he reviews work as illustrations. But if this were all, we would have to dismiss the essay or catalogue it among the multitude of minor studies, despite what remains a strong "historically explanatory affect." On the other hand, if we accept the latter, we will have to consider the possibility that his initial proposal relates to evidence and argues in ways not ordinarily thought to be part of the logic of science or of what Thompson has called "historical logic." This is essential if we are to take him seriously as a historian of society and ourselves seriously as readers of historical studies.

Let us say that Thompson's initial statement must *have* evidence even as it cannot, strictly, *be* evidenced. Whether one operates from the assumption of a uniform nature or from that of a meaningful nature, the available conceptions of social protest, Thompson's included, do not imply the empirical relevance of anonymous prose materials; nor, in any case, are Thompson's letters sufficient in number or quality to constitute even the most flimsy of samples; nor again do the letters come bearing sufficient indication of authorial context to point as directly as Thompson says they do to events of social and political significance, though their manifest content often contains explicit reference to the practices of their victims in regard to workers and the poor.

Despite this, his exposition seems, at a number of points, to assume: (1) a definite uniformity in the nature of protest; (2) the relevance of these letters to said nature; (3) that there has been, somewhere if not here, an adequate depiction of authorial context; and (4) that these letters make an authentic statistical sample.

The fact that these assumptions are not and cannot be met would be fatal if we were to apply criteria appropriate to induction or hermeneutic interpretation to Thompson's essay. They are not if those criteria are irrelevant. Therefore, in order to preserve the essay's explanatory affect (ourselves as readers), we need to treat the inconsistency between what the concept of protest mentioned in the first paragraph of the essay seems to require and what Thompson actually provides as if it were deliberate, as a way of saying something that requires precisely this inconsistency and expository extravagance if it is to be said. The question is, then, what is the aim of the essay if the inconsistency is its constitutive feature? Perhaps it is not too tight a short circuit to say that Thompson is teaching us about a special historiologically pragmatic relationship between certain sorts of proposition and certain sorts of evidence that is necessary if history is to be about society.

From this point of view, what is at stake is not so much the settings of the letters as the discourses appropriate to Thompson's initial passage itself, in particular the discursive conjuncture that his apparent extravagance has made suddenly vital as a problem in reconciling historiological obligation with historiographical competence.

Thompson does not merely draw conclusions about the anonymous letters. He *displays* in his presentation—its tropes, mixture of voices, and ratio of conclusion and comment to evidentiary material—a sense of the historian's obligation to go beyond the arbitrary idealization of "the information given" (though he presents tables and figures) and declare the perspective of its reality as information.

This must not be thought of as an expression of the author's psychology, an instance of a bias or style, or something that he explicitly, programmatically, or personally intends. It is a feature of the writing itself to the extent that we recognize it as historical writing and therefore, one might say at this stage of our inquiry, part of the pleasure of this particular historiological text. The essay displays obligation and perspective, and a particular obligation and a particular perspective, as an internal commitment of the text that must be read as thoroughly as one reads the words, sentences, and paragraphs. As such, it constitutes for us who read history an unmistakable pedagogical vitality and source of motivation. What does it teach? Something about historical writing surprisingly other than what Thompson calls, in another context, "historical logic"; something about what it means to make too much of too little; something, after all, about the too much that must be made.

The proposition stated in the first paragraph of "The Crime of Anonymity" must be admitted regardless of the adequacy or relevance of its "evidence," though not regardless of reference to some sort of exhaustible "factual" matter. It follows from what history is about and is reflexive to the project of reconciling "history" and "society" for the sake of a historical sensibility and communicative understanding of human affairs. The proposition—the assertiveness of this sort of proposition—is a necessary ingredient in showing what it is to recognize history as the history of society and society as historical. What needs to be specified in this formula is "society"; and, as indicated in my introduction, this will depend upon what can be made of "the people." For now, we need to explore further the methodology that underlies the possibility of conceptualizing the relationships among "the people," "society," and "history," particularly Thompson's use of evidence and his clarification of the way in which "the people" is "society." Along the way, we will discuss the significance of "evidence" as the historian's occasion rather than the historian's material, and touch upon the related problems of the exhaustion of sources and the expansion of concepts, and the particular separation of concept and object that is a feature of the diversity of claims made upon language such that referents must be found, specified, and given over to one appropriation or another.

Evidence

That there must be evidence is part of the nature of the enterprise. Whether or not this is because of some epistemological truth or simply a discipline-defining norm is not important. What is important is that the *being* of evidence is the occasion for the historian's reflection to be of the most general understanding of human affairs possible. "Objectivity" in this sense breeds the discursive "heteroglossia" that (1) every disciplined enterprise whatsoever presupposes, that (2) gives "educated" speech (the speech of topics, issues, and problems) its conjunctural character, and that (3) the writing of history uniquely addresses as a conjuncture.

"Evidence" is the "too little" that must be forced into design, and in being so forced must be expropriated from the design that originally made its prominence problematic. But it is only too little in relation to the obligations of design. No body of evidence points unequivocally toward a particular theoretical realization. It could not, since any such realization must communicate across the boundaries of the discipline within which what has been found can be considered evidence, and since every theoretical realization is as much a repudiation of an alternative as a realization of the evidence's value. On the other hand, evidence must be part of a recognizable exhaustion of "sources" if the historian is to speak beyond his or her own texts (if his or her activity is to be seen as producing texts as products for distribution and purchase/use), and if the work of the individual historian is to enter the collective historian's discursive realization of a yet more general collective project.

Without making too much of too little, without seeing too much being made of too little, one is left with the idealization of theory as "no more than what the evidence can bear." Surely no one would claim either that historical writing is or could be a strict (and beyond that what are the limits?) reflection of what "the evidence can bear" or that there are no rational limits to formulation other than evidence and the logic of its explication. History without the inter-discursive excess of exposition is, at best, record or almanac; history where exposition is without bounds loses its referential character and its relevance. Where, then, is the middle ground? What mediates the relations of prose and evidence, sense and information, concept and fact is project against alternative projects, in a word, the politics of heteroglossia that Mikhail Bakhtin calls "dialogue" (1968). Which is to say that writing history is an instance of society; which is also to say that there is no middle ground, but there is a dialectics of historical knowledge.

If we were to reject Thompson's characterization of the relation of the anonymous letters to social protest on technical rather than project grounds, we would have to purge from history itself what must nevertheless remain its most disturbing presence—the intentional rebellion that must accompany a certain type of difference, the protest implicit in any regularity of domination, the element of what we already view as life in any controlled process or externally mediated structure, the dialectic inherent in anything that can be called "social."

The anonymous letters occurred, and their presence was certainly remarked upon by those who knew of them at the time and those in authority, and at least some were received and recorded publicly in newspapers for one reason or another. Our problem is not to discover the reasons why their authors wrote them. Nor is it to establish their immediate significance to their contemporaries in the practical activities of their everyday lives. Both are impossible even to approximate. It is, rather, to describe societal events in such a way that the letters, or something similarly dramatizing the active and intentional underlife that must have existed if those events are to have been historical, must have occurred, that *these* letters (as part of sources to be exhausted for the reasons of disciplined communication) might have had some bearing on the events such that any account of the period without reference to them or their sociological type could not be plausible.

It almost goes without saying that the historian must treat as ideological any account of events that favors what *already* appears to be momentous, glorious, and memorable. Part of this obligation must involve, then, making too much of too little. It is to this extent only that the writing of history can be said to be an act; and it is in this way that historical prose is both reflexive to society and, given the mediation of the political dialectic, able to avoid the perils of chauvinism and the easy expressibility of particular and dominant interests.

Writing and Reading

How does Thompson's writing display this obligation and realize the relation of "society" to "history." Consider the first passage in which the reader encounters "evidence." There, Thompson quotes an anonymous letter in the context of a series of notices and announcements in *The London Gazette: Published by Authority*, no. 10752, late August, 1767, the letter having been published not "by the letter's author but by the Secretary of State in order to apprehend the author":

> Thus in no. 10752, . . . we have notices for an election of Scottish peers to sit in the house of Lords; of a review in Madrid by the King of Spain of his garrison; of the movements of the Papal Nuncio; while from Berlin it was announced that "the Marriage of the Princess Louisa-Henrietta Wilhelmina of Brandenbourg with the Reigning Prince of Anhalt Dessau was solemnized in the Royal Chapel at Charlottenbourg by the Reverend Mr. Sack . . . After which the French Play called Turcaret was acted in the Orangerie. . . ." The gardens were illuminated, and there was a ball, attended by the King of Prussia, which lasted until the next morning. Immediately following, cheek-by-jowl with Princess Louisa-Henrietta Wilhelmina, there appears a rather different notice, addressed to Sir Richard Betenson of Sevenoaks, Kent:
>
> Sr: "Your Baily or Steward proper is a black gard sort of fellow to the Workmen and if you dont discharge him You may Look to Your House being sett on fire if Stones will not Burn You damned Sun of a hoare You shall have Your throat cutt from Ear to Ear except You Lay £50 under the Second tree of Staple Nashes from his house at the frunt of the Great Gates near the Rabbit Warrin on Wedsdy Morn next." (p. 256)

This is the third paragraph of the essay. It immediately follows the initial statement and a brief description of the source of Thompson's "evidence," *The London Gazette*. The first two paragraphs establish that there is a text, a point to be made in regard to a specific subject matter; but the administrative flatness of their affect gives way, in the moment of a sudden phrase—"Thus . . . we have . . ."—to the text's interior and therefore to acts and their subjects.

- One can almost feel Thompson's pleasure at the sound of the well-placed "Reverend Mr. Sack" and again at the reversal of fortune in the second passage, the letter itself. But there are also the pleasures of a certain conspiracy to which the reader is joined by the ironical shift of voice and tenor in the series: "Thus . . . we have," "it was announced," "cheek-by-jowl . . . there appears," and then, catastrophically, "Sr: Your Baily . . . ."

"Thus . . . we have . . ." and "cheek-by-jowl with Princess Louisa-Henrietta Wilhelmina, there appears a rather different notice":[2] The passage bracketed by these two phrases and minus the letter is virtually self-contained. Its specific accomplishment, as we will see, is the occasion for and a condition of the fulfillment of the essay's project. Yet this is not, at first, obvious to us who wish to gauge the significance of the essay as a whole, though it *must* be to a self-conscious reader of the writing.

What makes the bracketing obscure and in any case seem inconsistent with the claim that it constitutes a relation of moment to project is: (1) The ostensible object of the passage is the letter (and therefore the passage seems merely to point beyond itself); (2) the reader's movement is ostensibly nothing more than the vehicle through which that object is put into place (and therefore the reader seems only to be the impression of the object); and (3) Thompson is ostensibly the engineer of this schedule and deviser of this fate (and therefore authorship seems to be external to readership, of the essence of the text, and an instance of the domination of matter by mind).

This apparent dispossession of the reader in favor of the administration of objects must be taken as a parody. As such, it undermines the supposition of a naturally invidious relation of author to reader on the order of the relations of estates that constitute, we are beginning to see, the very fortune that will suffer reversal in the "notice" of the letter (and then, as well, historiographically).

The dispossession takes place only if we ignore the poetics of Thompson's prose. If we do not, then the reader as constituted lives with and through *what* is read. If we ignore the poetics, then the reader is only the arbitrarily appointed register of local facts, motivated at best by accident or the burden of duty, and under no obligation to *read* in order to get the facts.

That is, the administrative order that obscures the catastrophic shift from the first to the second passage and the bracketing, which makes that possible, mark the first passage as an imposition from the standpoint of an unassailable authority (the idealized author beyond all questions of authority) neither recognizable through reading nor able to be part of the reader's self-recognition. We need to explore this paradox further to appreciate what Thompson has done and, for this appreciation, to rediscover reading in the midst of critique.

Reading that fails to recognize authority lacks motivation; it is the trivial or self-reproducing subjectivity of instinct, imitation, habit, obedience, or calculation. Reading without self-recognition is merely consumption, and therefore the denial of the reader as subject. Either a trivial or absent subjectivity would disqualify the form of Thompson's essay, one might say its strategies. Either would, as well, invalidate any but a strictly "literal" content.

But we can only establish the significance of the essay to the understanding of history if it can be said to have form and content, and it can only "have" both if it is more than the play of techniques and objects, if writing and reading are more than the exhibition of codes and the reception of messages. Otherwise, any attempt to understand the essay's significance would seem irrelevant, arbitrary, or self-serving, and the essay would be something that did not have to be written, something altogether asocial and ahistorical: It would not be an authentic text, and there could be no authentic reader but the commentator whose history is not bound to the history of the reading of a text, whose commentary is an autonomous objectification whose connection with its own object must be mediated by a third party whose subjectivity is both the real subject that comments and another false subject in need of its own third party, and so on. At this point, "we" who are attempting critically to grasp the relation of reading and writing history (the "us" of Hegel's "for us") have found our way back to the self-consciousness of reading and forward to the movement of history itself.

The bracketed passage, then, introduces the objectivities in relation to which the essay can be read and the reader can develop as a subject. It anticipates through the progress of its irony the anonymous letter as a moment of a text—not, as Thompson claimed in his immediately preceding methodological statement, as "evidence" (it is not presented, from the standpoint of the poetics of Thompson's prose, as a document, a part of a larger reality beyond the text that the letter indicates, or even an element of a sample). In that anticipation, it establishes the reader's practical position (positioning) within and in regard to the text that corresponds to the moral problematic of reading "history": the *essential* freedom of being confined by the text and the *existential* bondage of being subjected to what the text signifies as a whole, beyond itself, the freedom to follow and the obligation to decide, the false freedom of the passive agent and the volatile situation of the active subject.

This contradiction between intension and extension, being ruled and being social, motivates this reader/subject's work. It is a condition of that praxis. To be above what one is nevertheless within is to experience both the temptation and the futility of privilege: The one disposes toward demonstrations of power, the other toward an unhappy and ultimately self-serving cynicism.

But there are two privileges at stake—the one, of the aristocracy in the text, and the other of the reader him- or herself as one who reads about privilege and is therefore privileged yet about it. The reader will, therefore, witness fortune and its reversal in the transition of the two quoted passages, and will finally experience as reader both fortune's form and the form of its reversal. This experience places the reader in the midst of the problematic relating history to society, and is essential to his or her final transformation into a reader of history.

On the other hand, to be within (and therefore subjected to) what one is nevertheless above (and therefore subject of) is to experience the timidity of waiting and an ambivalence toward the textualized materials (structure) on which essentialist (false) freedom depends. The first disposes toward passivity or apathy, the second toward self-denial and ultimately resentment, anger, or unconsciousness.

But there are two positions of subjection that combine in this situation, that of "the people" who had to write anonymous threatening letters and that of the reader who must be anonymous in a one-sided relation to the inscribing and inscribed authority of the text. Therefore, the reader will not only witness fortune and its reversal and experience their forms, he or she will also witness the agency of the reversal ("the people" seen from the standpoint of one subjected to a different but analogous domination and aware of it) and experience the ambivalence of that agency in the unrealizable temptation to be partisan: After all, the only real subject (and the only real perspective of need) presented in the two passages is the anonymous author of the letter; one is tempted to say anonymity itself.

To be partisan is to become lost in the text. When the only legitimate object of partisanship cannot be named for its own subjectivity, to be lost in the text is to experience the text as, in a sense, a noumenal presence—real but sensibly beyond all grasp. Therefore, the frustration of this temptation through the acknowledgment of the uneasy privilege inherent in reading redirects the realized threat of reversal to the authority of the essay and engages the reader in a critical relation with it.

But that too is cooperative: Both the privilege and its challenge must be sustained and enlightened if there is to be reading and texts and authors. This is why the reader has the advantage, over the anonymous and individuated letter writer, of a possible conspiracy with the author of the text, the center of privilege, the principle by which the various voices are ordered within the text for the sake of the reader's development as reader. This is the reader's possible labor of cooperation. But it must be shown within the text as a practical realization. How does Thompson produce this humanization of the reader?

To answer this, we need to return to the quoted paragraphs and follow the movement of voices. First, the "we" in "Thus . . . we have" is virtually royal.[3] It operates with the confidence of total immunity and the certainty of the judge or satirist. But while there is foible to be ridiculed and malfeasance to be corrected, this "we" temporarily suspends the higher law on which the judge and the satirist normally depend. It carries the force of an absolute indifference, if only for the moment, and a formal condescension that notices its objects, but only in passing.

The arrogance of this indifferent condescension is there to comfort the reader (soon to be discomfited) from within the context of a privilege already presumed. Comfort is necessary if the normal awkwardness of being subjected to a text is to be assuaged so that the reader can work with the author, reading with the intentionality of the textualized material.

On the other hand, arrogance is not, finally, to be the tone of the two passages taken together, nor are "we" ultimately to remain immune. The move from the second to the third voice, from "it was announced" to "cheek-by-jowl . . . there appears," establishes the privilege within a limited and problematic conspiracy of authorship and readership and then gives it the paradoxes that stimulate the reader's labor.

"It was announced" is no longer royal, though it still speaks beyond any concrete speaker and any community of interest. There is, on the one hand, the hint of a clerk's detachment, devoid of responsibility yet efficient for all practical purposes. But the efficiency is undermined by the inconsistency between the phrase and what "it" refers to, and this establishes the actual pleasure of a subject's diversion of its object. The newspaper did not "announce"; it merely listed events and news. An announcement, by its tone, intends to command attention and matters as much to the announcer as to the announced. It conveys a certain command over the total range of mentionable objects (and not merely the momentarily concrete set); it is not complete until every one appears and is violated by any interest that concentrates on a single instance. It is an intentionally ordered set that expresses itself as law rather than need or disposition. Through this device, Thompson gives the reader superiority over this subtext, a momentary equality with the author himself, and the right to entertain an attitude where the "source" material might have denied it.

To transform a list into announcement is to give something nonhuman the power to proclaim, and to serve as a vehicle for the reader to experience that power as his or her own. The *Gazette*, by virtue of its power to announce, now overwhelms the items of its news just as the newspaper that announces and thereby becomes the reader's vehicle overwhelms the subtext in favor of the new equality of author and reader.

The announcement of events is, in any case, greater than the events. So, it will appear momentarily that it is not the nobility but their celebrations that gives announcement its voice. This is ensured, finally, by Thompson's sudden personification of the marriage of the princess in order to allow the anonymous threatening letter to coexist "cheek-by-jowl" with the aristocrat/celebrant that it threatens.[4] Indeed, by the time we read the letter, the nobility has become virtually all "cheek" and "jowl," as 1930s' cartoons of plutocrats dressed the airs of wealth in shuddering corpulence. That it is the letter which is "cheek-by-jowl" with the princess merely establishes equal standing, a momentary equality of estate from which vantage point the letter carries all manner of challenge, including betrayal, though its capacity to betray (dependent as it is on equality) is fleeting, a flourish intended to amuse. But even as fleeting, betrayal adheres to the letter's threat, as part, almost a latent feature, of its power. And, of course, by now we are aware that the letter's power is constructed within the text and that this rhetorical construction is consistent with Thompson's preamble. At this point, we begin to understand the intent of that preamble as other than interpretive and inductive and to understand the importance of the poetics of theory in the realization of the essay's project.

The passage voiced by "it was announced," completed by "there appears a rather different notice," and appended by the anonymous letter, is a single rhetorical gesture that, at one and the same time, elevates the reader, establishes the text as the object of reading, subordinates the nobility both to the subtext of the passage and to the possibility of threat and betrayal, reverses the order of hegemony between the classes, and establishes a certain competence of what would otherwise have been a rabble, a competence of "the people." The nobility's fortune is held up to ridicule within the text for the sake of our sharing the anonymous letter writer's pleasure of his threat; it appears, now, as a fragile sham—which it was not while backed by real power but is when taken in isolation and as one intention pitted against another. Fortune's reversal is the result of two conspiracies: one of the reader and author, established rhetorically, and the other of those parties and the letter writer whose newly found power makes possible the pleasure of the second conspiracy. The fortune of the aristocracy has become dumb inadvertence, a taking of things for granted, an idleness and ease that is, by its nature, liable to disturbance and violence, like a gourmet's meal that cannot tolerate the imprecations of schedule or the small voices of children.

By these means, the reader's partisanship to society has already begun, though it still depends upon power, status, and idea; still represents the aspirations of those who can have little hope, and relies on irony and burlesque to control its own ambivalence and insecurity. These can be dispelled, or at least put in their place, only through further work. But it is work that can now be initiated since the reader has entered the confinement of, and embraced, the text.

The threat of the anonymous letter is not spoken from its words alone. We have seen that those words lend themselves to various interpretations and such a letter can serve many purposes. The threat is constructed in the work of Thompson's text. But it is no less real for that. "Threat" implies vulnerability, and this is created ironically; it implies power, and this is created by a subtly savage burlesque; it implies risk and therefore equality, and this is created through the juxtaposition of a way of life (the parodied way of life of the nobility) and desire (the blackmail)—the former unconscious but complete and confident in the fullness of its celebrations of self, the latter conscious but incomplete and overbearing as if it could never be confident of the future.

This is the way that this letter appears in Thompson's essay as "evidence." This is how it comes to reverse so many fortunes without yet having one of its own. "The people" as a formal operation upon the logic of nobility—desire versus confidence, the conscious incomplete versus the unconscious complete, dialectic versus the positive—makes its appearance as precisely the danger that was known by the nobility and the gentry; and, despite the partisanship so cunningly concealed beneath the words of these passages, the reader also appreciates the threat—"a rather different notice" heralds the reader's surprise—and experiences something on the order of a reversal of fortune in the intimation of a general challenge to all privilege. The pleasure of entertaining this dread depends, of course, on the immunity of the reader derived from the "aristocratic" immunity of the author, Thompson. The whole presents us with a series of commitments and removes, with apparently limitless opportunities for pleasure.

From that complex position, we read items, the contradiction of items, and our own immunity—of time, perspective, and epoch—and we begin to read ourselves in the context of predicaments. And some of those have to do with the perspective of desire. The letter is rife with intention, its specific intent deliberately (even if the data had allowed for the empirical sense of context) divorced from possible settings: It is one of several items, and it is preceded not by a description of oppression but a summary of luxurious living.

This free malevolence, this artificially concentrated will that engages our partisanship in what we nevertheless observe from a position of privilege analogous to that will's enemy also cues the more abstract negation of order by desire (including the orders of reading and writing that are, for the moment, combined). Ultimately, this ambivalence must be reduced in the text. Thompson does this by listing in an appendix a collection of the letters organized by type of grievance but singular for their excess:

> we have suffered so long that we are detarmied that sun shall suffere as well we you are not alone by night or day we will seek revenge.

> Whe REsolve before you shall say & the rest of the heads of that bloudy and unlawful act it is finished to have your hearts bloud if you proceede in the aforesaid bloudy act Whe like horse leaches will cry give, give untill whe have spilt the bloud of every one that wishes to rob the Inosent unborn it shall not be in your power to say I am safe from the hands of the Enemy for Whe like birds of pray will prively lye in wait to spil the bloud of the aforesaid Charicters whose names and plaices of above are as prutrified sores in our Nostrils.

> The Farmers friends and the Pasense enemy Wee have taken the liberty of riting this few lines to you to inform you of our intention and that is to let you known our determanation is to live or Die.

> We have inquired into your tithes, and we have determined to set fire to you in your bed if you do not lower them. . . . Deem this as friendly, and consider that we would not burn you up without notice.

When combined with the sometimes scatological and Rabelaisian invective of the rest, this excess is often more hilarious than representative of unequivocal rage. The appendix gives us something of the hilarity of relief, and so leaves us reading.

But before that, there has been something like a radical rehearsal. One has had to be conscious of many relationships and has had the experience of a possibly universal interest against the multifaceted precariousness of privilege. Despite the fact that this is so far negative and reflects the limited perspectives of momentary desire and artful conspiracy, desire and conspiracy are there and with them facts that are irrepressible and democratic. Need and conspiracy confront, in this subtext and in reading, the falsely judicious order for which need is irrelevant, society incompetent, and "the people" immaterial.

We are, therefore, on the side of the historian who appreciates the relation of society to history, though he or she has not yet solved the problems of their conceptualization and practical realization. We have discovered "the people" as need, have understood some of our own ambivalence when confronted with need and the privilege that suppresses it, and have engaged in a labor of cooperation, limited though it might be at this point. These are sufficient since the problem is, at this moment, theoretical—no less important, certainly, for that. We have laughed at the authors of threatening letters, but with them as well; we have felt the virtues of patronage, but ended by patronizing the patrons. We have enjoyed the reversal of fortune, as well as the ambiguity of our own fortune, as an intimation of a social universe.

Thompson has extracted what appears to be a blackmail letter from its author's condition and concern, and from the confidence of class with which it must have been received, and delivered it to *us* (who lack that confidence) amidst a larger text that, by dint of all that, becomes our object, the letter merely its part. We are privileged by this presentation; it would have been melodramatic and would have suggested an interpretive possibility that could not be realized for Thompson to have presented this material in such a way that the writer of the letter, its recipient, or the readers of the newspaper, were privileged. He has made what might otherwise have come to us burdened with significance, "too little" (and thus prepared us for "too much"), an order of presentation that itself duplicates his own introduction of the letter. He has made us parties to a project rather than its victims.

On the page following the passage quoted above, he introduces the full set of his "data" in a similarly ironic tenor:

> the *London Gazette*s lie, like so many bi-weekly lobster traps, on the sea-bottom of Namier's England, catching many curious literary creatures which never, in normal circumstances, break the bland surface of the waters of eighteenth-century historiography. (p. 257)

Here, we are not only privileged above the parties to the letters and their publication, but above eighteenth-century historiography and its readers. And we know both from the content of this passage as well as its tone that that historiography errs and that its errors are both legion and ideological. Legion because the metaphor indicates a general inability to penetrate the depths of the social seas; ideological because a bland surface is one that desperately avoids the turbulence of knowledge; ideological again because it is clear that registering the curiousness of the literary creatures of the deep is a mind's way of noticing and moving on. Privilege has prepared us for metahistory and a new sense of evidence.

It remains the case, however, that the metaphor goes beyond Thompson's intention. This is indicated by the qualifications he makes on the evidentiary use of these creatures. The lobster traps do not in fact catch complete or even completable organisms, nor can we be certain of their integrity as traps.

Yet, the excess is forgivable because of the message it begins to deliver and because there are not so many ways that the message can be guaranteed reception. Something more than the errors of eighteenth-century historiography is at issue, and Thompson does not mean merely to redeem the literary creatures. He means to dispel blandness, to redeem history and historiography. And so, we sense that more is at stake when we read of "the grim and conscious humour of these letters," and ponder with Thompson the fact of the letter writers "racking their brains and embellishing their style in the hope of striking maximum terror into the minds of the great" (pp. 279–80). The serious intimations of the first phrase are somewhat dispelled by the tone of the second—"racking" and "embellishing" are too much to be anything but burlesque, and the elevation of voice that can speak "the minds of the great" is ironical, all the more so in regard to the obvious futility of the hope of actually striking maximum terror into such minds.

This momentary invocation of the pretentiousness of the aristocracy and gentry concurrent with the lower order's pretense to convey danger and the prospect of violence is, to say the least, wry, almost Augustan in what appears to be high reflection upon foibles. But there should be no doubt where Thompson's sympathies lie, as well they must if he is to invoke the historian's authentic society. So he says that "there is no doubt that some of the authors enjoyed their stylistic extravaganzas" (p. 300). It is clear that Thompson did: He gives voice to the desire that the great might have been, in fact, terrorized. At that point, he has moved beyond the discipline to the adjacent discourses that it must join—moral, political, social, domestic, etc. And, by way of figuring those connections, he makes his final statement:

> It would now seem, Richard Cobb tells us, that half the valets of pre-Revolutionary Paris, who followed the nobility servilely through the suave *salons*, were nourishing in their reveries anticipations of the guillotine falling upon the white and powered necks about them. But, if the guillotine had never been set up, the reveries of these valets would remain unknown. And historians would be able to write of the deference, or even consensus, of the *ancien regime*. The deference of eighteenth-century England may have been something like that, and these letters its reveries. (pp. 307–8)

This seems more precise and focused, less moralizing, and somehow more epistemological than Thompson's earlier self-evaluation in *The Making of the English Working Class*:

> I am seeking to rescue the poor stockinger, the Luddite cropper, the "obsolete" hand-loom weaver, the "utopian" artisan, and even the deluded follower of Joanna Southcott, from the enormous condescension of posterity. Their crafts and traditions may have been fantasies.

Their insurrectionary conspiracies may have been foolhardy. But they lived through these times of acute social disturbance, and we did not. Their aspirations were valid in terms of their own experience; and, if they were casualties of history, they remain, condemned in their own lives, as casualties. (p. 308)

Thompson sought to inculcate in his reader the sense that those stockingers, croppers, and weavers were human and lived society as we are and do. But his own passion overwhelmed the effort, and that alone was sufficient to sear the mind with "memories" of familiar oppressions, courage, and the hopes or despairs of people who, like us, had to be caught up in events whose boundaries were infinitely beyond their ken.

Here, the suppression of passion in favor of the more subtle and philosophical emotions of humor and interrogation serves to set the tone for a more radical epistemological turn; he does not merely show that the *ancien regime* lacked consensus and an internal norm of deference, but that a historian's conception of society could not conceivably allow for them.

Thompson not only has made "too much" of the letters, he has used them to remind us of everything. Lest there be some doubt that his use of them has nothing to do with inductive argument from statistically representative or typical cases, lest there be some doubt that there is deliberation behind the move from too little to too much, we can review his own characterization of the body of letters on which his essay appears, at first, to be based. He notes that the "study is based in the main upon eighteenth-century evidence" (p. 255); it deals only with letters that were published (an average of a little less than five per year between 1750 and 1811), the vast majority of which did in fact have "social" content. He admits that "an attempt has been made, sometimes on slender evidence, to break these 284 letters down into matters of 'private' or 'social' grievance" (p. 257); yet, there is no "absolute line of definition," nor is there any way of knowing how many letters were actually sent or how those published were selected for publication (p. 258).

Hence the figures give only an erratic indication as to the extent of this kind of activity. What survives in the *Gazettes* is only what is left after much else has drained through the sieve. And undoubtedly scores of threatening letters were received by persons who never bothered to inform the authorities. (p. 263)

But why "undoubtedly?" Why are these survivals of a larger population of letters rather than, as is certainly possible, all or most of what there was or no more than there had ever been.[5] There is an apparent deception in the "hence," since it suggests that, having qualified his evidence, Thompson still may use it without further argument as "best" evidence, an adequate indication of a greater phenomenon that might, but for the loss of even better evidence, eventually have been proved. This would be a lapse on Thompson's part since the qualifications and his use of the evidence amount to denying that an induction is at all possible and to admitting that any interpretation of the letters is possible if one treats them as data and waits for them to speak or if one fails to include them in a greater design.

It seems better to see his qualifications as asserting that these letters are evidence only if the design is already in place. In that case, the design could not be validated if it is a "model," by reference to "the" evidence, though its use as an account would require evidence; it could only be validated through its relation with a larger project and the adequacy of its partial realization of that project. That project's validation for the historian depends upon the conceptual, discursive, and communicative problem of reconciling "society" and "history."

Now it is certainly possible to argue that, far from making too much of too little, Thompson has just fit one small piece (the "history" of the anonymous letters) into the picture of greater struggles about which current knowledge requires just that piece, just the final indication of the existence in the oddest or most out of the way places of politics *sub rosa*. In that case, Thompson's essay is a work of detection in which the seams of the garment were tested for the missing stitch and the weakness repaired: The evidence on the history of social protest was of such high density and good structure that the knowledgeable and diligent historian could find a precise point at which the insertion of these materials would reinforce the whole.

It scarcely needs saying that the evidence on social protest lacks these qualities, and, if Thompson's earlier work is correct, must always lack them. In *The Making of the English Working Class*, he shows that it is only possible to forge an adequate conception of social protest if it is seen as part of a sub-formal, inchoate, dialectical rather than fully structured and repeatable, and essentially untranslatable (though able to be indicated) everyday life. It is not methodology that has prevented the evidentiary specification of protest. Empirical unspecifiability is of the nature of the phenomenon itself. *The Making of the English Working Class* demonstrates (by its exhaustion of material) the historiographical principle that records, documents, and preserved accounts of events can never yield the image of a society that is the overwhelmingly necessary condition of the evidentiary reputation of those materials in the first place. It also demonstrates two corollaries of this principle: (1) that an attempt to limit theory to those sorts of material necessarily distorts their historical significance in favor of contemporary images; and (2) that one must, in some sense, narrate underlife since the latter is on the order of what social scientists now call "oral culture," is itself ceaselessly interpretive of even the materials it leaves for posterity to mull over, is interactive in the antistructural way suggested by current discourse analysis and anthropology, and consists of acts so local in their intensity that it is inconceivable that they could reveal their participation in an extended design as explicitly as the empirical methodology of "historical logic" seems otherwise to require.

In fact, the very study of social protest, no matter how formalized and restricted by "hard" evidence, testifies to the validity of Thompson's historiography. One must now admit that social conflict has no phenomenal reality for the historian unless reference is made, with whatever "evidence" can serve as a point of entry, to the most minute and/or undercover infra-activities that must occur if there is to be such a thing as conflict much less "structure." It is only through this reference, and its corresponding narrative obligations, that the historian can convey the sense of society that is historical, and, in doing so, convey *the experience of Necessity beyond thematization*" that is the sense of history as societal (Jameson 1981, 102). Thompson was therefore obliged to extend the history of social protest to cover significant *sub rosa* activities of the sort presumably embodied in the fact of the anonymous letters, though such activities could not have been proved significant by any existing evidence, just as he was obliged to "extend" (formulate) the history of English society to cover social protest.

Thompson's discussion of the letters is not then merely speculative. Nor is it, strictly speaking, hermeneutical. It is constructive, an aspect of a project in which past and present must be shown as of the same order of human reality if the future is to be conceived as capable of "production" through the activities of people. It attempts to *display* the fact that any account of class interactions and political life is "complete" only when it takes account of the possibility of underground activity, inchoate resistance, and the whole panoply of minor events and unregistered acts that must be a feature of any event or outcome if history is to have occurred and to have been part of our own history—if history is to be conceivable as human action such that we too could have acted.

All of that is implicit in the very concept of social protest, not to mention politics, and hence allows us to see why an older historiography had been wholly unable to deal with anything like protest and unable to provide a nonideological history that was more than a record of events, an ordering of epochs by their dominant representatives, and a listing of possible causes of a total movement beyond cause. Thompson has given us a sense of the necessity of that intentional and interest-constituted underlife for any formulation of socio-historical significance, as we know that it is essential in any activity in which we participate for the sake of the sociality of that participation (and therefore for society).

The force of his essay is, then, decisively methodological. It urges a style of historical writing that allows for the combination of voices that is, after all, history. It distinguishes between evidence that is the occasion for a historical construction and evidence that might, on any given occasion, be taken as incorrigible (records, documents, testimony, etc). And it shows in what way "the people" must be conceptualized if "they" are to be "of" society and capable of history.

The essay displays as a whole, in its formal operations, in the rhetoric, the recognition and acknowledgment of which mark the reader as one who understands historically: (1) that any account of the history of "the people," "social structure," and "social process" must leave room for subjectively valid forces and events for which there can be no decisive evidence (and for which the nature of the forces and events precludes such immanently objectified traces); (2) that any account of regularity (of form and content) is false unless and until it includes as a constitutive feature intentionally constituted irregularity—in Thompson's case a literary underground; and (3) that historical writing cannot and must not attempt to evidence its total claim by reference merely to obvious and objectified forces and events (material from the record) despite the temptation to do so that is encouraged by the normal, and positivist, historiographical programs. In this regard, Thompson is clear:

> Hence the historian who encounters such letters as these, and then turns back to the licensed press or to the papers of the great, has a sense of double vision. On the surface all is consensus, deference, accommodation; . . . We should take neither the obeisances nor the imprecations as indications of final truth; both could flow from the same mind, as circumstance and calculation of advantage allowed. It would now seem, Richard Cobb tells us . . . (see above for the remainder of the passage; pp. 307–8)

Thompson's presentation of what "may" lie beneath the surface brings us back to history, not merely to those people whose acts are still only technically problematic. In doing so, he raises the question of what sort of surface it is whose primary constitutive features lie underneath that society which is historical, and how different from what it had been must now be the description of that "surface." The *plausibility* of his work *is* the evidence that any period must be described so as to make room for an underlife: (1) without which it could not have been comprehensible as a historical period in the first place; (2) without which it could not be part of *our* past such that our understanding of it is part of our self-understanding; and (3) therefore that our attempt to understand, our *interest* in understanding, is itself comprehensible as *of* society. What still needs to be done is to clarify what "making room" must mean for the "design" that had been forged without inductively adequate reference to the constitutive underlife. For the moment, it is clear that the anonymous letters are only a means for grasping the *significance* of the underlife on which history depends; they are not evidence in the usual sense at all.

If one had read nothing else that Thompson had written, one would see in this immensely witty and only apparently speculative exercise an attempt not simply to inform historians about facts they had momentarily overlooked but to redefine and relocate these and other materials (the major evidentiary materials, no doubt) in relation to a dialectic of "social being and social consciousness" whose recognition must remain problematic and even opaque within the discourses that still insist on the difference between history as a human accomplishment (the dynamic of society) and history as a temporally organized and causally determined array of facts. Thompson's accomplishment is to engage us in that struggle within the field. That is what will survive his "hypothesis" and "factual accounts and interpretations." It gives radical direction to what Peter Burke calls "the discovery of the people," and makes it a discovery of society *and* history.

Making too much of too little is difficult to do well, but it is necessary to the task of knowing human reality through historical study. It is a moment of a theoretical intervention, in this case in the historiography of "people's history." As such, it establishes a basis for a more general intervention of "people's history" as an entire enterprise in the still more general debate over the propriety of all sorts of concepts, theories, and practices to a historical analysis of society.

Above all, Thompson's making too much of too little reminds us that the overwhelming fact of the vital underlife, the ordinariness that makes up society, is not what is brought to mind by the usual sociological and historical renderings of the concept. "The people" is not this, that, or the other group; it is not the same as "the population"—it is precisely what "society" must signify if we are to retain it as a concept.

Ultimately, making too much of too little for the sake of being constructively skeptical about the meaning (appropriation) of "what has happened" is part of a debate of more than "theoretical" significance, one to which Thompson, among others, has mightily contributed. That is the debate over *historical agency*—not who or what is the agent of history, but whether there is to be conceivable history at all if there is society, and conceivable society if there is to be history. It is this that brings immediately into question not only the nature of history, historical research, and social science, and not only the significance of the work of the people's historians, but the organization, direction, and possible appeal of socialist scholarship and critique, and socialist movement.

3

Issues in the Historiography of Communism, Part One: Identifying the Problem

I

"History," says Fernand Braudel, "seems to me to be a dimension of social science: they are both aspects of one and the same thing" (1980, p. 69). Moreover,

> It can hardly be denied that history and sociology come together, identify with each other, and merge often enough. . . . The vocabulary is the same, or is becoming the same, because the problematic is becoming increasingly the same, under the convenient heading of the currently dominant two words *model* and *structure*. (1980, pp. 69–71)

In fact, a great deal of contemporary historical writing is fundamentally sociological. This is perhaps too explicit in George Rude's early study of *The Crowd in History*, in which the "riot" was analyzed by a standard "structural-functional" theory of "collective behavior" (1964); less so in E. P. Thompson's *The Making of the English Working Class* (1963). Thompson enriches the key sociological distinction between formal and informal principles of human association in order to make explicit the overlapping forms of rationality that account for the development of a distinct "class consciousness" among British workers at the dawn of the industrial revolution. The post-Thompson "people's historians" have begun to reckon even more broadly with societal institutions in their popular as well as elite/segregated forms and as articulations of what Talcott Parsons called "parts" of authentic "social systems" (cf. Burke 1978; Samuel 1981; Parsons 1951). And, as reluctant as many practitioners of an older type of historiography are to accept a newer type, it has become clear in the work of writers like Williams, Jones, Darnton, and Abraham that the fruitfulness of the socialization of historiography depends on coming to terms with Marxian theory, structuralism, and the semiotics of discursively realized culture (cf. Williams 1977, 1980; Jones 1971; Darnton 1985; Abraham 1981; Brown 1986).[1] Occasionally, this reluctance becomes transformed into attempts to suppress the new historiographical intention altogether. Historians no less than social scientists have always fought desperately, and occasionally unscrupulously, to protect the methodologies on which their claims of objectivity seem to depend. Even Thompson, in the formidable polemics of his critique of Althusser and the British Althusserians, shows precisely this intent (1978). It is in that regard that his discussion of what he calls "historical logic" fails to enhance our understanding of his own work, so similar as it is in many respects to the work he condemns; and it fails by the passion of its animus to contribute as one hoped it would to the rational discussion of the serious problems raised by structuralism for the human sciences (cf. Anderson 1983; Williams 1977).

What sociological thought, if not sociology, has added to historical research is considerable: substantively, the emphasis on social structure with its essential distinction of informal interactive processes and formally rationalized procedures that underlies all analyzable unities; the systematic analysis of "everyday life" with its dialectics of norm and activity, product and process, and culture and discourse; a distinction between what processes can be attributed to nation and what to society; the articulation of institutions and the proper level of their interaction; the identification of social movements in contrast to institutions and organizations; the distinction between popular life and regulated life; the articulation of time in collective projects; the relationship between processes of bureaucratic rationalization and limitations imposed by interaction, novelty, externalities that are themselves more or less structured, and power; the distinction between structures of power and authority; the relationship between organization and legitimation, a consecrated word in the field; the interpenetration of demographic status and the institutional and extra-institutional circulation of types of people; and the interconnection of expressive and instrumental social action.

Methodologically, it is clear that the use of statistics, the identification of suitable quantitative techniques for the analysis of records that had been used descriptively, the treatment of documents in ways that presuppose their imbeddedness in discursive contexts, and even the determination of interpretations of "social facts" have benefited by the association of historians with sociologists as much as other adjacent disciplines.

Thus, it is difficult and I believe not useful any longer to distinguish the two disciplines by object, method, or theory. That they remain separate departments in the university is a problem, to be sure; but that should not confuse the issues pertaining to their shared intellectual content or theoretical viability. It is precisely this state of affairs that has become unnecessarily, though not unnaturally, volatile in current debates among historians about how the history of socialism and communism should be rendered, which is the topic of this chapter.

My discussion assumes that socio-historical studies can only be understood in their own contexts, and therefore, so far as concerns their meaning and significance, by reference to the greater discourses, curricular as well as extracurricular, of which they are part. It also assumes that this relation is *constitutive* in the sense that socio-historical works draw upon a discursively realized "lexical field" that embraces but is by no means exhausted by the discipline as such, for their capacity to be relevant to our understanding of society. This is why current historiography emphasizes the rhetorical, discursive, even poetic aspects of historical texts, and why it now understands those aspects as constitutive rather than incidental, accidental, flourish, or style (in the sense of manner opposed to content).

These assumptions allow me to discuss differences expressed in current debates over the relevance of the new historiography to the history of socialism and communism as *differences in project* (and hence types of rationality) rather than technical differences or differences in ideology. In order to proceed, however, I need to discuss a preliminary implication of these assumptions—namely that it is not possible to evaluate such debates by examining specific texts apart from their contexts, including especially the contexts in which they are read and reproduced as conveyable knowledge (what Marxists and structuralists might call their "value").

There is by now an enormous literature on how historians arrange their materials according to criteria of plausibility, with particular reference to two aspects: (1) the development of the research material in regard to the debates over interpretation that are the occasions for research, and (2) the presentation of their material in a way that guarantees that what is being read exemplifies some conception of history—in other words, that what is written can be seen as being about the *possibility* of writing historiographically. The former I refer to as technical aspects, the latter to metatheoretical or discursive aspects of history writing. The latter can focus on rhetorical devices, including much of what breeds imagination in specific texts, genres, and literatures; poetics, including all the elements that give a particular work its manifest integrity; the empirically oriented constraints by which a given text or set of texts is constituted as a recognizably historical investigation of society; or the types of analogy by which historians reduce the range of plausible interpretations of given material.

The more successful of such treatments of history writing, and Hayden White's *Metahistory* (1973) is as good an early example as any, attempt to show a text or set of texts as continuations of other noncurricular discourses that embrace them and make them socially available as part of a more general, and generalizable, "social stock of knowledge." This is in sharp contrast to those studies that focus on texts separated from their extracurricular contexts and end by attributing to them and their authors intentions or projects that could not, if we consider a text a communicative device, in fact have been their reason or occasion. Thus, such a history of historical ideas might see a given text as attempting to correct an error of prior texts, rectify a problem implicit in a specific line of literature, or cover a segment of a subject matter laid down by other writers or a tradition. This decontextualization of text tends, more often than not, to promote strictly technical criticism rather than knowledge-constituting dialogue precisely because the discursive contexts, in which the critic and the historian participate independently of their discipline and that are essential to dialogue, are eliminated from consideration at the outset.

In fact, the extraction of texts from their contexts in this way tends to elide some of the essential ambiguities and inter-textual, inter-discursive features of history writing that make it debatable in the first place and hence a significant topic for critical reflection. Moreover, it tends to draw attention away from what seems so obvious a characteristic of a great deal of history writing that it *should* attract attention: its moralism, its sense of lessons that must be drawn from the study of the past if the present is to be enlightened, that is, its relevance to the self-reflection of human affairs that makes such writing so compelling.

This is important to notice because studies of history writing often attempt to attribute texts to a decisive "historical period" and to identify interests, attitudes, and projects that presumably provide their frameworks of relevance. But this is misleading unless and until the texts are "deconstructed," by which I mean situated in and made continuous with their embracing discourses (including those within which the necessity for the *textualization* of a piece of writing is taken for granted). This is, of course, what many historians do to their own objects of research; and all historians write to be read for their interpretations as well as the information they provide, thus for the relevance of their work to what else can and must be said about *society*. All historians, in other words, write for the connection of their discipline to its extradisciplinary contexts. That is the sense in which history writing is a praxis and how it is possible for such writing to be communicative. But then what is at stake in such writing may be very much like what is at stake in anyone's giving accounts about life's affairs.

In any case, it is difficult for readers to read history books as if they are nothing more than technical exercises or the intellectual products of the secret crafts of their discipline. Most interested readers read such books as part of a more general participation in the self-reflective processes of their society and therefore in the light of various "received" projects that give significance to all that they speak, hear, and read. And writers must be understood as taking that for granted as a constitutive feature of their writing. It follows that any piece of history writing must display in one way or another the ambiguities of value, norm, and project in this relationship between socialized reading and socialized writing.

It follows as well that the critical study of historical texts, including debates among historians, can take two fundamentally different paths: one that is essentially technical and/or discipline-bound, with all the problems implied by the difficulties of removing texts and disciplines from contexts, and the other that is essentially a reflection on projects, with all the problems implicit in any attempt to interpret materials both for their self-constitution and their participation in sociological contexts—including politics, discourses, and the rest. The first attempts to criticize in order to settle issues, the second to criticize in order to display the movement of thought in encounters with intellectual works, the need, as it were, to continue the dialectic of surmounting the limitations of textualization (transcending the moment of objectivity and that of theory/consciousness/subjectivity). The first intends to show the grounds of any work in "nature" (by focusing on techniques for representing what "nature" affords as grounds of knowledge); the second intends to show the grounds of any work in the expansive processes of work itself.

It should be clear that the second critical attitude is consistent with our recognition that history writing is constituted by (though not mechanically, simply, directly, wholly) the discursive contexts that give it its significance as a whole and make it possible to see in its terms and formulations the sort of greater meaning it must have if it is to do more than merely designate, if, in other words, it is to convey the significance of events much less identify them, and if it is to find its *meaning* in the circulation of signs and concepts that allows it to be *meaningful*.

For this second attitude, it is necessary to formulate projects to which specific works can be taken as rational (as expression or realization). Initially, and only then, the formulation is adequate if the interpretive *assignment* of works to projects is plausible, and if the works *appear to be included* within the project(s) and its (their) discourses. These criteria are, of course, familiar in the actual studies of most historians writing today (see Chapter Two). It is nevertheless important to recognize what this excludes: among other things attempting to show how a text or work taken by itself defines, rather than participates in, a project or projects, and treating points of criticism as no more than errors that could be corrected and still leave "the text" intact.

In practice, it is difficult to maintain the distinction between the two critical attitudes, and this becomes one basis for the critique of the critique itself. In any case, what is to be avoided as much as possible is the attribution of the project to text or author as a self-consistent intention, since it is assumed by the second attitude that the intentionality of works is to be found in the mobile and expanding contexts that include them. And, it should be remembered, if the critique of history writing is to be consistent with how historians themselves treat their material, it is necessary to insist on this assumption as a foundation for critique. It should also be kept in mind that the critical practice that I am advocating appears, despite its consistency with the practice of historical writing, to be exempt from its own assumption—it appears to be an independently motivated intervention. Perhaps it is begging this important question to state that this would have to become a problem only for the critique of the critique, as indicated above; but I believe that having stated the terms of the critical attitude it is possible to proceed on the assumption (guaranteed by the "fact" that writing is partially socialized through reading) that my own critical intervention is (will be) the object of yet another.

Thus, I can say without fear of being held to account for the apparent inconsistency, that my purpose in discussing the works mentioned below is to show how what appear to be technical errors or misjudgments of fact and inconsistencies must be seen as rational features of a project or projects, and that my criticism aims to show the incompatibility of certain projects with certain others as the foundation of debate. What is gained through this procedure is the ability to recognize that historical works are parts of greater constructions that must be made objects of orientation in their own right for what they mean to our understanding of ourselves as critical actors participating in events with an eye to the possibilities of social progress (cf. Brown 1986).

Another reason why I have chosen to deal with the sort of conflict among authors and commentators that seems to focus on "errors" and "lapses of judgment" is to establish a way out of the seemingly incurable repetitiousness of technical debate by showing that debate is itself a feature of something ongoing and therefore implicitly beyond *debate*. Thus, the received debate must be taken as part of a new topic rather than allowed to dominate all topics.

An example of the incorporation of this sort of critical reason in research itself can be found in the writings of quite a few modern historians, notably E. P. Thompson's essay on anonymous letters of abuse (1975; cf. Chapter Two). There, Thompson deals with letters sent anonymously to members of the British gentry at the end of the eighteenth century, threatening, always colorfully and often with Rabelaisian humor, to do them harm if they do not change their ways (such as paying excessively low wages). Because the letters were reprinted in newspapers of the time and their numbers are too small to constitute a sample (even if it were possible to specify a "population" for which such letters could be taken as a "sample"), and because they lack adequate evidence about their conditions of authorship and are accompanied by altogether weak evidence of context in the full sense of the term (so far as establishing intentions and reactions that could only be established at best circumstantially and not, strictly speaking, as probable in any case), discussion of Thompson's means of interpretation (necessary within narrow limits, to be sure) would generate endless and repetitious debate without useful outcome.

It is better to say that Thompson's study attempts to show that whatever the letters meant at the moment of their writing and reception (and reception by the newspapers' audiences), they need to be represented as part of a yet larger intention tied to some sort of historical dynamic, in this case the conflict of incipient classes. Thus, Thompson cannot be understood as having tried to settle the issue of what they meant to their authors, addressees, and audiences at the moments of their preparation, execution, delivery, reception, reproduction, and acknowledgment. That would be impossible in any case. Rather, he must be understood as having shown what they must have meant (what sort of authorship, addresseeship, and audience they must be taken to have constituted) if we are to represent those events as features of the "historical dimension" of human interactions on a sufficiently large scale to make what we can recognize as a historical difference within a "society." His only alternative to operating within this project would have been to eschew the letters as material for history writing—and it follows that this would have been the only option for anyone dealing with materials of similarly precarious empirical status. To try and take them into account at all can be rational only within the project of displaying how we identify the historical dimension of any "society" (and hence how we identify any ensemble, including our own, as a "society" in the first instance). Thompson has shown how we must represent events historically (and therefore how we do so whenever they occur) if we are to represent them historically at all, regardless of the inductive adequacy or inadequacy of the materials themselves.[2]

It is clear that not all studies require this sort of self-conscious reflection of historical consciousness within the material itself. Taking "facts" to speak for themselves (directly or indirectly) is part of (a moment of) what is required for self-reflection and therefore what Alan Blum and Peter McHugh call "theorizing" (1984). The issue of reflection (metatheory) does not arise of its own accord. The subjectively naive objectivist stage in the human sciences operates upon what it constitutes unreflectively as *facts in the midst of debates* that seem to require direct answer in terms of those facts. The discursive context is necessarily taken for granted. When the debates come to reiterate themselves, and their segregation from their context seems to account for what at that point may appear to be a lack of mutual understanding, the discipline is forced to confront itself and its debates from a more inclusive and self-critical point of view.

This is what structuralism and post-structuralism in the human sciences have shown to be necessary today: Historical study must now be understood as not only about something other than itself, it must also be able to recognize its own possibility in its "object" and at the same time the possibility of its own context. At this point, material taken as factual is reconstituted in terms quite different from those appropriate to establishing "models of reality" that demonstrate causal or structural contingency analogous to the analytic procedures of the "natural sciences." Instead, that material, those sources, are occasions for interpretations intended to display concepts of history in connection with other concepts thought to be essential to a plausible understanding of human society. It is at this point that discipline lines are obliterated or redrawn; and we can see this happening today in all those human sciences that have avoided being co-opted to ruling interests, the needs of administration, or the exigencies of control.

II

The first part of this chapter was written as a response to what seemed to be a certain repetitiousness and lack of connection among proponents in current debates over the historiography of writing about socialism and communism in the United States, similar in many respects to debates now raging over depictions and interpretations of the Soviet experience since the Russian Revolution. It is not only that the debates have become heated virtually beyond the endurance of reason, they have. When otherwise cautious and sensitive scholars declare that "socialism never became important in the United States because of disillusionment with the October Revolution," it is obvious that their discourse has reached a dead end. Who among us would try and answer so specific a question about so general a history in regard to any other experience? Who would defend this sort of mass psychological and simple and sovereign account of something so complex, and an *absence* at that, in regard to any other topic? Who would assume a post-historical position so definite to account for anything historical and therefore in process if anything other than these events were at stake?

Nor is this curious regression simply a result of prejudice. It is related to the prejudices that would characterize anyone who writes as a participant or ex-participant—and all of the literature on the socialist and communist experiences in the United States reflects those experiences, at least those books that have dominated the field of study until very recently. But it is neither heat nor prejudice that can explain one important aspect of the debates: the apparent intellectual incompatibility of the writings of one group of scholars with those of the other. Earlier debates over the depiction of the American Communist Party and the Left in general essentially involved claims that authors' selections of facts were biased, that their use of facts often tendentious, that their applications of standards uneven and inconsistent, and that the works themselves took incorrect or unjustifiable positions.[3] Witness Daniel Bell's characterization of the "American New Left" in his 1967 preface to his book, *Marxian Socialism in the United States*:

> What is lacking in the American New Left is any precision of analysis (therefore its reliance on such vague terms as Power Structure,

the Establishment, or simply "the system") or any discussion of political philosophy. Some of this lack derives from the emphasis on "gut feeling" and emotion (and a consequent strong anti-intellectualism); some from the inability to locate the sources of power and change in a society where three or more criteria (property, technical skill, and political mobilization) have become the bases of class and social mobility. (p. xi)

It goes without saying that this is the statement of someone whose prejudices have gotten the better of analysis and whose confidence in his own conclusions supersedes respect for dialogue, but also someone who is immersed in the kind of objectivism within which self-reflection, and therefore dialogue, is difficult if not impossible to attain—and this is the most important point about this example.

Two types of social scientist/historian, loosely divided by generation and therefore experience in relation to the events for which they hope to account, are currently engaged in a debate in which there is only an ostensible possibility of resolution. "Only ostensible" because underlying this debate over what appear to be technical issues—the sufficiency of information, whether interpretation is or is not premature to the facts, what sort of evidence should be taken as "best evidence," and so forth—is yet another encounter of discourses even less compatible than merely technical discussion can convey. To appreciate how difficult it is to see beyond the given terms of the current debate, it is worthwhile to review some of the most prominent attempts to regulate it by appealing either to a higher method or a higher morality.

Thus, Sean Wilentz writes, in response to two articles by Theodore Draper attacking the new histories of the American Communist Party:

It's sad how the history of American Communism can still provoke gang warfare in the intelligentsia. In 1985, half a century after the American CP reached its peak and more than a generation after American Communism all but died, it should be possible to approach the subject with something like detachment. Not, to be sure, dispassion, which is neither attainable nor desirable when studying Stalinism; rather, the kind of distance that informs historical passions and turns them into good history. But where the CP is concerned, memories are long, and old loyalties and grudges live on like folk traditions. (1985)

But this insufficiency of "detachment" can be and has been a claim that all sides make, and it is difficult to know precisely how to adjudicate the issue unless it involves accusing some of the parties of writing to satisfy a special interest (as one might charge scholars in Soviet Studies of writing under implicit constraints of government contract, or scholars who study the American Left of writing to satisfy organizational and institutional loyalties that interfere with their ability to argue judiciously); and even then, since all research has its connections with interest, does it follow that no research can be what Wilentz calls "good history"?

In any case, as Wilentz would have it, the debate can indeed be regulated by parties' willingness, in good faith, to put their personal experience and passions behind them for the sake of the sort of detachment that presumably allows the facts to tell their story as it happened. Not that Wilentz would care to see his comment reduced to this, but in the context it attributes to itself, "gang warfare," it is not unreasonable to see him as suggesting just this sort of easy balm for so extreme a disorder. Wilentz has not transcended the debate but only constituted his own voice within it, and to that extent he is not much different from Draper, though the latter's moralism aims at a still higher principle. For example, in his response to a series of letters criticizing the same two articles discussed by Wilentz, Draper says:

> Yet I cannot resist raising a question that has long puzzled me. Markowitz is at least as much a professional pro-Communist as I am a professional anti-Communist. Is professional pro-Communism more permissible in principle than professional anti-Communism? Is professional pro-Communism legitimate but not professional anti-Communism? (Draper, August 15, 1985)

Both writers have been provocative, though to me Draper's comment seems essentially dishonest in its systematically misleading use of terms and the fact that an inference to principle seems to have been made on the strength of that verbal trick (if you can find names for arguments that allow them to be presented as absolute positions, and if the words that name those positions insinuate a sense of their being parallel, as in "professional" and "pro" and "anti," then it is possible to demand equal justice for both duly constituted positions). But whether or not one agrees with my evaluation, it should be clear that this, like Wilentz's, attempt to transcend the debate fails because it merely perpetuates it, as any accusation must.

At any rate, Draper's commitment to the debate goes beyond his characterization of Markowitz. He has undertaken, virtually single-handedly, to defend the historical tradition of which he is an important part against what he takes to be an indefensible onslaught by new scholars whose works he believes are fundamentally inconsistent with what he and his colleagues have found beyond a shadow of a doubt to be the case of the American Left. Since I believe that the ensuing debate has become both unmanageable (and unregulatable) and destructive (consider the case of David Abraham, who was forced out of American academic life by a concentrated assault disguised as a technical criticism on his intellectual project), I want to explore the debate a bit further, apply the principles discussed in Part I of this chapter to it, and use this to try and find a position from which the debate itself can be put in a different perspective and some higher order conclusions can be drawn.

Put more simply, if it is to be possible to free the study of American socialism and communism from the ungovernable yet highly specialized polemics that surround it, the public political language (not discourse proper) that has made it impossible to be anything but utterly conclusionary and certain in one's position on such topics, defensively certain, one needs to add, in the case of scholars who are expected (and may expect themselves) to know better, and from the ideologies that have so thoroughly infected this topic that debates about it are more memorable than even the research, then it is necessary to re-examine the sorts of project—beyond what is ostensibly constituted by any particular text or author—that might underlie the various works now offered for our consideration.

In this way we will be better able to appraise the rationality of these texts and the degree to which there might be something far more fundamental at stake—call it a view of the world, of humanity, of self-understanding—than otherwise appears to be the case. If that is so, then the historiographical departure, which I believe is set in motion in the mainstream literature on the history of the Left, is of considerably greater significance to our evaluation of the human sciences and their role in the socio-political/historical life of our society; and the opposition to it represents a more general type of opposition that must be re-evaluated and given its own place in the dialectic of our own developing self-consciousness.

My procedure will be to establish a simple, but hopefully useful, typology of projects derived from the possible relationships of the events depicted in works to the socio-political circumstances of their depiction. I treat these as attitudes, or occasionally as predicaments for which certain attitudes are most appropriate and rational. I will develop the typology through an extremely general and overly simplified reflection on the history of history writing. What justifies the simplification is, I believe, the fact that the typology refers not merely to projects within the discipline but those of which historians were and are a part but which they and their discipline could and can never sufficiently make clear. On the assumption that the typology is adequate to its purpose, I will examine some of the most important historiographical principles involved in the works under consideration in order to evaluate them as features of one or another project. Finally, I will attempt to show something of the significance of mixing essentially incompatible projects disguised as technical criticism, and suggest some directions for an adequate study of socialism and communism in the United States. Some of my own project will carry over to Chapter Four.

III

Consider the plight of the historian writing about the French Revolution not two generations later. The witnesses that remained were old and becoming fewer day by day. The prospect of the death of a "last witness" is emblematic of a distinctly modern reflection on the possibility of reconstructing the past, the writing of history (Huet 1985). What could it be if it could no longer rely on the cross-examination of testimony? If the possibility of interrogating witnesses no longer exists, how can the ambiguities of their accounts be resolved? How can missing details that could only reside in individual memory be recovered? How, then, is it to be possible to account for the past with any degree of validity whatsoever when those who knew it in all its singularity and intensity are gone? What, then, is the writing of history to be if it can no longer defend itself as the summary of the "best evidence" about events?

These are problems that are extracurricular, there for all, not just the historian who has his or her own professional problems as well. Since accounts of the past had, by the early 1800s, become particularly significant for the ways in which people were beginning to know "the" present as "theirs," something on the order of a project can be attributed to the work of historians that corresponds to a similar project among all those who needed to speak to a scale, degree of prospective integration, and vast movement appropriate to the new centering of "society" by law, property, administration, and trade. How could such a society that encompassed all particular territorializing activities with the authority, or so it must have seemed, of its own imperatives beyond any individual or group claim to power be understood without being shown to be accountable to its past and therefore part of a secular development?

If this is so, then it is reasonable to suppose that questions of evidence and the relative significance of testimony must have been general to the public that knew "society." And since "The Law" was paradigmatic to the evaluation of evidence where accounts of events were at issue, it seems likely that the testimony of the eyes and ears—direct observation—would be thought far and away the "best" evidence for resolving the ambiguity inherent in events accounted for by those who did not witness them. So it was that at least some nineteenth-century historians were reluctant to relinquish the idea that it was possible to account for the past by an essentially empirical evaluation, despite the momentary discomfort caused by the loss of witnesses. Like "The Law," they operated on the assumption that beyond the "best evidence" (the examined testimony of those who were there), second and third best evidences might be accumulated that could substitute for the missing witnesses.

On the other hand, it was still possible to hope for something to replace the "direct testimony" of witnesses; so methodologically conscious historians turned to "documents" and, with the determination of the *document form*, to the development of new technologies for authenticating signatures, dating materials, and interpreting statements of intention (cf. Huet 1985). The modern question—history without witness—had not yet generated a modern answer, as historians continued to grade evidences by the standard of direct testimony. It was still necessary and possible to account for events of the past.

Nevertheless, some who began to think of history as a social science attempted to reckon with the possibility that the writing of history was only incidentally an exercise in recovering the past as such and primarily an attempt to construct conceivable pasts from agreed upon "sources"; and this entailed recognizing that these were at least constrained by and perhaps grounded in what the present (and therefore "interests") offered as models of accountability. This suggests that reflecting on the death of witnesses ultimately had to raise questions about the ways in which evidence itself was to be determined, therefore about the validity of the narrative form as well as evolutionary and causal models of social change. It also had to raise a question as to whether the "past" was something that could speak in its own right and on its own behalf or something the present constituted as part of its own field of self-reflection.

Thus, it may be said that history writing in the wake of the loss of possibility of participating in the determinative features of testimony (interrogation and dialogue) takes a distinctive, one might say modern, turn. But what of the moment before, when the witnesses were there but dying, the historian desperately aware of the fading of a last chance? And what even of the moment before that, when there was no dearth of first-hand testimony and speakers of that testimony, witnesses whose words could be subjected to the discursive rigors of interrogation?

The death of the witnesses meant that historians had to reconsider the possibility of giving accounts according to scientific legal theories of evidence; writing history while the witnesses were dying meant that accounts had, finally, to be settled; writing in the midst of discussion by those who had witnessed the event must have been something quite different still, since there would have been time for accounts to expand, differences to be resolved, and credibility to be determined. And for each of these conditions, the "historian's voice" stands for altogether different subjectivities. Each of these idealized "periods" of history writing can be thought of as realizing different interests or attitudes. Writing in the midst of a plenitude of "testimony" moves between advocating one position or another and attempting to keep the event itself alive by registering as much difference as can be found. Narrative would have, in this case, the look of what we call journalism, with its apparent momentary tolerance of fragmentary accounts ("fairness") and the summary articulation of debate ("judiciousness"). The position of the writer would most certainly be registered ironically, or even satirically, as if he or she is momentarily elevated above events now permitted to swirl beneath in their expressions of human foible. This writer will speak for a humanity taken as survivors of an order higher than events, which still have to be convincingly portrayed, but only as instances of a primitivism against which readers/survivors might be by their own elevation inoculated. Above all, this writing presupposes the continued existence of the witnesses, though not necessarily the participants for whom no voice can or even need be found.

Writing as the witnesses are dying is an altogether more desperate venture, one that sacrifices the elevated perspective of the survivor for the final, impatient and virtually administrative, settling of accounts. Final decisions need to be made about the validity of testimony, the credibility of witnesses, and the significance (or meaning) of what they claim to have observed. Accounts must be settled so that those writing in the future will have no doubt about what happened in what they *then* can take as their past, and why and about what eternal lessons need to be drawn from these finally inscribed events.[4] The aim of this attitude is to grasp something fully that presumably cannot, after the witnesses die, be grasped at all. Writing in this attitude is combative, employs the debators' wiles, and often appears more moralistic and self-righteous than its authors intend.[5] It settles for terms that resolve ambiguities in favor of a putative discursive order taken to be the moral order itself.[6] Indeed, terms, and therefore their imagery, must be taken from discourses beyond and above the witnesses' own in order to guarantee the sort of concession from general audiences that makes so otherwise particular an exercise as accounting for events socially worthwhile.

Consider what writing in this attitude has meant for conceptions of civil society, education, and useful knowledge. It allowed (allows) the declaration of a body of knowledge in history and therefore in the human sciences beyond any previous empirical certainty. It constituted (constitutes) the human sciences as such as a stipulated accumulation of knowledge from one certain grasp of a bit of the past to another. It established (establishes) those sciences as *nationalized* disciplines capable of yielding "true" histories of "true" peoples whose newly constituted "identities" would finally have been (are) inscribed, and made as ancient as they were (are) made new, in the settled account. It constitutes, in other words, precisely what our schools strive even now to take for granted, "authentic" national histories. It also means that secular education can be justified by demonstrating citizens' obligations to a shared past and its permanent aspirations regardless of whatever differences might once have been thought to have constituted events and aspirations. And it means that one can actually learn from the past because the last word was actually spoken by living witnesses and summarized by those who presumably could themselves testify that the testimony of *those* witnesses had been duly sworn, delivered, interrogated, and recorded.

Writing after the death of the witnesses is a modern (not modernist) attitude in that it reflects, *in principle*, upon its own grounds. It is not only historiographical but historiological, not only technical but methodologically self-critical, not only "empirical" but theoretical and metatheoretical. It undertakes not only to make the past accountable but also to show how the terms of that accountability are determined in the "present." It is simultaneously a writing of (and in) history and a necessarily philosophical discipline. Despite the unevenness of this development and its occasional mixing of attitudes (cf. Chapter Four), its most thorough expressions to date, among historians, are in the works of the social historians and the post-Thompson cohort of "people's historians," influenced at their most philosophical and metatheoretical by the major critical traditions of European and North American thought, particularly Marxian theory, structuralism, and discourse analysis. This is the attitude that informs the work of scholars who have raised questions about who and what are the proper objects of historical accounts, the role of ideology not to mention the poetics of discourse in those accounts, and what different models of transition, passage, coherence, difference, and the rest can mean in different discursive, political, and social structural "contexts" (cf. White 1973).

A great deal of writing about the history of communism and socialism can be understood in part by referring to these three attitudes, in particular in the ways in which the various texts resolve ambiguities whose possible resolutions are not capable, as presently formulated, of rational adjudication, at least as we usually think of it. I want to use these distinctions of attitude to explain some features of those writings that might otherwise seem peculiar and in any case are methodologically and conceptually problematic for anyone trying to read them in the general context of today's social sciences and humanities. While my concern in this chapter is the history of the American Communist movement, I will introduce the problematic from another, related, field.

An appreciation of *attitude* makes it possible to evaluate the limitations, as well as the accuracy, of Stephen Cohen's and Moshe Lewin's criticisms of Soviet studies (Cohen 1985; Lewin 1985). The errors and biases they note seem so eminently correctable that it is difficult to believe that anyone could have been so foolish as to commit them. On the other hand, if we treat them not so much as errors but as ways of doing work that are difficult to avoid when writing in a certain attitude, that may even be obligatory, they appear far more rational in their analyses and far more conscious of the theoretical needs that define that rationality. If, in other words, we ask what makes such writing necessary, we might be able to evaluate the extent to which its frame of reference overlaps our own and thereby further develop criticism to the point of self-criticism and critique. Moreover, to declare that the problems noted by Cohen and Lewin are nothing more than errors can make obscure the modern attitude in which Cohen and Lewin themselves are writing and which is now so important to us.

Let me list some of the "errors" they mention and hope by their own works to correct. Cohen lists specifically, missing or underused data, a failure to analyze and appreciate changes that were taking place in the USSR, ethnocentrism, "obsession with the Soviet 'threat,' " and use of inappropriate concepts (1987). Moshe Lewin comments, in addition, that "the study of Russian society in our century is still an underdeveloped, even barely developed field" (1985, p. 4). He criticizes its "politicized" character (p. 6), and concludes:

Their characteristic reaction: "What difference will this kind of study make?" One suspects a widespread sense that there is nothing much to be added to what is already firmly understood and can be expressed in a word or sentence. (p. 4)

It would probably be enough to say that any literature so naive must be dismissed, that it can only be taken seriously as a documentation of the Cold War and its circumstances. I believe that this is only partly correct. Soviet studies has often not been a credit to the academy and is as a field beyond reasonable determinations of validity precisely because of the involvement of so many of its scholars in affairs of state and a system of patronage that make it difficult if not impossible to evaluate the credibility of their work. From this point of view, it has conceptualized its subject matter in a way that defies reconciliation with the greater body of work in the social sciences and therefore can be said to express attitude even before topic.

But it is still the case that much of that writing, as well as writing about American Communism, when viewed other than technically, has achieved what Hayden White might call an enormous degree of "explanatory affect." It seems to register an unusual agreement among scholars to correspond with a certain common sense about communism, and uses a language—the cynically ironical language of dispositional inevitability—that fits well with the most commonplace prejudices often used to regulate ambiguities in everyday life. Let us examine these properties: agreement, correspondence with common sense (and hence discourses that operate across various domains and topics), and the use of a language and logic of disposition. Clearly, the evocation of dispositional traits is eminently suited to the settling of accounts; correspondence with the discourses of other disciplines and common affairs is essential to guarantee that accounts once settled are unlikely to be reopened; the registration of agreement among specialists provides an additional guarantee that the issue of accountability will not replace the account itself; and that the knowledge produced will be indeed *received*.

Key to this attitude of writing in order to settle accounts before the witnesses are gone, before a new generation of scholars will have to look at everything *but* testimony (and must, in principle, reject every factual claim that relies on testimony), is the use of dispositional language. It is necessary to say more precisely what this means. A disposition is an imperative tendency, normally said to be present within, and possibly as a part of, some totality (society, personality, system) and to operate upon it as a whole. Many attributions of identity through, for example, the use of labels, express this logic of disposed totality. Its use indicates a relationship between something that can be imperatively oriented (e.g., motivated) as a whole and something particular that has general effects.

While there may be many things that can be disposed in this sense, given to manifestations that emanate from dispositions, the convenient use of this logic to explain the social activities of human beings and collectivities in their "normal" operations has been sufficiently criticized that we can take it prima facie as not competent to the problem of explaining such behavior without satisfying a heavy burden of justification. Otherwise, its use must be taken on its face as misguided or possibly mischievous.[7] On the other hand, the attribution of disposition can be taken to reflect a different attitude from that which characterizes the human sciences today. Nor is it merely that such work is anachronistic; clearly many attitudes may coexist, leading to different problematics, expressions, and formulations in regard to what might otherwise appear to be the same subject matter. Nevertheless, it is possible to identify a dominant attitude in particular cases. The literature on the history of American communism is one such case.

From this, it follows that it is necessary to consider the persistence of dispositional reasoning in the human sciences as indicating that attitude of desperation in which writing is intended to settle accounts. A further qualification is necessary: One must distinguish between a given piece of writing, what might be taken as a "text," and the mix of discourses and literatures to which that piece, by its words, images, metaphors, and semblance as text, appeals, invokes, reinforces, reinstates, or in some other way acknowledges. This distinction is important if we are to account for what would otherwise be taken as exceptions or alternative programs if their situation and attitude were left out of discussion, as in the Cohen and Lewin criticisms. And even works that do offer authentic alternatives can only operate as works, contributions, recognizable texts on the topic, to the extent to which they either participate self-consciously in prevailing discourses and literatures or establish a sufficient ambiguity in their relation to them to raise the question of alternatives at all.

The evidence that allows us to identify an instance of dispositional logic of course varies; but the following must be taken prima facie: where behavior or policy, organization or process, are analyzed as stemming from a prior and unmediated determination (disposition) that, by virtue of the lack of specific mediation, must appear to supersede both responsiveness to situation and deliberation; where specific sorts of experience or prior behavior are taken as sufficient to explain and interpret something subsequent without reference either to process or mediation; where the use of a specific term or label both denotes its referent and places it in a context of analogy with other possible referents already taken to be essentially disposed rather than responsive to situation or deliberative. Examples abound: to interpret behavior as direct "expressions" of "canonical texts" or even prior statements of intention; to explain present behavior on an analogy to past; to use terms (e.g., totalitarianism, party line) to identify a phenomenon with something else about which there is some certainty of tendency or the assumption of such certainty.

These indicate, on the surface, and as a strong case, the historical limitations of such works (by indicating attitude), but they do not imply that those works are simply wrong. They are wrong or useless only from the standpoint of a position that cannot avoid the specific ambiguities those works must in their own attitude unselfconsciously resolve (without having to justify that resolution so that writing may proceed). They are only wrong, in other words, from the standpoint of a position absolutely beyond the testimony of witnesses (and therefore even the *need* to interrogate), the contemporary historiological position, a position that attempts to integrate a method of analysis independent of witnesses' testimony with a theory of the combinatory possibilities inherent in historical "data" consistent with developments in the human sciences in general, including metatheory and methodology.

_ This sort of literature, itself so unselfconsciously and therefore un-methodologically criticized (in the case of Soviet studies) by Cohen and Lewin, corresponds to the "period" (the "problematic") in which the witnesses are dying (and in which theories of evidence correspond to legal theories of "best evidence"): they are still here, at least some are and some that are have not yet been discredited (such as those who did not leave the Communist Party) or have for various reasons been rehabilitated as "reliable" witnesses (have defected, are born again, show regrets, etc.). With their deaths, their testimony vanishes, and with it vanishes the theoretical possibility of organizing historical accounts by reference to testimony (as, e.g., a chronicle or narrative of intentions rather than a structural or process analysis). With their deaths, accounts will be forever unsettled, and the principle of settling accounts will itself be lost. Once they are gone, the events, collectivities, and societies they presumably knew (in ways no contemporary historian would ever claim some person or persons could "know) will forever be objects of debate, discussion, reformulation or "revision," and shifting significance subject to fundamental contemporary concerns.

This attitude of desperation characterizes most obviously the literature on socialism and communism in U.S. history. Theodore Draper's classic *The Roots of American Communism* is exemplary. It attempts to settle accounts with the Communist movement of which he was once part. His later bitter attacks on the "post–New Left historians" are yet more transparent in this attitude, though they are burdened by either an apparent lack of knowledge of or interest in the current state of historical research that provides those historians with their methodology and empirical focus: He attributes the emphasis on non-elites and everyday life to ideological bias, political and psychological disposition, and even status greed, the latter he delicately phrases as "professional rewards,"[8] and the others to a "party line of the post–New Left historians," their desire to "keep the faith," and "the singular political symbiosis . . . between the present generation of post–New Left academics and their Communist predecessors" (1987).

The Roots of American Communism was first published in 1957, in the heat of the Cold War and tumult of McCarthyism. Draper says:

> The historical problem is not merely to establish what position the American Communists have held at any particular time but to seek

out the dynamic forces that drove them from one position to another—and back again. The Communists have held so many different and conflicting positions that at first glance the total effect may be one of incredible inconsistency and confusion. They have been so inconsistent that they have even hopelessly confused themselves. But when the reasons for the changes are looked into, when the conditions that made them necessary are analyzed, a number of basic problems and forces appear—a pattern emerges.

This pattern began to emerge at a very early stage. Once the Communist movement matured, it became the prisoner of its own development. It gradually created precedents, traditions, rituals. . . .

The deepest, the most important secrets are hidden in the formative period. (p. 4)

Historians also have some reason to give thanks that so many early American Communist leaders were expelled from the party. A few of them have been consulted personally in the preparation of this work. (p. 9)

A few critical points can be noted at the outset: (1) The privileged testimony of those who "were expelled" or even left the party is less compelling when combined with the testimony, or recollections, of those who stayed. The point is not that he has selected his witnesses according to his own judgment but that he does not seem to appreciate the problem, even within the context of the attempt to settle accounts, implicit in that selection. (2) The use of terms like "precedents," "traditions," "rituals" has the virtue of pointing to the fact that every developing movement or organization confronts its own traces. But those particular words carry the weight of things fixed beyond experience, properties of cults or sects, and while Draper, or indeed anyone else, may prefer that image, it is nevertheless not one whose validity can be taken for granted though it is certainly a convenient attribution. (3) In any case, that a movement becomes "the prisoner of its own development" is not a distinctive feature of the Communist movement unless *its* imprisonment is more than a "situation," and there is no reason presented by Draper beyond his own assertions to believe that the imprisonment of the Communist movement by "its own development" is any more than we find for any instance of social action, including the literature of which Draper's work is a part. (4) The use of the term "they" and "the Communists" and the identification of a common condition of "confusion" is tendentious even by the standards of desperation, and it is certainly one of the gains of the current round of studies to have shown differences within the movement against Draper's unsubstantiated assertions of uncommon unity. (5) Indeed, to portray shifting adaptations or shifting positions as inconsistency and confusion implies that character rather than situation is responsible. The possibility that Draper is correct cannot be absolutely dismissed, but he has given no evidence and no good reason to decide in favor of character. His own choice resolves an ambiguity that at the least needs to be made more rather than less vivid, because the discovery of variety and deliberation in such a movement may open precisely the sort of inquiry the newer historians claim must be done for history writing in general and which Draper has so completely opposed as a matter of attitude.

Taken as a whole and in the context of Draper's book, the quoted passages illustrate as well as anything the dispositional logic of writing in order to settle accounts. Here is the attempt to identify a "pattern" that repeats itself in many and sundry disguises, much as any deep disposition makes itself felt in all that follows its establishment. One wonders at Draper's capacity to have removed himself from so forceful an impulse as to be able to write objectively about it. Perhaps some of those who did not leave the movement or were not expelled also have this capacity, in which case Draper is derelict for failing to have included their "testimony." The elevation of his own voice above the impulse to which he presumably was once attached is no less a problem than the elevation of his account above the differences it hopes to settle. In both cases, we need to go back to the differences rather than avoid them as he later counsels in 1987, *even if the settling of accounts remains the primary project.*

Even the conflation of "reasons" and "conditions that made them necessary" reinforces that logic. Draper's reference to "deepest" and "most important secrets" instituted in "the formative period" is extreme even by the standards of historical interpretation prevalent in 1957. It confirms the logic of dispositional analysis in a way that registers the desperation of his prose: The text aims at finality in the context of ambiguities that must not be permitted to survive its account. Such a reference also reconfirms the elevation of the author's voice—such depth and patterning is neither visible to the observer nor evident from any facts yet put in the record, though it is not illegitimate to offer them as hypotheses. Draper's reference to such implies that he has already, problematically, settled accounts, that in fact it is his own testimony that is embodied in his book, that he is the final witness whose knowledge of the facts is a result of a "direct" experience for which reviewable evidence could not exist and is in any case simply beside the point. It is a feature of this logic that the voice that realizes it displays in that realization its own privileged access to information that he or she can choose to disclose but that no one else can fully know apart from the author's right and capacity to settle accounts.

But desperate writing needs the elevated voice, the privileged access to patterns and secrets, the resolution of ambiguity without regard for the conditions of ambiguity, and a studied indifference to reasons and causes. This is how accounts are settled, by conclusion and illustration rather than an attempt to make clear what is problematic in the events and their actors. But these are defects only for those now interested in understanding the testimony as well as the events and their actors rather than using the first to evaluate the second and third. Draper's book is, of course, a

classic in its collation of material; and it is a classic instance, in its interpretation, of its attitude. This is shown even more clearly in a representative chapter prologue:

> Another Russian specter came to haunt the American Communist
> movement as it struggled to be born.
> To their American disciples, hurriedly catching up with decades
> of Russian revolutionary history, the Bolsheviks seemed to have pre-
> pared for power by spending most of their time fighting among
> themselves or against other factions in the Russian Socialist move-
> ment. The Bolshevik-Menshevik split of 1903 had been followed by
> innumerable other splits, always justified as the way to strengthen
> the revolutionary movement by removing foreign excrescences.
> If this was the school of revolution in Russia, what self-styled
> disciple of Lenin dared say that it could be otherwise in the United
> States? (p. 164)

It is not too much to note that only an intention to settle accounts can explain such remarkable language. A movement that struggles to be born is already in the throes of its deep secrets, subject to its final pattern. "Disciples"
in this context hardly refers to *people* in the sense of actors whose ambivalence, sociality, and insecurities are constitutive features of their decisions.
"Self-styled disciples" are even less like people in this sense since they not
only follow but claim to want to follow, and make that claim only because
they have found some *one* to follow. And Draper's reduction of so complex
a relationship as existed between the USSR and the American Communist
movement to a pattern of imitation and passive acquiescence begs the very
questions of organization and deliberation that must be addressed if the relationship is to be understood at all (cf. Naison 1983; and see the run of issues of Draper's own *New Masses*, which presented the Russian emphasis
alongside virtually all the topics that have now become accepted as politically and morally significant in modern American history). Again, studies
like Paul Lyons', among others, show in the analysis of the everyday lives of
activists precisely the ambivalence and sense of problem necessary if we are
to appreciate how such a movement could have subsisted at the base even of
a party organization (1982).

Nevertheless, this critique of Draper—and it would apply as well to the
related works of Irving Howe and Lewis Coser, J. R. Starobin, and Daniel
Bell—draws its force from the perspective of the post-testimony historio-
graphical/historiological attitude. The more obvious and conceivably correctable errors and excesses aside, the inadequacies of these texts lie in
their incompatibility with modern historical practice, in the fact that their
rationality and intelligibility is a product of the sufficiency with which they
fit their material to the knowledge-constituting attitude with which they
are interdependent. Thus, it is possible to imagine accounts being settled

differently: Many other writers comprehended the same material within this attitude and came to utterly difference conclusions based on equally plausible interpretations of the same and other "facts." Within the same attitude one often reaches, as all these other authors did, the limits of adjudicability: Ultimately, debates among authors writing in the desperation of settling accounts by an appeal (explicit or implicit) to witnesses soon to be lost are endless and repetitious. It is only from a point of view that takes the debate itself as part of its object that the new sort of knowledge adequate to the present state of the human sciences can be constructed and evaluated—in, it goes without saying, the contexts of its own debates.

Thus, it would be wrong to attribute the peculiarities of these works to personal animus (cf. Wilentz 1985), though it is there, wrong even to argue that the attitude itself is no more than prejudice since the writing of history from within such an attitude is both itself historical and, one might argue, even necessary if the perspective that comprehends the debate itself is to be rational in that comprehension. Certainly we see the same attitude, at least in part, among those more sympathetic than Draper with the Communist movement: for example, in recent studies that rely on "oral history" (cf. Lyons 1982). This conjunction, of "oral" and "history," is problematic from the standpoint of current "historical logic," since it attempts to fix testimony before it is lost. In this manner of fixing testimony, one again loses the dialogic and discursive aspects so necessary for it to have been considered testimony in the first place. There are treatments of these materials as instances of discourse—as in Jean Franco's study of "The Mothers' Movement in Argentina and Chile" (1986) and Gayatri Spivak's studies of the "subaltern" (1987)—but these works do not claim to be dealing with the categories of "witness" and "testimony" in the usual sense of those terms. Sympathetic uses of "oral" materials, no less than unsympathetic accounts, attempt to create a fixed voice for every witness (and how many are necessary?) as a permanent testimony beyond the sort of doubt every voice must display if it is to be recognizable as "voice" rather than "record." The sort of "witness" whose "testimony" consists of these tapes and transcriptions is vastly different, altogether different, from one whose speech is truly discursive, modulated by intrinsic dialogue and therefore self-reflective and authentically social (and therefore authentically "speech").[9]

The problem we have in trying to fit works like Draper's into the body of literature that has grown out of the methodological and theoretical developments of these past few decades is like trying to use bricks as furniture. They attempt to organize a given sort of material for a given sort of purpose; and present purposes are and must be different in regard to the same topics and require attention to different sorts of material and a different handling of all the material. Above all, it is in their nature, from the perspective of those attempting to write history without witnesses, that they are desperate works, eager in principle to settle accounts, and hence unable to transcend themselves in the form of a self-critical methodological program (and thus unable to do the kind of theory, which is also metatheoretical, that we now require). They are, in other words, instances of received rather than chosen projects, victims of their own pasts rather than participants in their own presents (to reverse Draper's criticism of the "post–New Left historians"), bound to external discourses over which they do not attempt to exercise control and in ways that are difficult to gauge but clearly essential to appreciate if the works are to make sense beyond whatever animus they do express.

Our use of them as texts cannot depend primarily on what they say about their topic, not simply on evaluations of their "truth" or "coherence." Rather, it depends on the ways in which a more historiologically conscious attitude must define them: as documents rather than analyses. Aside from the sources they make available, we need them in order to ask how their (and such) writing became and becomes possible and even necessary. What they are as books and what their writing constitutes is not "knowledge" of their topics in the usual sense of the term so much as material for the study of how certain claims to know everything that needs to be known about socialism and communism were made plausible.

The newer literature on American communism is in principle quite different, and not simply because of the particular sympathies or the disposition of the authors, as Draper would have it, that would presuppose that the new works share Draper's project and are intended to participate in the work of settling accounts. It is different because of how it delineates its object (as social movements coterminous with other aspects of life and inherently multifarious and layered), how it selects "empirical materials" and determines their significance (including the debates of which Draper is part), how it formulates concepts and uses terminology, and how it describes events as mediated processes rather than exemplifications of dispositions for the sake of moral evaluations of the history of the Communist movement as a whole.

If this analysis of the relationship between one literature about communism and another is to be useful, it is necessary to develop further the character of the "newer" writing and to use the explication of its attitude to generate the dimensions of a project. It is not merely that we know more now than earlier writers on the American Communist movement did—we may or may not. It is that we need to cultivate an altogether different perspective in order to connect our understanding of those pasts with our understanding of the present. Our agenda is now simultaneously theoretical and methodological, and this means that concepts need to be rethought and methods made suitable to those reconceptualizations. It means, as well, that we have to find ways of transcending the debates intrinsic to settling accounts.

4
Issues in the Historiography
of Communism, Part Two:
Some Principles of Critical Analysis

I

The British historian Eric Hobsbawm has attempted to clarify the significance of a radically democratic, or Left, approach to the writing of history by distinguishing between "orthodox history" and something broader in scope and more responsive to the conflictual nature of society (1984). For want of a better word, I will refer to the latter as "critical history." By "critical" I mean immanently self-reflective and oriented in detail to the changing character of human affairs. Such an approach is, then, likely to be suspicious of received categories, any appearance of a unity that can be removed from its original context and still remain the same, and any implication of repetition in description. Toward the end of the chapter, I exaggerate differences among historians in order to emphasize some critical principles now familiar in those fields (e.g., literature, cultural studies, sociology, anthropology) in which practitioners have had to make the idea of history consistent with changes in the conception of their subject matter (see Chapter One for references and discussion). Radical history aims to repopulate society with "the people" and their activities and to show how popular life articulates the apparently unified formations and determining processes taken by orthodoxy to be the substance of legitimate historiographical concern (cf. Samuel 1981).

Briefly, "orthodox history" means, according to Hobsbawm, "the great actions, the great public actions," including especially such events and affairs as "battles, treaties, cabinets, and so on" (1984, p. 41). This is unquestionably a gross simplification, but it is a useful characterization for gaining insight into some problems posed for the disciplines of researching and writing history by the study of Left social movements and their formal associations: because it is in regard to this topic, with the remarkable heat that it generates and its special relevance to us, that the adequacy of historical orthodoxy is most sorely put to test.

Two of these problems are particularly important. First, how does the study of the Left fit the more general socio-historical interest in understanding complex societies? Second, what historiographical problems are singularly brought to mind in the debates over the conduct of research on this topic? Specifically, what do these debates and the works to which they refer teach us about the difficulties of determining what can be taken for "data" and "evidence," and in deciding how those should be treated in order to produce the "explanatory affect" required of historical knowledge? And in what terms and from what perspectives—conceptual and practical—is it possible to evaluate materials that must be seen at the outset as inherently ambiguous residues of the events of which they are presumably evidence? For, until recently, most work on the history of the Left has exemplified "orthodox history" in its extreme and thus can be held to whatever criticisms have become possible by virtue of newer works based on new principles of research and interpretation.

As things stand, there seem to have been two empirical strategies employed by students of the history of the Left, each with its own rules for selecting, combining, and even interpreting information, and each, and this is less obvious but nevertheless fundamental to the reasonableness of the procedures, with its own ontological frame of reference. The results are different understandings of what is objective, capable of cohering and of generating agency, structure, process, and development, different ideas about what comprises a "society" and a "population," and, indeed, any ensemble of social activities, and therefore different ways of reflecting upon the task of the historian and the nature and significance of "historical knowledge."[1]

The first strategy is essentially Hobsbawm's "orthodox history," with its assumptions about the irreducible objectivity of institutions, the virtually exclusive role of elites in the deliberative process of society and its ensembles, the importance to the historical narrative of univocal decisions and the perceptions on which they are presumed to be based, the objectivity of societal continuity, its natural *durée* guaranteed by the identification of societies with nations, and the legitimacy of evaluating evidence by reference to the standard of direct observation and the testimony of witnesses.

The reduction of "society" to "nation" in the sense implicit in the idea of the nation-state (of a social to a juridical entity) cannot be justified as an approximation of the type of integrity implicit in the concept of society. In fact, it does a special mischief since it entails reducing societal action and its products to the activities of a relatively few agents able to compose a unity of decision, and a corresponding tendency to attribute historical significance only to events of great scale and prominence, but, paradoxically, to see them as if they were small, analogous to a family, a group, or a firm. This is encouraged by a bias toward taking biographical narrative as a standard for research, but it applies at least to some extent to most orthodox historical studies.

This reduction sees the unities in and of events as products of special elites capable of reflecting upon their joint activities, as if in soliloquy, and providing the continuity of consciousness commensurate with the assumed continuity of action and manageability of conditions: as if one were to treat a complex economy on the model of a small, family-run shop or as a network of barter. This is clearly a stereotype or idealization, in keeping with Hobsbawm's intention to simplify in order to explore the difference between two approaches to history. It elides the complexity of orthodox historical research, but it has a kernel of truth adequate to understanding the general "explanatory affect" of such works and the image they ultimately establish as their parahistorical conclusion. The stereotype is most accurate when dealing with historical studies of the Left because of the special circumstances of its being selected as a topic and because of its grounding in debates beyond the discipline over the same issues that form the topics of those studies.

When the Left is studied from the first point of view, using the assumptions, inclinations, and strategies of orthodox history, the result is a study of policies, leadership, rational organization, debates, and canonical texts, in other words products of unformulated productive processes; and interpretation not only seems to be aimed at settling accounts, as if the writer is trying to adjudicate the testimony of immediate witnesses on the strength of a privileged insight, but, consistent with that aim, involves the attribution of dispositions to actors then seen as epiphenomena of their groups and ideologies. This resolves diversity in a set of related tendencies and begs altogether the question of deliberation. This is what Theodore Draper has done in his own books (1957, 1960) and defended in the debates recounted in Chapter Three.

Later followers of Draper, notably Harvey Klehr, have departed significantly from his procedures, and even from some of his interpretations, but have nevertheless remained within the mechanistic framework of elites and fixed dispositions, though with appropriate qualifications. The result has been an elaborately simplified idealization of Left history that lends itself more to moral evaluation than to an appraisal of its significance to the history of society and our understanding of socio-political change, regardless of the amount of information uncovered or the complexity of the analysis. The one-sidedness of this work's strategy reduces the value of both its treatment of data and its conclusions, though certainly not its enormous accomplishment of accumulating usable material; and it leaves one, after all the reading is done, with a sense of events out of the space and time of conceivable society, an independent and therefore curious history outside of history itself and outside of the society that is the object of all historical research.

The second empirical strategy, what I am calling "critical," has been informed by recent studies of "the people" and "popular life" in historical societies and by research on social movements and collective behavior. Its emphasis is on essentially extra-institutional forces and processes (cf. Samuel 1981). Both strategies, the orthodox and the critical, deal with each other's theoretically primary empirical material in one way or another: in the one case instituted arrangements and elites, and in the other the situated movements of populations. They differ in their points of departure and, consequently, in the kinds of conclusion they substantiate. Orthodox histories of the Left have emphasized the tendencies or dispositions that cause people to do what they do, and thus have substantiated an image of the Left that is mechanistic and the design of appetite rather than one of conviction and responsiveness to situations.

The critical histories deal from the outset with the volatile relations of unity and diversity within an ambiguously historicizing situation or conjuncture. The orthodox picture is one of a homogenous political formation whose direction, and relative success or failure, depends upon an initial state of being. The critical picture is one of deliberation among diverse agents vulnerable to the interactions implicit in their diversity and sensitive to the vicissitudes of situation. It is predicated upon beginning with social movement as a process bearing no inherent unity at the moment of its appearance; and it introduces leadership, parties, and other unifying projects only at the point at which context and mobility are established. The orthodox strategy treats the Left as something inserted into otherwise self-sufficient situations, while the critical strategy treats it as a feature of situations that are themselves anything but self-sufficient.[2]

Each position has to resolve ambiguities and deal with uncertainties too great to allow for an uncontroversial approximation of a final or settled account of events. Hayden White has argued persuasively that the "explanatory affect" attached to successful history writing is a result of the use of literary devices coterminous with other apparently settled discourses, and only secondarily related to "scientific" criteria of accuracy, comprehensiveness, and corroboration (1977). This is not because of an inherently ideological foundation that makes it possible to receive some historical accounts and not others, but because of the singular character of historical uncertainty, the immensity of the spaces inevitable in information about matters of action, collective will, self-regard, sociality, and the rest, and the fact that socio-historical discourse operates at a scale that necessarily elides the qualitative complexities of the matters subsumed by that scale.[3] The latter is what historical knowledge has in common with ideological language—it often employs concepts at a scale too great to complete accounts of the motions at that level that are taken as events, actions, and arrangements. It is not that this is its flaw; on the contrary, this is its peculiar fascination. But it is the most important reason why we can only think of historical knowledge as constructed artfully from indeterminate materials minimally constrained by their own character.

We notice these aspects of history writing most clearly when the subject matter is obviously controversial. But any historical account must provide evidence of them since plausibility depends upon an appeal to an unresolved and perhaps irresolvable mix of validating discourses—moral, political, experiential, etc. This is why it is legitimate, and necessary, to examine historical texts for the adequacy of their conceptualizations to the requirements of that appeal.

Not that what can be said about human affairs at any particular time has no independent validity beyond its apparent consistency (beyond the fact that certain discourses are treated as settled for certain purposes, as in moral discussions that presume upon economic, political, and even historical discourses as though each is settled and can be taken for granted); but it seems beyond question that dialogue, and hence social science as a critical discipline, depends upon a willingness to consider human affairs as shared and shareable topics.

This is what makes social science texts, including historical ones, different from sacred texts. The latter establish only the particularity of the collectivities for which they purport to speak. The validity of the former requires a discursive realization (a socialization) that must be, in principle, unlimited and therefore continuous and at least putatively universalistic. The essential insufficiency of the facts and the inherent ambiguities and uncertainties in the historical enterprise, so far as it is concerned with accounting for human affairs at the level of "society," are only part of this problematic; another part is the intrinsic connection between what can be called historical knowledge and those processes of reflection that are essential to anything considered from the standpoint of its historical dimension, including the writing of history itself.

These considerations apply most obviously to controversial matters like histories of the Left, and so it is appropriate to consider what universes of discourse are implicit in each of the two strategies, particularly governing their ways of resolving doubt and uncertainty. Orthodox historical accounts must deal with the fact that the course of realizing tendencies is, on its face regardless of the amount of evidence adduced, uneven, and the steadiness and identity of established formations are insufficient to leave any account of them beyond fundamental challenge. The use of dispositions both resolves doubt in favor of tendencies and established formations and provides an adequate foundation for selecting corroborating information—as when one assumes a leader's tendency to carry out the dictates of a position beyond examination (dogmatism) and substantiates the assumption by showing how past associations of the leader are consistent with it (cf., e.g., Starobin's discussion of Earl Browder's decisions over the reorganization of the American Communist Party in 1944, in connection with Soviet policy and the role of communiqués from Dimitrov and Duclos [Starobin 1972, pp. 73–75]).

The explanation of events in terms of fixed dispositions of their actors reduces uncertainty in favor of a theory of Left history in which anything associated with the CPUSA appears to be the direct and exclusive expression of leadership. Agency, in turn, is reduced to a rationalistic model of decision qualified by personality (dispositions evidenced by circumstance) and the demands (treated as cues arousing the appropriate dispositions) of situations. The further accumulation of information is, then, subject to this theory as a set of selection rules further confirming the original explanation and its metatheory. The accumulation itself provides, as a feature of its own explanatory affect, a sense of a more qualitatively complex and comprehensive, as well as conclusive, historical ordering of events than is apparent in the actual model employed by the historian and therefore the universe of discourse to which that model appeals.

The moralism inherent in the model and its universe of discursive validation is particularistic and hostile to the principle of dialogue precisely in the absoluteness of the boundary it establishes between those who must judge with the historian and those who are judged (and on that same side those who fail or refuse to participate in that final judgment). This is how orthodox historical texts finally enter the lists of the sacred against the profane, by appealing to a universe of discourse that is inherently inexpansive and ultimately hostile to dialogue, absolutist in this sense of the term. Thus, Draper concludes in the last passage of *The Roots of American Communism*,

> This book has tried to reconstruct the birth and early childhood of the American Communist movement. It was a difficult birth and an unhappy childhood. Like most people with unpleasant memories, the older Communists would rather forget them; they prefer to give the impression that the real history of the movement started much later. But something crucially important did happen to this movement in its infancy. It was transformed from a new expression of American radicalism to the American appendage of a Russian revolutionary power. Nothing else so important ever happened to it again. (1957, p. 395)

And Klehr begins his summary chapter, "The Party's Over," with the following assessment, consistent with its orthodoxy of account though less so with the more elaborate historiography of its research:

> Sooner or later, Communist parties begin to repeat themselves. The rhetoric and tactics of an earlier era reappear, and Party lines are far less interesting the second time around. (1984, p. 410)

The ambiguities and uncertainties present to the second strategy are not simply those posed by missing or unsubstantiated information; that strategy is also constrained by the obligation to extend and intensify the "data base." But in this case, the obligation is to provide material against which an increasingly rich sense of the ambiguities and uncertainties of historical experience (including the writing of history) and a yet more self-reflective theorizing become available as features of the progressive socialization (universalization) of critical history. The ambiguities and uncertainties are features of what critical history takes as its primary data, since only then can it establish the relevance of the concept of human social action, and that of society, appropriate to its subject matter, to its own activity as well; that level of identification is minimally required if the writing of history is to be "about" human action and society. Such "data" alone are capable of establishing the deliberative processes, self-reflection, regressions, and learning that are common to experience and writing and hence constitute the decisive bond between historiography and its subject matter (see Chapter Five). This metatheoretical observation means that historical accounts are necessarily sociological, though only if it is agreed that all adequate sociological accounts display the historicality of their own subject matter. The connection between history and sociology will become clearer in the following analysis (see also Chapter One).[4]

I will discuss the dialectical aspect of critical history briefly in regard to an essential problem of critical analysis, one that is inherent in both what is taken to be "information" and the concepts that, for the moment, make information historiologically and sociologically significant. It has to do with the relationship between the "formal" and "informal" aspects of social organization as a fundamental formative and self-transformative tension, essential to all accomplishments of human ensembles. The special relevance of this relationship to the critical historical project lies in the form implicit in the distinction itself—that it constitutes a *contradiction* in the sense of mutually incompatible activities mediated as a relationship, nevertheless, by what must be identified as factors of situation. This is how I interpret Marx's account of the contradiction of socialized production and universal exchange (his most general expression of the relationship between labor and capital), and Freud's account of the psyche in terms of diffuse, irrepressible movement (energy) and specifically suppressive control. Both are, from this point of view, examples of critical historiography.

The contradictory and history-constituting character of the relationship between formal and informal aspects of organization, and its implications for the critical project, can be appreciated in its application to the sociology of organizations and its possible extension to other ensembles. The main point is that such unifying formations cannot be understood as merely resolving momentary differences of interest or perception, but must be seen as increasingly complex sites of certain irresolvable tensions responsible for whatever appears to be their identity (of form or project) and course of self-transformation in regard to their historical and historicizing situation. The alternative, characteristic of orthodoxy, is to see human ensembles mechanistically and as passing through rather than constituting historical time.

II

Perhaps the turning point in the modern literature on formal organizations is James March and Herbert Simon's *Organizations*, published in 1958.[5] Its importance was guaranteed by the elegance of its formulation and by its use of an idealization of decision-making derived from "administrative science," in particular the "theory" of the business firm. Both aspects were encouraging to sociologists who were eager to bring rigor and applicability to their field consistent with the growing technocratic entailments of the American hegemonistic project called "the Cold War" (see Lazarsfeld et al., 1967, for the most complete summary available of the influence of that interest on the discipline from the point of view of its proponents). Both were consistent with the single most compelling feature of "structural functionalism," the prevailing frame of reference in sociology at that point, namely the emphasis on the incessant movement of social formations toward the increasing "rationalization" of increasingly multifarious (what was called "complex") organization through the elevation of "exchange" to the theoretical position of a concept essential to identifying "social action."

Subsequent research, drawing on earlier traditions, in particular those that emphasized "human relations" in industry, explicated the March-Simon model of "rational" problem-solving in terms of its possible application to all organizations, not just firms, for which could be claimed a superintending task, goal, or instrumental project. The result was a more critical and historical picture of such organizations than had originally been intended. The following summarizes this literature in order to clarify the theoretically historical character of the relationship between "formal" and "informal" aspects of organization. It will provide, as the last section of this chapter attempts to show, one basis for distinguishing a critical historiography of the Left from orthodox historiography.

The model was deployed as a theory of oriented or focused ensembles. As such, it implied that any such an ensemble survives only to the extent that it solves two fundamental problems—*given its integrity or "identity" as an organization*. First, it must provide arrangements among types of participants, including a clear chain of command and active channels of communication, that are capable of being modified by whether or not they are efficient and effective for the attainment of crucial organizational goals. Second, these arrangements must facilitate a specific type of deliberation— task-oriented, mindful of technical to the relative exclusion of nontechnical considerations, rigorously oriented to instrumental satisfactions rather than concerns over issues of substantive value. But, and it is an unstated assumption, this type of deliberation is uniquely competent to address only those problems that arise in an environment of competition already rationalized by institutions that promote the universal comparability (exchangeability) among things, people, deeds, and affairs (such as "the price-making money market," and the credential-making system of grades and licenses).

These two, the mechanism (the formal arrangement) and the operation (experiment, calculation, and evaluation), constituted the primary constituents of the model and provided several important insights into the operations of "real" organizations, seen exclusively from the standpoint of the instrumentally rationalizing project.

For one, it was possible to identify sources of interference with the "structure" and "course" of rational action, since everything excluded by the model fell within the category of nonrational, and thus virtually obstructive, activity. This had obvious implications for the selection and training of personnel, the development of sanctions for encouraging "performance," the insulation of specialties, and the hierarchization of coordinative operations. Theoretically, it substantiated a "deep" opposition of rational to nonrational or irrational factors that would have to systematically be taken into account by research on any economic, social, or political process. That is, both factors would be *necessary* for any adequate account of events. Historically, it meant that one could identify processes of secularization explicitly with the kind of rationality (and rationalization) presented by the model, further justifying the sort of "cultural lag" hypothesis implicit in the standard distinction between the modern and the traditional.

Not that March and Simon had established this identification; only that it was necessary for any but the most restrictive empirical interpretation of their model. Their work was only the most visible of what was, by the early 1960s, the dominant sociological frame of reference—one in which instrumentally rationalizing patterns were articulated on other patterns taken as qualifications of rational action, substantiating in turn a technocratic notion of a "social system" that moves between unattainable equilibrium projects and insupportable conditions of disequilibrium among externally related juxtaposed patterns (e.g., culture and polity; cf. Smelser 1963).

On the other hand, and despite the fact that the model provides interpretations of a variety of phenomena—social movements, business firms, voluntary associations, manufacturing concerns, and political interactions—its limitations make it unsuitable for the critical historical project. Further explication is necessary if it is to be possible to confront those limitations for the sake of such a project.

Particularly troubling were:

1. *The fact that the model seemed to imply that ordinary activity outside of "existing" organizations of its type was by definition nonrational and therefore virtually disruptive of a certain kind of*

progress. This implication made it impossible to reconcile the mechanism by which the model worked with the fact that all of its operations had in one way or another to depend on the interactions of individual actors or groups of actors who were (a) limited in their access to information of sufficiently good quality to reduce those ambiguities of situations that are likely to stimulate nontechnical, hence nonrational, social activity, and (b) incapable by the nature of their positions and specialties of evaluating the superintending goals (and transformations thereof) to which the requisite degree of task involvement required them to submit (see Blum and McHugh, 1984, and Blum, Brown, Dallmayr, Roche, and Wolff, 1987, for discussions of the impossibility of "social action" on this condition).

2. *The assumption that the environment is itself essentially rationalized.* While this was one condition of the model's coherence and interpretation—that the environment lends itself thoroughly to "rational" problem-solving (and the establishment of its appropriate mechanisms)—it found no basis in existing historical or sociological accounts, and indeed was not consistent with those accounts. The result was that the key question of how organizations are articulated by and in environments was begged; and, with that, one was again confronted with questions about the fundamental concepts of the model itself.

3. *The fact that organizational change, other than technical modification, could only occur by virtue of "problems" introduced to the technical apparatus from outside the model.* This rejection of a dynamic, historical perspective made it difficult to reconcile the model with what else was thought to be conceivable in human affairs, specifically with even a minimalist account of "social action." The idealization of decision made it impossible to take account of the deliberative process itself, much as technical accounts of profitable investment beg the problems posed by production for exchange.

4. *The elimination of any concept of sociality, and with it the possibility of a dialectical, self-transforming, interaction of unifying and differentiating tendencies.* This is inconsistent with the claim that the model provides access to what is normally meant by social organization, and marks the limits of the model's application to the rare and theoretically uninteresting situations in which planning is univocal and can presume upon an established, compliant, and unself-critical corps of executants. Attempts to generalize beyond that, as in rationalistic theories of social organization, beg the questions that provide the concept of organization in the first place.

5. *The description of operations such that the possible patterns of their implementation are complementary rather than contradictory.*

This is not just to say that the theory must refer to problems that arise in practice, contradictions presumably being of the exclusive province of the latter. It is to say that the nature of operational interdependence, the socialization of effort within and across the operations themselves, is unaccountable as a *social* composition. One result is a tendency to research the model by studying positions in isolation from one another (each held be "controlled" in relation to the other) or as analogous to a mechanical process (e.g., "role performance" or "role set"), or by focusing on elites taken to be the executive, or practical, idealization that corresponds to the theoretical idealization of the model.

Two moves were available for dealing with these limitations, among others. The first was a radical rejection of the model as inappropriate to the study of the social dimension of social organizations. This solution was adopted with considerable success by some phenomenologically oriented sociologists and social psychologists. The second attempted to explicate the model further in order to force it to confront the very nonrational activities that were presupposed within the activity of theorizing yet excluded from the model that was the result of that activity. Within that explication of the model, these presumably nonrational factors include a continuing process of value determination and a self-socializing base of participation. This base, such as it is, corresponds both to inexplicit aspects of production and decision-making and to continuing conditions of ambiguity and uncertainty that constitute a minimal specification of such a base (see Simon 1983), and a degree of historicizing tension that shows any apparent unity of decision or action to be, at best, both provisional and self-transforming (inherently ambivalent). My emphasis is on reform by critical explication because of the problematic to which this chapter is directed and because an immanent critique is more instructive than substituting one model for another. The more radical solution is explored to some extent in Chapters Two, Five, and Six.

The rational model purported to be a theory of organizations, but it now appears as an ideal corporate problem solver whose "structure" is derived solely from an already idealized "process" of problem solving. However, this can only be imagined practically and historically as a *project*, something to be realized, with all the politics this entails. Thus, when the effects of concrete interactions among participants are discussed, and with them the capacity to implement plans by the use of concrete labors already appropriated as an abstract value, the conclusion is inescapable that both sociality and the process of work are noisy factors, essentially irrational (obstructive) to the accountability, focus, and abstractive evaluation required of the ideal problem solver.

The concept of organization that emerged as an attempt to account for both the directive functions of ensembles and the sociality of their constituent actors was essentially a social machine unfortunately inhabited by people and embodied in their sociality, the ongoing, self-reflective, and contradictory relations that are implicit to actors in each moment of action as a matter of the nature (conceivability) of action itself. This solution to the apparent paradox posed by the conjunction of operations and sociality succeeded only if it eliminated the latter from theory and reformulated it as a problem of management conceived of as either "social control" or "resource mobilization."

Sociality was then seen as a kind of abject or irrepressible nature against which rational problem solving and its special corporate technocratic practical agency must impose themselves as "conditions of rational action." Thus, all that the human sciences had identified as historical and social, except for what could be simulated by a mechanical composite and its iterant processes, had to be disregarded and eventually replaced if the March-Simon type of model was to be deployed as a general theory of organizations. Moreover, it was necessary to see "real" organizations, those conceivable within comprehensive characterizations of society, as *tending* toward the rationalistic model and containing or eliminating, as a matter of adaptation, all that had to be identified as irrational.

The actual determination of goals and their implementation in the sphere of production were simply excluded from the analysis of decision-making that was taken to be the essence of what could be meant by organization (and hence, one must add, all those ensembles and processes thought to be instances of organization—societies, groups, social movements, and enterprises—now understood in terms of a task orientation in which tasks were essentially analyzable to simple complements and in any case taken for granted).

This meant (1) that task orientation itself was no more than a state of agency oriented to reduce the distance between an initiating condition (problem or need) and an ideal end state (solution or goal), and (2) that the initiating condition had to be taken for granted as fixed (and therefore knowable by rational actors as well as sociologists) rather than as the continually changing and ambiguous product of a historical process. This led researchers to advocate policies in regard to efficiency (in the use of "resources") and effectiveness (in meeting quantitative standards of valuation) that were neither adequately supported by research nor valid in terms of prevailing concepts of social action, the latter requiring a more complex view of deliberation, participation, and interaction than was possible within the framework of the rationalistic model (see Lazarsfeld et al., 1967, for examples of this sort of advocacy and its presuppositions).

Consequently, sociologists were forced to distinguish between what they called "formal" and "informal" aspects of social organization, both of which were seen as necessary even for efficient and effective problem solving. The most radical conclusion possible under the circumstances was that the relationship between the two aspects was *mediated* by the overlapping situations (environment) in which it could be identified as a relationship, and *dialectical* in the sense that each aspect could only be constituted by the other. The difficulty of further specifying these characteristics—mediation and dialectic—was due to the limitations imposed by the original definitions of "formal" and "informal." Formal organization represented the design aspect of social action and hence presupposed what needed to be included, what Talcott Parsons called a solution to "the problem of power"—that goals were unequivocal and univocal. Informal organization represented the sociality or solidarity of action without adequate theoretical regard to the fact that its interactional and productive bases were embodied in what Marx called concrete labor, the activity of implementation in contradiction with both the terms of its appropriation and the abstractive standards of its evaluation.

This had to be conceptualized as more than merely the execution of a plan; it had to be seen as a self-defining activity whose objective focus posed as much a problem of self-identification as of dealing with materials and conditions. Thus, in regard to the limitations of the rationalistic model, the relationship between formal and informal aspects of organization became a minimal characterization of what could be meant by "organization" if it was to be conceivably historical and sociological.

When the dialectic of formal and informal aspects was taken into account, it provided a critical perspective on organizational life, making it possible to discuss social change without positing either an ideal state to which organizations tended of their nature or a mechanism that elided production in favor of product. It also allowed one to study the process of collective orientation as an ongoing and highly problematic process of self-definition, orientation being intrinsic to what must now be meant by organization, rather than something extrinsic and fixed as a constant condition of implementation and evaluation. Finally, it established that the sort of rationality appropriate to social organizations was not one in which the human components, the ordinariness and polyphony of action, were irrelevant but one in which those components were both necessary and constitutive. This conclusion marks a key difference between orthodox and critical histories of the Left so far as they depend on a concept of collective action and social movement.[6]

– Two intellectual traditions were particularly relevant to the extended critique of rationalism: (1) social phenomenology, represented in the work of Alfred Schutz (1967), and (2) the neo-Marxian critique of state structures (as instances of organizations that disguise power) by C. Wright Mills, the Frankfurt School of Critical Theory, and other more political, economically inclined critics of the institutions of power and hegemony.

The first tradition, enriched in the United States by symbolic interactionism and social linguistics, found its voice in the literature on organizations in the work of Egon Bittner. Bittner argued that it was not possible to conceive *simultaneously* of rational organization (in the above sense) and the base of sociality and "participation" upon which it must depend, that those who "implement" design cannot by virtue of the subjectivity inherent in and limited by that activity *intend* that design or any approximation or component thereof (1965). And it found its program of research in the works of Erving Goffman and Harold Garfinkel. They showed that no operational position in what was reputed to be an organization can be understood independently of all the others *but that the interdependence of positions is an "ongoing accomplishment" rather than a totality in the sense of a system* (Goffman 1961; Garfinkel 1967). Garfinkel's research showed in addition that no set of technically rational procedures in a given setting can be coherent without being inconsistent with the social forms by which the setting was defined.

The upshot of all this was a more radically historical theory of organizations (crucial in the available histories of the Left) as unifying projects rather than completed or completable formations, and as historical in the sense that agency is defined in the very encounter with something momentarily beyond itself rather than as a set of dispositions that "develop" along a fixed or rational path, as in "modernization." The first means that organizational form is always contested terrain; the second, the historical dimension, means that both informal and formal aspects of organization have to be featured in every determination of a researchable unit, in other words are analytic. It is this that is relevant to understanding the historiography of critical studies of the Left. It implies that every ensemble, every instance of social organization, including social movements, must be understood in terms of both formal and informal aspects and that each must be identified in regard to the problems posed by the other such that their relationship is both intrinsic and contradictory and hence a constant occasion for movement. Above all, at no point can the aspect of socialization be eliminated, or what had appeared would no longer appear to be an ensemble (cf. Brown and Goldin 1973).

Analysis depends then upon what can be made of informal aspects of organization more than merely exchanges or celebratory manifestations of solidarity among people as members of a task-oriented group. This is where the work of Goffman and Garfinkel is crucial, in their emphasis on the productive aspects of social life (in the Marxian sense of contradictory but mutually constituting operations), and hence the vicissitudes of self-definition and collective action. Despite the fact that their work has not been explicitly associated with problems of historiography, its bearing on the historical sociology of organizations is unmistakably fundamental to our enterprise.

Briefly, Goffman and Garfinkel illustrate the ways in which social reproduction occurs in those most ordinary and extraordinary cases elided by the rationalism of modern organization theory: as "an ongoing accomplishment" directed at, but not by, unavoidable contradictions of instrumentality and communication and mediated by a similarly tense and unformable environment that nevertheless appears, always ambiguously, formed (cf. Goffman

1961, 1963; Garfinkel 1967; Brown 1986). Interaction among people in definable, mediated, apparently totalized settings appears in this analysis as a continuing process of self-redefinition by way of a politics of objective orientation (*work* within the dialectics of unity and diversity, including the appropriation and expropriation of "the value" yielded by such work).

In the course of this process, both self-definition (never univocal or resolved) and objective orientation (similarly polyglot and contradictory) are continually reconstituted in the activities of what Garfinkel calls "members to a setting," by which he seems to mean instances of collective enunciation and collective action (1967; see also Garfinkel 2002). In this, interaction—hence sociality, hence production and reproduction—continues as such only if interactants ignore the determinations of design (formal aspects), taken then as the terms by which activities show themselves to be accountable without having to be accounted for, in favor of the productive work of interaction itself. A simple, but possibly misleading way of saying this is that interaction continues in the form of what Goffman calls "an encounter" only if the parties pretend to agree on certain basic terms of interaction in order to deal with the issues at hand, and only if that pretense is such as to leave the "basic terms" subject to revision in the course of the interaction (Goffman 1963).

Thus, any account of social organization (including historical accounts of all such ensembles, social movements, parties, and the like) must now refer, in ways far more complex than envisioned and involving indeterminacies originally thought inconceivable if organizational activity was to be understood, to (1) a "*formal*" *aspect* formulated as a project, rather than a "structure," or "system," momentarily taken for granted and mediated in both respects by a divided context, and subject to constant revision in the course of the activity of the ensemble as the latter's terms of solidarity, obligation, and value; and (2) *an* "*informal*" *aspect* in which every noticeable activity must be seen as projecting its meaning to its participants ambiguously and polyphonically,[7] making the course of that activity *essentially indeterminate* both for interactants and observers.

This implies that such an activity cannot leave *traces* of itself, facts that allow for the reconstruction of the process by either an outside observer or a participant reflecting after the event. Any such attempt at reconstruction must therefore be understood as an appropriation rather than a factual account, record, or recollection. It does not follow that records, facts, and the rest are irrelevant, but only that they are material for a dialogue (an instance of interaction in the same sense as the interaction now subject to "research") among historians (and others composing the reconstructive interest), the terms of which depend upon the self-reproductive processes of a different setting with mediations that may or may not be consistent with those of the events subject to reconstruction.

What is significant about this for critical history is what it requires of an adequate historical account of societal events. Specifically, such an account (entered into dialogue) would have to refer to activities that could not be traced as such through any available evidence—not because such evidence is difficult to find, essentially perishable, etc., but because *it is the nature of the subject matter to be accounted for that it produces meanings and significances implicit in the events themselves and not separable from the course of their movement*. Such events were not and could not have been determined in a way that allows their residues to be interpreted as traces from which the events can be reconstructed, after the fact, as they occurred.

Thus, any critical sociological study or historical research must demonstrate in every ostensible unity a productive moment in relation to which that unity can be understood as a momentary compromise within an uncompletable dialectic of dispersion, reconciliation, and so on. It seems to me that this remains the single most important insight of critical sociology for historical research, though its principle appears most generally applied in literary studies. Perhaps this is one reason why such studies seem to be most immediately influential in recent treatments of historical documents as instances of informal processes and "discourse." This influence is particularly evident in the work of historians whose metahistorical richness transcends traditional disciplinary boundaries (see Chapter One).

E. P. Thompson's discussion of the "pre-political" aspects of class development in England is a preliminary version of this insight, continuous with still earlier works in the same vein and now taken virtually for granted. Thompson's study of the incipient class movement of pre-capitalist workers demonstrates the need to posit and then illustrate a volatile underlife to (and in contradiction with) any noticeable historically unifying formation *if such a formation is to be imagined and apprehended*. On the other hand, it is a requisite of any such effort and of its plausibility to readers that there be some historiographically induced sense of commonality between readers and those about whom they read, in Thompson's case artisans and workers of the late eighteenth and early nineteenth centuries (1963). Thompson establishes the possibility of this capacity for empathic understanding by his own rhetorical undercurrent of polemic against practices (e.g., child labor) thereby rendered morally analogous to practices deemed problematic in the contemporary world (1984).

Robert Darnton pursues a different strategy to the same end. He attempts to reverse his readers' attitude toward a massacre of cats by French workers during the late 1730s (1985). To disabuse readers of an empathy-defeating revulsion toward the massacre, and the possibility that the incident would overwhelm the account he wishes to make of the relations between workers and masters at that time, he places it in a context that subordinates it to other historically significant affairs, as an incident rather than a complete historical event (the working out of social antagonism in the social economy of the day), and then uses the latter as the foundation for seeing the massacre as a joke played by the workers on their masters—by this time in his text something like putting spiders in the bed of a despot:

Yet it strikes the modern reader as unfunny, if not downright repulsive. Where is the humor in a group of grown men bleating like goats and banging with their tools while an adolescent reenacts the ritual slaughter of a defenseless animal? Our own inability to get the joke is an indication of the distance that separates us from the workers of preindustrial Europe. The perception of that distance may serve as the starting point of an investigation, for anthropologists have found that the best points of entry in an attempt to penetrate an alien culture can be those where it seems to be most opaque. When you realize that you are not getting something—a joke, a proverb, a ceremony—that is particularly meaningful to the natives, you can see where to grasp a foreign system of meaning in order to unravel it. By getting the joke of the great cat massacre, it may be possible to "get" a basic ingredient of artisanal culture under the Old Regime. (pp. 77–78)

This subordination of cruelty in favor of an embarrassment of power is a classical ingredient of a type of humor that we use to appreciate our own circumstance. Its evocation by Darnton was not imposed by the material, since that was inherently ambiguous. It was required by the critical project of his historiography if readers were to disabuse themselves of an attitude of dissociation, inconsistent with the recognition of the "others" (the "natives") as like ourselves, necessary for the account to be a historical one in the sense that I have discussed in this chapter.

Darnton shows by his analysis how historians empathize with those they study such that the events of those lives can be seen as products of the type of human agency recognizable by us for whom human agency has become fundamental to the knowledge we call, at once, sociological and historical. Darnton and Thompson establish the significance of the informal in all that would otherwise appear as design, as a matter of being able to appreciate, and therefore analyzing, events as instances of historical movement. Both writers express a current of social thought that is critical of apparently fixed unities in favor of the dialectical aspect of human affairs.[8]

This, then, is one metatheoretical foundation of what I have called, following Hobsbawm, critical or extra-institutional historiography. It is necessary now to bring these observations to bear on the historiography of the Left, in particular of communism in the United States. I will present a list of propositions that I believe are necessary, though by no means sufficient, to account for this historiography. In the light of these, I will make some suggestions about what sort of "information" is needed for historical analysis, beyond that provided in most instances of "orthodox" studies of the Left. In other chapters, I explore these metatheoretical considerations through textual analyses of studies of the Left.

III

My discussion of orthodox histories is intended to highlight what I believe is added to historical study by the new historians of the Left and by recent theoretical developments in the social sciences and humanities. The difference described by Hobsgawm is exaggerated in the history of communism. This allows me to simplify the discussion in ways that would be inappropriate if another literature were at issue. Thus, my intention is programmatic rather than strictly analytical. Paradoxically, "orthodox histories" of the Left have tended to over-rationalize the organizational experience of Left political movements. This is partly a result of exaggerating their unity by systematic reference to indices of disposition revealed by selected testimony and documents. Above all, they have tended correspondingly to *underrationalize* participation and its constituent activities—taking them either as trivial, as Theodore Draper did, or as reducible to the same irrepressible tendencies (e.g., toward "Stalinism") presumably exemplified by selected elites, as Draper's original research further illustrates. In satisfying the requirements for identifying social and political movements as "organizations" (in the rationalistic and formal sense of term) and by way of that with leadership and texts, orthodoxy retains the view of rational action enunciated in earlier uncritical theories of social organization—one that we have seen is decisively ahistorical and mechanistic.

What, then, comprises the singular move in Left historiography, tentative and of mixed orientation though it remains? The first key element is *a reversal of the normal order of orthodox analysis*. The latter begins with the delineation of the unifying projects (the character of the party, etc.), with a corresponding emphasis on elites, structures, policies, and design, and uses that as a frame of reference to understand the mobilizing activities involved in "participation." Critical historiography, however, orders analysis precisely in reverse, beginning with the informal, inchoate, interactional bases of social movement that must underlie any attempt to unify people under the auspices of a definite project. This means that it situates those bases, since they can only exist in situations, within a comprehensive view of the history of society and its conjunctural features, which requires, in turn, concepts consistent with so comprehensive a view. The second key element involves *description and analysis of all ostensible unities (formations, ensembles, texts) as epiphenomena, expressions, or residues of a dialectic of formal and informal aspects of the radical project as it takes shape in regard to its conditions*. The following propositions are numbered and presented with only the briefest of commentary, on the assumption that they clarify some implications of the discussion so far and given the fact that their significance is clarified in other chapters.

1. *The history of the Left, including communism, begins as the history of a social movement, and hence with the historical conditions of social conflict evident within society, in this case the*

society indicated by *"The United States."* This situates the study amidst a set of more or less interrelated problematics and establishes it at the outset as an examination of something inherently diverse, polythematic, arrhythmic in its motions and perturbations, and governed by principles of collective behavior rather than institutions as such.

2. Consequently, *it deals with a situation, and conjuncture, conceived of as able to provide occasions for social movement—better, as unable to avoid provoking such occasions.* Because of this, critical historiography is committed to examining the sort of diversity that emerges in and is embodied by informal and undesignable interactions whose tendencies are no more than momentary and in constant flux. This implies a search for a certain type of evidence—of such interactions and movements of participation—and a willingness to place that evidence in the context of the only type of conceptualization capable of yielding an account of a social movement as such. This means that interpretation must both go beyond the "given information" and, at the same time, display the conceptualization that gives the elements interpreted their significance to a history of a social movement.

3. Thus, *the conditions taken to be such occasions are not treated as causes or as stimuli of rational problem solving in the Weberian sense employed by March and Simon, but as genuine occasions constantly being appropriated and reappropriated as conditions and constituents of the social movement in the course of its own history within the history of its society.* It follows that the identifiable forms of deliberation must be social rather than merely technical, responsive in the sense of reforming the apprehension of conditions according to the experiences involved in apprehension rather than reactive or tendentious, and innovative rather than symptomatic. Moreover, those forms of deliberation have as essential features the interaction of attempts to create design, a project or unifying formation, and the essentially subversive aspect of informal organization with its built-in ambiguities of orientation and constant and momentary reflection upon its constant and momentary motions in regard to its constant and momentary mix of problematics—a subversion that reveals the essentially indeterminate features of interaction and the essentially determining or totalizing features of the attempt to achieve the forms of unity *given the demands of diversity as such.*

The most general conditions to which the emergence of a Left in general and communism in particular must have responded, if they are to be understood in regard to the social conflicts inherent in a capitalist process of private accumulation on the scale of a society, are fairly well known: the development of private property in the means of production, the universalization of exchange, the commodification of labor in the form of "labor power," and the establishment of exploitation as the foundation of capitalist wealth. Thus, one begins with the notion of a historically volatile society, and the Left appears as part of all that expresses the contradictions of that society and its conjunctures rather than as something foreign, something engineered, or the expression of the traits of its leading figures.

4. Given this, *it is then and only then possible to ask several important questions that are preliminary to a valid account of party formations, ideology, and power struggles within the ensembles of the movement and between the movement so constituted and projects of control on the scale of society—e.g., the state.* Specifically, one is in a position to inquire as to the contours of the movement: Who were initially attracted to it, and in what forms were they aware of dominant social forces, and how were these communicated among participants and between them and their possible constituencies? What regional, political, economic, and social factors need to be taken into account? And in what sense can they be said to have been conditions of the movement and its various converging elements? What ambiguities in the situation and among interactants and participants must be imagined, with whatever evidence is available, if their activity is to be understood as social action? What facts can be identified that indicate an interaction of informal and formal aspects of organization and indicate the sort of deliberative processes inherent in that interaction under the identified conditions? What composes the diversity of the movement such that the elements of that diversity can be seen as at least positing the problem of unity in their own activity? What relationship can be established as able to pose the problem of representation and hence leadership and ideology prior to as well as during the period in which diversity is part of the "self" of the self-consciousness of the social movement? What is the history of unifying formations in regard to the relationship between the movement and its situations and in regard to the inner diversity (including that occasioned by interactions among different people in different locations under different circumstances and in regard to different interests and perceptions) of the movement and its changing character under the changing conditions that make up its continuing set of occasions? Given all that, how are the decisive features of unification (policy, procedures, ideologies, discipline) related to the indeterminate features of its informal base and with what consequences?

It should be noted in regard to this last question that merely to ask it affects one's interpretation of the vicissitudes of policy and "line" in studies of concrete parties such as the CPUSA. Rather than a result of expediencies governed by established and fixed dispositions, they must be seen as part of a process over which no full control could have been asserted even if leadership had desired it. It is at this point that it is possible to consider the "history" of specific parties, as Mark Naison has done in such detail in his account of Communists in Harlem during the depression of the 1930s (1983).

This ordering—from conditions and occasions to movement, unifying projects, parties, and the tensions implicit in the continued interaction of these "phases"—is missing altogether in Draper's studies of the Communist Party, and insufficiently represented in accounts by others of that tradition discussed in Chapters One and Three (cf. Draper 1957, 1960). When this order is respected, it is possible to come to terms with the peculiarities of party development in relation to participants, functionaries, constituencies, and opponents, and in relation to formal institutions and the state. Only then can we address politics as a feature of society and Left politics as one manifestation of it. It becomes apparent that the "prepolitical" and the political are two aspects of a single, though complex, diversified, and constantly self-reconstituting process, rather than complementary phases of a process understood rationalistically and as if only the formal aspects count. This is the condition under which the issue of power can be intelligibly discussed within the context of party formations, and questions can be asked pertaining to power struggles taken as attempts to establish form and content on what might now be considered, from the point of view of a centralizing formation, "the masses." Ideology, from this point of view, can be seen as a contested determination of policy, political action, and obligation.

The fact that historians like Naison have written in regard to these sorts of consideration is what makes their work appear to orthodox historians to endorse (or apologize for) the Communist experience, rather than to be what it is, a sociologically informed historical study of that experience. The difference between a Draper and a Naison is not between one who sees that experience negatively and one who sees it positively, as innumerable commentators have claimed, but between one who sees it ahistorically and one who sees it historically. Draper attempts to set the record straight, and Naison attempts to provide a historical account of it both as a record and as a referent. Draper's is, then, a work of advocacy intended to settle accounts (quite different from the sort of advocacy found with historians like E. P. Thompson), Naison's is responsive to the sensitive connection between the concept of society as something human beings do and the account of the social movements within which what they do has societal and historical significance for addressing questions about the history of society.

Critical histories of the Left further place into perspective the activities of propagating ideology, formulating policy, and initiating action through agitation and coordination, and the mediations of those activities including the instruments of social control and the technical aspects of negotiating difference in the context of pressures to unify (cf. Przeworski 1986). These are, of course, essential components of any account of the relative autonomy of parties and their claims to autonomy, and necessary for a dialectic of autonomy rather than the orthodox view of an independent, though externally regulated, unity present at the outset and forever after resistant to the complexities of experience inherent in the development of a social movement (see Keeran, 1980, for an account consistent with this notion of dialectic).

What sort of information must be used in such a history of the Left, including the Communist Party? It must be said in advance that the materials of orthodox historiography are not to be underestimated in their importance to the historian's enterprise, but that they need to be rethought in terms of critical principles at the moments of their identification, collation, and use. This means that the orthodox texts are themselves documents and sources, but they cannot be taken as accounts upon which to build further historical interpretation.

To some extent, Harvey Klehr has done this with Draper's materials using the same orthodox frame (Klehr 1984). But Alan Wald's study of the "anti-Stalinist" Left and the turn to the right by some of its key intellectuals is to me a more satisfying exercise in historical conceptualization, based as it is on a return to sources thought by many already to have been plumbed sufficiently for their bearing on those events (1987), and on a re-examination of their bearing on a more dialectical view of the history of this part of the Left, particularly the relationship between the ambiguities of situation and the ambivalence of response. While the following concluding discussion is intended neither to be exhaustive nor to preclude the materials favored by orthodox historians, it is intended to show what more is involved in critical historiography (see Chapter One).

Participation in social movements, in regard to their dialectic of unity and diversity, reconciliation and dispersion, involves somewhat different evidence, as well as a radical difference in its use, from that involved when participation is reduced to "membership," and hence visibly role-determined conduct within the ordering projects of an established and relatively fixed organization. For the latter, documents describing plans, formal expectations, reflections upon success and failure, and the like are of primary significance for analyzing participation as functional to the organization, as the activity of functionaries. The clarity with which this allows one to distinguish between participants and nonparticipants seems, then, to account for the origin of internal criticism and defection in terms of suddenly apparent marginalities of position or interest—as, for example, in accounts of Communist Party manipulations of certain constituencies whose participation is established *by* *those attempts to manipulate* as marginal to the organization and hence able, and motivated in one variant of this, to generate a critical scrutiny difficult for members as such. This is one tack that is taken by some orthodox criticisms of "the popular front," Communist activities in ethnic centers of large cities, and the involvement of the CPUSA in unions (see Keeran, 1980, for a critique of that application of orthodoxy).

Such criticisms presuppose (1) a sharp and easily evidenced distinction between member and nonmember constituencies, or between functionaries and those momentarily participating for reasons of agreement with stated goals or principles but not subject to party discipline as such; and (2) a notion of organization in which the boundaries are the same for all members, like juridical citizens of a state who are presumed to know and accept the law by which they are regulated.[9]

In fact, there are few unequivocal examples of such membership organizations in the sociological literature. Rather, most of what have been claimed to exemplify the model have been licensed or named collections of various groups defining participation (and "the" organization itself) in vastly different ways. One can only see this error when sufficiently elaborate conceptions of informal aspects are introduced into analysis, specifically if a collective behavior/social movements perspective is brought to bear on what would otherwise appear to be an instance of the rationalistic model of organization. Then and only then is it possible to take the problem of participation as requiring the investigation of irreducibly qualitative differences in its manifestations. The point is that one must not assume for anything momentarily labeled "an organization" that there is a corresponding statistically relevant "population" of entities called "participants." This is true whether one studies an enterprise, a religious formation, a school of thought, a party, a social movement, a "public," or even a society—witness the use of public opinion surveys that presuppose an authentic population, capable therefore of being "sampled," of members having among themselves some unstated and theoretically unstatable uniformity as a kind of nature.

It is not that the "data" from such studies are uninformative, though the key questions are begged when the collection is referred to as "a data set." It is merely that the assumptions underlying both their collection and interpretation—first as a set corresponding to a sampled population and then as a foundation for analyzing interrelationships among "variables"—have become questionable. Statistical studies of the "student Left" of the 1960s shed no clear light on the movement as such, though they continue to be useful in refuting claims about it made on the strength of similar procurements and analyses of such "data" (see the whole issue of the *Journal of Social Issues*, July 23, 1967, for an example of the critical usefulness of such studies). A number of histories of American communism describe participants essentially as members in the quasijuridical sense. Therefore, interactions between leaders and *such* members are contaminated at the outset by the assumption of a model that takes participation to be a uniformity controlled by an inorganic and non-negotiable commitment to those norms and that discipline.

The study of participation begins within the context of the problematics of social movements, including the analysis of situations as capable of providing occasions for the sort of critical activity necessary for a social movement to exist and for participation to be an issue for those moved by such occasions.

But because of the inherent ambiguities and uncertainties of such situations, the different ways in which they are articulated, and the vicissitudes inherent in any developing set of responses, the historian must search, archaeologically as it were, for residues that indicate this multifaceted, diverse, and therefore self-critical process, though they cannot be sufficient to a determination of what indeed constitutes the concrete events and terms of participation, nonparticipation, and rejection. This allows one to examine acts of leadership within the dialectic of which they must be a part if they are to be considered meaningful to participants.

For this, interviews with contemporaries can be helpful, but only because they substantiate the fact that there must have been informal processes that could have included the events referred to by the interviewee, precisely the sort of reference to "daily life" and "rank and file" activities that Draper dismissed as irrelevant in his criticisms of the "new Left" histories of communism (1987). It would be inappropriate to treat such materials as direct testimony, corroboration of other evidence taken as an approximation of direct testimony, a form of documentation itself, or as capable in any way whatsoever of providing material relevant for a final adjudication of past issues, a resolution of difference by recollection that could not conceivably have been possible in practice.

Not that adjudication of this sort is altogether illegitimate, but it cannot be part of a critical historiography since it aims to end the sort of dialogue that critical histories must both find in their objects and display in their own accounts. It would not be possible to treat interviews as evidence of the validity of an interpretation even with apparently corroborative materials, since corroboration itself assumes a degree of coherence and objectivity in the testimony that cannot itself be corroborated. This is why Darnton advocated an anthropological and ethnographic approach to understanding the significance of such data, and why interviews must be clearly limited to the tracing of incidents (dating, specific occurrences, etc.) and indicating (through incidental references, the discursive aspects of speech, etc.) the fact *of* but not the *facts* of informal aspects of the life under investigation.[10]

Some suggestive ideas about interrogating interview materials as instances of discourse rather than sources for interpretation come from "ethnomethodology" and post-structural literary analysis. The former aims to show that, and how, parties to an encounter act in ways that make the continuity of that encounter possible; the latter aims to demonstrate the inherently self-dissolving aspect of every apparent communicative unity (text, author, meaning, etc.).

In each case, the key questions are: (1) *How is the continuity of this series of utterances, gestures, references, etc., made possible within the series itself as enacted, or within the setting that features this series?* Here, analysis cannot avoid the problematics of the relationship between interlocutor and testimony, and must consider what terms or referents appear in the discourse that give the speaker a sense of its possible coherence and permission to continue speaking without having to review "the point" of the encounter. (2) *How might those communicative and self-reflective references fit a generative model of informal processes at the time at issue such that those processes could be a part of a dialectics of "formal" projects known by virtue of still other concepts and evidentiary material?*

For the first, what is being said will not be assumed to be analyzable as an integrated content but instead to be an unintegratable set of materials consisting of figures that account merely for the socially significant continuity of the discourse. Whatever structural integration appears in the light of this will appear as the momentary product of interactional work. Those figures indicate what might have been taken for granted among participants in the events described such that one can account for whatever formal project seems to remain in place as a continuing product of "an ongoing accomplishment" (cf. Garfinkel 1967; Blum and McHugh 1984; Blum, Brown, Dallmayr, Roche, and Wolff 1987).

But such interviews are rarely available since transcription is seldom adequate for this sort of investigation. In any case, they could be, at best, only one of several sorts of material useful in reconstituting informal aspects of social movement. Goffman has shown the usefulness of taking account of certain properties or furnishings of what, for theoretical reasons, could be taken as the daily life (and hence possibility of enactment) of participation (1961), as have a number of urban ethnographers (Suttles 1968; Kornblum 1974. See Brown, 1978, for a critique; and see Latour, 2005, for a detailed review of work related to these considerations). Records can be of considerable importance in establishing these features of participation. Indeed, it is by virtue of the emphasis on the informal aspects that certain materials take on the historiographical property of being documents and records. Finally, the sidelines of sociality—recreational activities, humor, scrapbooks, etc.—can be taken, subject to criticism, to indicate the "thickness" of participation necessary if people are to act in ways that seem to them spontaneous and committed and yet subject to the sort of self-critical reflection that constitutes the phenomenology of freedom within their undertakings (but cf. Note 8. See Chapter One for references in the literature of historiography).

Shifts in what appear to be policy, "line," and obligation (a consistent theme in the historiography of the Left) can now be studied as features of a dialectics of reconciliation rather than as an expression of disposition and appetite—as Draper treats changes in Communist Party policy—if informal processes are taken to constitute the deliberation involved in such "shifts." Where evidence is missing, as it always is, the process must nevertheless be reconstructed with whatever material can be taken to indicate it in order that its dialectic and self-critical aspect be preserved in the historical account.

Thus, the "problem" of missing evidence, occasionally lamented in the introductions to books on the history of communism, as if such loss and such secrecy were a singular feature of Communist movements, should not be thought of as one that could be *solved* by further disclosures—those are certainly necessary, but only as possible sources of enrichment of the account, including the increased accuracy of its own references to incidents. It can only be momentarily *resolved* by an adequate portrayal of the dialectic of reconciliation and dispersion described above. In any case, it must be treated as part of analysis itself, one that encourages a self-critical conceptualization of its object (see Thompson, 1975, for an example; and see Chapter Two, for a critical analysis of Thompson's methodology).

These considerations apply to the study of elites—the informal as well as formal aspects of their interactions and deliberations—as well as to the relationships of participation and those of social action itself. This is the historical dimension of a social movement, indeed of anything that can be thought of as an organization; it is the aspect of production in the most general sense of the term, work considered as reflexive activity under conditions of ambiguity, ambivalence, and mixed interests and ideologies.

All such studies, in this case research about the history of the Left and American communism, therefore produce accounts that are open in a number of respects, beyond their openness to new evidentiary and indicative material: They are open as to their possible ordering according to their significance to *us*, principles of selection and presentation that bear on why *we* find it necessary to conduct such research in the first place, the questions *we* feel are necessary at this time. They are open in that they resolve ambiguities against other possible resolutions and hence must account for the temptations of the latter as well as the attractions of the former—must be, in other words, self-critical in the display of their own deliberations; and they must be open in their respect for the difficulties of achieving the kind of "distance" that allows us to account for events, and attempt to transcend them, in the first place.

5
Ideology and the Metaphysics of Content

B y and large, the key question in the modern study of ideology is "What are the implications of *what* people read, hear, see, and speak for what they think and do?" The "what" that is read, heard, seen, and spoken may exist on the surface of communication—as speech or message—or in the textured and driven depths of something one now calls "discourse"; but the issue remains in either case the relation of an extra-subjective content to the control and management of receptive, vulnerable subjects.

The problem with this orientation is that it feeds upon an empiricism that constantly threatens to idealize content, control, vulnerability, and its own position. One is in danger, at all points, of having to choose between the reality of content and the reality of subject, at best treating the one not chosen as an external modifier of or influence upon the other. Yet as long as the study of ideology presumes an external relationship between control and the controlled, and correspondingly presumes that the former operates by delivering definite and exclusive contents to definite and distinct subjects, it must invoke theories exceptional to historical materialism to account for what must appear as effects: Subjects contain ideas, at once complete and vulnerable, that dispose them to action; individual consciousness is modified by information that it receives and processes, on its own account, as cognitive structure; thought occurs through the integration of sociologically typical coded materials—presentations—with the psychologically typical codal formations of the mind; the psychodynamics of total personality is the stable base for a mental superstructure of orientations, either of action or attitude; experience is the group speaking through the person.

None of these hypotheses can be defended by historical materialism. Yet all and more are presupposed in one way or another by contemporary studies of ideology and "communication." To that extent, they lend weight to a certain social psychological exceptionalism that has developed in the theoretical discussion of culture and consciousness, and a consequent loosening of ties between that discussion and the main body of Marxian theory and critical practice.[1]

That this metaphysics of content has secured itself within a theoretical tradition firmly opposed to any metaphysics is curious enough. This paradox is not fatal in and of itself; it tells the truth of its own historical experience, the confrontation of Marxism with the established academic disciplines. What is critically significant is the consolidation of this metaphysics and its elevation as meta-theory beyond the imperatives of its original historical circumstance, the concrete situation that takes it concretely into account. *There*, it served as pretheory, as an instance of practical reason within a particular politically charged setting. *Here*, it threatens to become an ideological disposition, a conceptual base for the further development of Marxism and for the proliferation of the "regional" Marxisms with which we are now so familiar—cultural, ideological, political, linguistic, etc.

In its "original" academic circumstance after the 1960s, Marxism was obliged to demonstrate that its scholarship was appropriate to academic discourse. This involved bringing Marxism itself into convenient connection with objectivities already identified within and defined by that discourse— society, the individual, conflict, status, values, institutions, organization. It also involved establishing a tradition of scholarship validated by the engagement of classics already firmly rooted in the general institutional histories of disciplines and departments. The metaphysics of content was, as we shall see, a necessary condition of that demonstration.

Marxism came to be, variously, a paradigm, a point of view, or a theory of a reality equally and equitably claimed by other such formations, with which it could therefore invoke the rights of cohabitation and dialogue; so it was that Marxism could be received by the family of disciplines as their prodigal niece, now chastened and humble, offering the small insights of her travels and the modest hypotheses of her insights. Its truth, in that circumstance, depended on the conditions of its acceptance. These were the curricular limits of what it could present as a point of view, a theory, even a paradigm. On the other hand, its capacity to remain the Marxism of historical materialism and to continue its engagement with socialism required an appropriation of objects—authentic and traditional works—beyond dispute on the Left as well as unarguably possessed of scholarly respectability within the academy. The success of this doubled membership, this coverage on all fronts, lay in its conformity to two principles: (1) that neither position disturb the classicism of the books for the other, and therefore, that the two determinations of "classic" be somehow combined; and (2) that the method of appropriation be competent to the immediate political problem, that of securing a position for an identifiable Marxism among and within the academic disciplines.

Marxism had to become both a collectible literature and a tradition of commentary. It had, in other words, to generate an essentially secondary literature. The books had to be constituted and reconstituted (academic work at its most representative) as texts, made explicit as authored things and subjected in obvious ways to abstractive transformations that would lead inevitably to argument and, with proper jurisdictional respect, application. The intensification of scholarly labor would become the means by which that capital was to expand itself, and the academy as a whole would increasingly dominate the assessment of the product's value. This drive for literacy in regard to both the sum of Marxian productions and all other institutionally related productions would finally establish the polarization of academic (what is often called "independent") Marxism and class struggle so tragically divisive of the Left today and so generative of endless acid debate. It would finally become one support for a continuing, antihistorical and self-destructive anticommunism within the Marxian Left itself.

The books had to appear internally consistent. This is an obligation of the things we call "texts." Otherwise they would be "merely discursive" or, almost as bad, in logical error. They had to be shown to be architectonically organized and connected by certain principles of affinity, isomorphism, complementarity, or inclusiveness to other texts, genres, and traditions. Above all, they had to conceal evidence of engagement, both on the side of "the" author and on the side of any conceivable audience, though they had somehow to remain "useful." Moreover, at the level of its own philosophy, that appropriation had to display itself as a serious and legitimate method of reading "primary" materials. There had then to be a certain *privilege* attached to the appropriation that could warrant the claim of serious intent, a privilege that could only be conferred by the classics themselves as established objects of scholarly work, and reinforced by the continual exhibition of their classicism.

As an object of inquiry, the classic book was both a Marxian object and an object of academic scholarship. As "found" in or for the academy, the book was already subject to being textualized, already a classic *text*. It therefore already signified the use of a methodology of containing content and an endorsement of a corresponding metaphysics. The legitimacy of the reading depended upon its conformity with that methodology and the substantialist claims of its corresponding metaphysics. This did not, however, seem to be the case for the Marxians, because the methodology and metaphysics were disguised by the practical identification of their project with the appropriation of the Marxian classics, an identification that had to lose sight of the special politics of Marxism's academic-scholarly circumstance even as it came to terms with them.

Because the privilege was grounded in an incorrigible philosophy—imposed in a situation but adopted with reason—it inevitably extended itself to all the questions that Marxism would have to frame if it was to remain both Marxian and academic, in particular the modern questions concerning ideology, consciousness, and culture. The disguise, settled by small successes, ensured that these extensions would meet little, if any, resistance, or that if they did, the opposition would fail to qualify as "intellectual." The key question about ideology was and remains, "How do messages influence thought and action without disclosing the interests that they serve?"

The problem for us is not to find the answer—that is a task without end as we now know. It is to do away with the question itself insofar as it remains tied to the original circumstance that required precisely this type of question. To dislodge this question is, first of all, to unsettle the source of its privileged status as "key," the methodology of containment and the metaphysics of content. And since the privilege and its source are bound to the reading of books and their appropriation as texts (as both an instance and an application of that metaphysics), we must begin with a discussion of reading. This return to the books is, I take it, on the order of what Althusser has called a regression to the object in the service, one must add, of the renewal of self-consciousness. It attempts to grasp what had been appropriated in such a way that the appropriation now becomes visible as a practical activity and therefore subject to renewed and critical scrutiny.

Text and Reading

To demand of anything that it be a definite content is to distinguish the thing as content from the thing as such. But, in this formula, the thing "as such" can only be the thing as object of a consciousness that cannot know content. The "as suchness" is not about a state of the being of the thing but about a particular subjectivity, namely that primitive, "natural" attitude that cannot reflect upon itself. It is the opposition of real knowing and primitive grasping that is formulated by the demand for content and the textualizing activity that makes the demand "productive." Marxism accepted this demand in its engagements with the institutions of the academy, and that acceptance has supported both the ideological disposition discussed above and conceptualizations of consciousness and ideology incompatible with a historical account of subjectivity, praxis, and the ideological disposition itself. The opposition of knowing and grasping is the reality of the demand and our problematic. This means that it can only be undermined from within. The first move, then, is to rehabilitate "grasping" by "turning the tables."

Let me approach this rehabilitation by clarifying a distinction presupposed in the first part of this chapter—between the methodic construction of "the content" of written materials, *textualization*, and the reading of those materials, a "primitive" *grasping* that takes place in an "objective" time (by which I mean the temporality of the materials themselves for the reader). The one has the aura of capital, the other of labor: One contrives while the other transforms and is thereby transformed; one is positive, the other dialectical; one denies process in favor of technique and application, the other is process and work. For the one, the materials are both an obligation of the act and an embarrassment to the product; for the other, the materials constitute a commitment that is intrinsic and immediate. The one aims at a cessation of tension, at completeness; the other aims at maintaining tension, at continuation. The one hides an essential unhappiness; the other knows, in its activity, neither pain nor pleasure.

For convenience, I will usually refer to textualization as "analysis" and to reading as "reading" thought of as a course of activity. The relationship between the two is antagonistic, on the order of a contradiction with a bias: Analysis identifies itself by its privileged and total opposition to the ostensible primitivism of reading. It approaches its materials as a puzzle, listing elements and grouping them according to the standards of its product—a definite structure the permanence of which makes it a content. The product, the permanent text, implicates a permanent and hence ideal subject whose work is technical in the sense of being governed by rules. The product as well as the work is infinitely repeatable: It can be represented, indicated, summarized, transformed, translated, recollected, used, modified, restored, and classified. As the concrete procedures of a practical moment, analysis reluctantly knows a beginning, a middle, and an end as its unavoidably human condition. As analysis, however, it is beyond time and the labor of application; its rules constitute a program rather than a map or recipe. It is as total as its product and comprehends both itself and its product spatially, in the order of simultaneous positions. *Reading*, like speaking, is, by contrast and therefore essentially, serial, following the order of experience rather than the order of program. It is historical in the dialectical sense of the term. It is what is happening rather than what has happened and might have happened differently. Reading, like speaking, is intimate with its materials: It savors and is cultivated by them. It does not release—alienate—subjectivity. If analysis requires a metaphysics of content, reading requires a phenomenology of mind.

The truth of each lies in its situation: Analysis has its situation in the legitimate struggle for academic respectability; reading has its situation in the need to confront analysis for the sake of a removal of historical materialism in the face of too academically positive a Marxism. Beyond its situation, Marxian analysis conforms, in the name of the reason of disciplines, to what it has on its own account identified as bourgeois ideological form: the twin idealizations of subject (the productive application of wealth) and object (the value that requires application) and an insistence upon a necessary contingency in their relationship. It is ironic that, at the moment when traditionally departmentalized academics find it impossible to avoid some redemption of subjectivity (through an acknowledgment of conflict in sociology; the differences between language, speech, and writing in literary theory; the significant creativity of myth in anthropology; the revolutionary moment in political science; the relative autonomy of popular life and daily experience in historiography), so many American Marxians, by the very methodic character of their scholarly work, still demand of one another an aged and infirm objectivism. This demand tends to remove them from precisely the intellectual circumstance for which Marxism seemed to have been waiting in the wings. More than this, it makes what had been a tolerable—historically accountable—practical withdrawal from the praxis of class struggle intolerable, especially since it involves, in a new situation, a retreat—often registered as a rejection of the "labor theory of value"—from the theoretical specificities of the intrinsic class locations that are the only vantage points available for the practical comprehension of capitalist development and the possibility of socialism.

The distinction between analysis and reading immediately challenges the former's metaphysics of content. It implies the possibility of restating problems and redefining concepts. It also implies a move from an objectivist criticism (a Marxism of this, that, or another topic) to a dialectics of critique, from criticism to self-criticism. In what follows, we should begin to see, at least, a basis for the redefinition of terms, and, at most, a recession from the category "ideology" of a great deal of what has for decades accumulated within its sphere of lexical convenience.

Book, Structure, Event

To draw a distinction is, subjectively, to settle an object. To make of the distinction a contradiction of the object with itself is to establish it for a dialectic of subject and object. The distinction between analysis and reading presumes upon the book, but their contradiction challenges its independence: it is material for and to two different but internally related activities. As an objectivity, the book is both structure and event, real for the contradictory figures of the analyst and the reader. This newly won volatility places that objectivity within the phenomenology of action, gives it an essentially historical significance, and provides for subjectivity a principle of and a basis for reflection. These remarks anticipate the following discussion of the reading of Marx's *Capital* (1967), much of which expands upon the preceding sections.

Anything written that has the authority and license of publication can be taken in two ways: for *what* it says about something else (as idea), and for *how* it can be read from a point of departure to a point of termination (as the realization of a subjectivity). This is not the familiar distinction between content and form, style, or method. Rather, first, there is the "objective" material (the written matter) taken as a communicative device that allows one to approach an idea. The written words are material to be structured by analysis and thereby rendered as text. Their materiality is merely the appearance of objectivity. The latter must be disclosed. Second, the material is already objective. It need not be worked upon for the sake of manifesting something of a different order of objectivity. The subject is engaged with it as the principle of both the material's *and* the subject's development. In this case the written material is not a total object known in advance, but a historical object in the process of discovering itself in a self-discovering subject. Analysis accounts for itself only before and after it has done its work. As a result, it confuses itself with its product or the idealization of its own work. Reading knows itself, through and through, to be engaged. To address the former is to interrupt; to address the latter is to intervene. Only reading can support a pedagogy that respects the subject. And only one who has read can teach.

To "read" for *what* is said, to *read falsely* for the sake of the analyst's truth, is to treat the written material as essentially unaccountable. It is to make of writing an abstraction of activity, an abstract labor confined only by the attribution of authorship (or, from a more sophisticated view, sponsorship). All that can be made accountable is the analyst's text, the product of an enforced cooperation. Successful analysis belongs to the analyst, either because the analyst alone can speak for the author (the priestly function) or because the text has been freed of its origin for the sake of the exchange-governed world of scholarly literacy. In either case, only the analyst deserves recognition and the prerogatives of ownership: only analysis can be *plagiarized*.[2]

As for *how* written material can be object to reading as an activity in its own right, we will need some way of noting the progress and inner time of the reading as the progress and inner time of its reader. This will be the task of most of the remainder of this chapter, initially as considerations on methodology. But it is worthwhile reminding ourselves at this point that Marxian theoretical literature is, as a received literature, almost exclusively analytic, especially in the United States and among many of the British philosophers who have turned their technology upon the Marxian books. Roslyn Bologh's work in "dialectical phenomenology" (1979) stands virtually alone in this country in its attempt to establish a reader's Marx, and its success depends, in no small way, upon work apparently far removed from the traditions associated with Marxian scholarship, that of Harold Garfinkel (1967), Alan Blum (1974), and Erving Goffman (1963). See also Scott McNall's collection *Theoretical Perspectives in Sociology* (1979).

From the work of Paul Sweezy to G. A. Cohen, and, most recently, David Laibman (2007) and David Harvey (2006), *Capital* has appeared as an authentic text, contained within boundaries and given the order of an idea, *a theory* in the most ordinary sense of the term. Propositions have been isolated from the "corrupting" influence of polemic, irony, style, sequence, rhythm, and method, and placed within the more elegant settings of definition, proof, and demonstration. This tradition gets to the point and then covers its tracks. The propositions, now cleansed and positioned, can be represented, taught, only as true or false, likely or unlikely, logically secure or insecure, fundamental or empirical, paradigmatic or suggestive, etc. The tragedy of this literature, now so uprooted from its original situation, and so unconscious of it, is that, in its desire to match what hostile disciplines call method, or in the mystification of that desire by its own idealization of reason, it has provided products without a hint of how that provision was accomplished as a praxis. This is the Marxism that, by itself, is so difficult to teach. It is the Marxism that is so relaxed in its institutional compartment that it tempts others to mistake its enemies, and consequently theirs, for good neighbors.

This publicly depoliticized literature is left, on the one hand, with an illusion of pedagogy, and, on the other hand, with an unrationalized nostalgia for the praxis of an idealized "experience" beyond what it admits privately and with embarrassment to be "mere intellectualism." Its journals become obsessed with the problem of using a putatively "ordinary" language to convey meanings culled from "extraordinary" texts, as even analysis scurries for cover. Teaching cannot avoid a presumption of the teacher's superiority in such a setting, both to the ignorant and to other interventions. Ultimately, it must reject all politics but a politics of the mind at the same time that it denigrates the analysis by which it knows itself as teaching. It is left with the dream of filling untutored minds, and therefore with the illusory politics of the innocent and the innocent politics of instruction.

In the face of that, the Left is as guilty as the bourgeoisie, its dream another form of control. From there to an ecstatically righteous and libertarian anticommunism is the smallest of steps. In other words, by itself, analysis lives in peril of a self-abnegating reaction that serves precisely the purposes it had begun by denying. That it has its contradictory other is its salvation from its own extremes. A textualized Marx must still be read, and this reading must still take place in the context of social movements, blocs, confrontations, and revolutions that Marxism's own presence seems so thoroughly to denounce. It is our task, then, to describe what is involved in reading.[3]

What is involved in the reader's reading? It is, first of all, a theoretical activity quite different from what analysis recognizes as theorizing. It arises, self-consciously and without extraordinary contrivance, within the often barely decipherable mediations of class struggle. Those mediations pose its occasion. Therefore, the attempt to make reading explicit in this dialogue with analysis is on the order of abstraction, no less but no more tolerably permanent than the abstraction of the interaction of worker and capitalist in volume I of *Capital* for the sake of a focus on the production of value and therefore society. Here, however, there is a privilege to be dislodged and tables to be turned.

In addition to knowing itself as mediated, reading constitutes an event rather than creates a product. The first is its modesty, the second its impulse. It finds itself, on its occasion, among indefinitely generated materials charged with signification but no *necessary* significance. These "found objects" are immediate to the subject in the special sense of having more the value of an icon than that of a concept. They are weighty but not measurable against each other. Reading moves, then, through, among, within, by, and with its objects. It is an event with the aura of a development motivated by its own contradictions and principles of progress. I will describe this movement, presently, as constituted by the motions of accumulation and investment, much as Freud described the intersection of the two processes of expression (need and control) and Marx that of the two operations of a social economy (production and circulation).

Unrepeatability and Memory

The *reader* is unimpeachably involved in a discourse that absorbs subjectivity, as work absorbs the worker in the self-transformation of material. This event, this discourse, this mutuality of subject and object, is *essentially* unrepeatable. Otherwise, involvement can be impeached, subjectivity retrieved and made a total foundation of a total object, and mutuality be replaced by the inequities of a positional order. Nor is this too much to say in any case since we are already prepared to admit, without those elaborations, that the very concept of an *event* precludes the concept of its being repeated. What is questionable here is only the depiction of *reading* as an event (rather than, e.g., a practice, a total act, behavior, or an instance of receptive cognition). If it is, then it too can be understood only in terms that show how it cannot be repeated. Moreover, for the sake of differentiating reading from analysis, unrepeatability must be displayed as a recognizable feature of a recognizable reading, and a positive feature rather than simply a lack of analytic substantiality.

Anthropological lore tells us of societies where gathering has its own integrity and is independent of distribution and consumption. While from an external point of view, gathering is a matter of economy; from the point of view of its possible integrity, it is an instance of "culture" or "society." The recognition of its possible integrity gives *us* access to gathering as something done and subsumed, spontaneously, in its event. Internally, if integrity is to be the activity's reflex, it must have the drama of a movement that cannot be repeated, something irreversible. Otherwise, it would know itself exclusively as *established* and as *a function*, as an *other*. This is why gathering has its own songs to sing and tales to tell.

Similarly, reading has its integrity and the drama of a movement. The mutual implication of subject and object, and thus the lack of an externally totalizing source of animation or control, gives it the aspect of gathering. This is also the aspect of spontaneity, humor, fluency, and mood so necessary to our belief in its possibility as our own. Insofar as it is a gathering *of*, its mutual implication of subject and object can be called "accumulation." I do not mean by this the pulling together of types or units of value, since that would detach subject and object and make of each a totality beyond its constitution. Rather, I mean to call to mind something on the order of collecting singularities in such a way that the fact that they were *found*, that their presence was surprising, is preserved. Thus, they are collected and saved *as* found rather than *as* subject to evaluation for distribution, exchange, use, or record.

The accumulation of found objects accomplishes an unordered collection of concrete, singular entities. All that these entities share is their surprise, and thus their *demonstration* of subjectivity. This means that the collection of objects embodies a mood but no principle of generativity. The entities are always arriving, but since it is not clear why they migrated, it is not clear why this bunch is a destination. The upshot of this equality among surprising things is, for any external or reflective view, a clutter, a mess demanding textualization at all costs. Without such a domestication, the gathered entities cannot share the peace and peaceful freedom of being relevant to a project; they cannot *exemplify*, and so they call to mind the wild subversions of jungle creatures and ships at sea. Left alone, they and subjectivity have no future.

This contradiction with the accumulative generativity of finding is the finder's predicament. Accumulation eventually runs up against the problem of meaning and the politics of meaning's determination. Those politics, however necessary to the fulfillment of any accumulation, nevertheless are governed by the occasions that distinguish a "given" accumulation from other activities. Politics are mediated as well as mediating. This allows us to formulate the relationship between reading as accumulation and what we often call "the larger context." More than that is a task beyond the purview of this chapter, though it is necessary still to say more about those politics of total signification.[4]

The determination of the meaning of a collection terminates its generativity for the sake of a new and more principled or self-conscious generation. What is the character of this intervention? To answer this question, let us distinguish between *accumulation* and *investment*, with the latter sufficiently inflated to include what is ordinarily meant by "reflection." Let us further assume that investment establishes a periodization of accumulation by which it can take what has happened to be a prehistory to the history it now wishes to constitute,[5] and by which it can know itself as the progress of a past. But this knowledge is, as well, the knowledge of itself as a principle of a further development, a future. The two, taken as aspects, complete what I am calling "reading." The finding of objects, accumulating, cannot see itself as a course of action since that would be to have taken a stance outside of itself. The generations still must have their cause, their reason for rebirth, and it must be our reason. Otherwise the occasion of reading and the necessity of reading *this* book must fail to sustain themselves, and reading would have no story to tell. Investment establishes the story, but the momentum it generates, in turn, makes the politics of that determination obscure. One can witness *reading*, then, only from the standpoint of investment. It is the force of our particular problematic—the distinction of reading from analysis—that gives that standpoint its special sense of contradiction and its access to the accumulation that it must, in any case, presume.

We specify our recognition of accumulation by assigning boundaries to that recognition within the course of accumulation itself. It is only in that way that we can be said to have taken an internal position. Then, and only then, can we understand the quality of focus that investment brings to reading. Accumulation recognizes itself in the periodicities instituted by investment. For if accumulation is to display the qualities of development, there must be moments of accountability, moments in which are asserted the periods of a diachrony, an order of *turns*. This crisis of internal transformation identifies and gives value to what could otherwise only have singularity. It dissolves the equality of the collected entities and enforces a collapse of their special relevance to subjectivity. Finding gives way to knowing, and knowing introduces the imperatives of utilization, definition, affinity, and rationalization. Because investment totalizes what had no immanent principle of totalization, it is analogous to policy and its process analogous to politics. Consequently, it produces, for reading, the burden of a certain arbitrariness that will give the courage of reflection to any further course of accumulation.

This move, this reflection, is qualified by its newly constituted object. The accumulation will be that object, and an occasion for further activity, if and only if it is rendered *unrepeatable*. The appropriation must guarantee the progress it has "discovered." But this is not solely for the sake of the accumulation; it is, as well, for the sake of the proprieties of appropriation, the projectivity that it envisions. Otherwise, it would be merely theft. It would have expropriated what must be, for expropriation, a past; it would have fixed its object outside of all activity and made of it an accountant's record. The guarantee restores reading to its larger context, the centers of its mediations. It retrieves, for that context, what had been done, and brings reading into direct relationship with the determinations of its own occasion.

This simultaneity of internal and exogenous reflection, the esoteric and the exoteric aspects of the event, gives to reading its sense of its own contradictions. There is, however, a semblance of analysis in this political economy of accumulation. But it is only that. Investment is a kind of textualization, but it is not simply analysis at work: It is analysis as political action, as appropriation that suits both its object and its project. It not only completes reading by allowing it to continue, it participates in the accumulations and investments of the larger context. It is in this light that we appropriate the "analytic" works of Sweezy, Cohen, et al. We read that reading lies, as I indicated above, in the fact that their methodology of containment, applied to the duality of Marx's classicism, confirms a privilege that belongs to Marxian scholarship only if it rests easily among the disciplines.

Memory

At this point, I will describe one reflective operation. The general theory of such operations would involve a poetics of discourse, what Harold

Garfinkel calls ethnomethodology and what in literary studies is partially realized as a "poetics of prose." The operation that controls this poetics is essentially *mnemonic*. It secures investment by (1) rendering accumulation unrepeatable, (2) figuring that accumulation upon the continuation of, in this case, reading, and (3) weighting its result with the obligations of the context, thereby restoring to reading its occasion. I will discuss three aspects of this operation: (1) what distinguishes it from other, essentially mimetic, conceptions of memory; (2) what it does within the political economy of the event; and (3) the internal division that marks its own contradiction and allows it to mediate the event rather than to stand as a mechanism of coercive control.

The difference may be thought of as the difference between *memory of* and *memory for*. The former refers to the retrieval of a definite content. It is the capacity of the psychological subject (the individual) to repeat a text or a sequence. Its image is that of mechanism rather than act; and, therefore, it is more easily understood in simulation of the human capacity it names than in the actual field of that capacity's putative exercise. If Foucault is correct that our knowledge of the embodied individual originated in the way in which clinical medicine freed the body from the mind, by making the corpse the essential reality for the study of life, there is an analogy to be made, hopefully with the same critical force, to the contemporary psychology of mind. In a curious Bergsonian twist, that psychology has modeled thought on the operations of computing machines. This encrustation of the mechanical upon the organic, so devastating in its more general application to human affairs (labor, education, psychotherapy, etc.), and so otherwise ludicrous, has made the decisive contribution to the extreme dehistoricization of the individual in so much of modern thought, that of discrediting the essential sociality and dialectics of experience. Such a psychology completes the person as "personality," makes of the skin an iron boundary shielding a privacy of soul that thereby excludes any access of theory or practice, and ultimately makes of this very privacy the principle of a failure that invites the practical imposition of the theoretically established and idealized machinery. "Experience" becomes, in that light, merely what happens to the machine under the "influence" of "role models," "family" and other "agencies of socialization," "norms," and "information." Psychological "practice" becomes a version of that "influence," and "therapy" imagines "retooling" and "specification of function" rather than the volatile dialectics of consciousness. The substitution of "conflict" for "contradiction" and "cognition" for "subjectivity," and the resolution of the sociality of experience to the automations of the motive, the attitude, schemata, and reinforcement, trap the human science in a proliferating idealism, the truth of which lies solely in the addition of real powers of enforcement. Like all idealisms, psychology rests on the purest of political determinations, simple and overwhelming imposition the reason for which fades at the moment one raises the question. "*Memory of*" is one figure of this idealism, and one obligation of its political practice.

"*Memory for*" is an operation upon discourse rather than the extraction of something from the past. Its demarcation of a *turn*, or turns, resembles punctuation. It has the force of a colon, asserting a before for the sake of a definite after. Unlike the simple conjunction, which previews what follows in the very mention of an initial phrase as conjoined, the colon provokes within a frame. But "memory for" not only marks a turn, it establishes the impossibility of a return, and therefore the necessity of continuation. This is the sort of "memory" that characterizes the movement of the subject/object relationship in Hegel's *Phenomenology of Mind*. It is memory in the dialectic of subjectivity rather than remembering at the end of a diachrony of thought. This mnemonic operation asserts a present and the possibility of a future. It constitutes a beginning predicated upon an accumulation now taken as complete. This means that it totalizes subject and object, thereby creating a separation that reintensifies the event. Its justification of itself is that accumulation has gone too far, that the clutter of equal entities threatens to dissolve subjectivity and its occasion, and that, therefore, reading will have had no sense from the outset: In that case, it goes on; the reading already done will have been no more than a lapse in the subject, like a coma. What this justification fails fully to acknowledge is that the mnemonic operation *constitutes* reading as an event and is, one might say, pregnant in each of its moments. That is, the justification merely comes to terms with an external, contextual stance; the operation itself is a *necessary* feature of discourse even though it conveys that necessity by its justification and defense. Justification is, then, necessary for the relationship of the event to its context, and is part of the rationalization of reading's occasion. Reading will not continue without *it*; but it cannot continue without *the operation*, regardless of justification.

For accumulation, *taken by itself*, memory is an eruption. Every element is reformed by a new principle of subjectivity. This eruption and reformation can be registered by familiar terms of experience: the shock of sudden transformation, as in disaster; the sense of profound misunderstanding, as in the first moments of betrayal; guilt, as in loss by implicit expropriation; relief, as in getting a clean bill of health after a routine checkup. In each case, one "discovers" that activity had unsuspected conditions and imperatives, issues *now* joined.

It is necessary to distinguish a *utopian* from a *practical* version of this operation. The first appears as an imposition, on the order of the State, the Gun, or the Law. It has the force of an unimpeachable authority. It is without humor or affection. Some of the phrases within discourse that register the utopian version are: "the point is . . . ," "what are we talking about . . . ?" "it follows that. . . ." Each *refers to* a subject, as well as *addresses* one. But each offers an external stance for which what is being held up for recognition is wholly objective. Each demands product or result rather than a genuine acknowledgment of work: The mood is one of final evaluation, the aim immediately to resolve the embarrassment of clutter.

The practical version is more interesting to us. It is intervention rather than violation. It preserves the necessity of the "past" by making its recurrence unnecessary and impossible: It is reading's self-respect rather than the utopian's dread of self. If utopia polemicizes against the present (against history), practical memory denies that any activity is routine and without significance. The angry wit of the utopian cognition of the past is in high contrast with the internal humor and respectful irony of practical memory. In fact, it is that humor and irony that provides us with the exemplification of the mnemonic operation in reading necessary to demonstrate the distinction between reading and analysis.

This has been a long way around coming to the issue of this chapter, which is the problem of reading *Capital* in the face of what has been an untroubled "history" of analysis. At least we have arrived at a case on which one might rest. In order to indicate the *reading* of *Capital*, it is necessary to attend to materials—polemical, ironical, etc.—that analysis had to reject but without which its own materials and therefore its text could not clearly be identified. Once these are put back into the encounter with the book, we will return to our initial questions about ideology and consciousness. But at that point and for the moment, we will have shed the metaphysics of content and its methodology of containment and will have dislodged the privilege of the traditional versions of those questions.

Capital: The Reader's Memory

Capital begins with the easy convenience of a conversation. The words tell us a familiar story, as if they are already our own:

The wealth of those societies in which the capitalist mode of production prevails, presents itself as "an immense accumulation of commodities," its unit being a single commodity. Our investigation must therefore begin with the analysis of a commodity. (Marx 1967, 35)

But why must it begin there? Is it because any investigation must begin with the analysis of the fundamental units of its phenomenon? Or is it because one must study the appearance of things before moving on to the things themselves? The ambiguity of Marx's proposal is not obvious at first because the words are familiar to prevailing discourses on human economy. Moreover, that familiarity favors the first impression. We are, then, involved in a discussion on the side of (our own) righteousness, though a precedent has been established (in the second possible impression) for doubt and insecurity.

The first page of the book is a simple recollection: Wealth is an immense fund. It has units. Its units are familiar in their singularity, objectivity, relevance, and dimensions. "A commodity is . . . an object outside us, a thing that . . . satisfies human wants. . . ." "Every useful thing . . . may be looked at from the two points of view of quality and quantity" (ibid.). So far, we are satisfied as well as righteous. We find ourselves, through the reading of these words and phrases, on the side of what is useful and serves humanity; and because the thing that "satisfies human wants" is the unit of wealth for our society, we can be loyal to the material order and take pleasure in its accomplishments. We have found what we expected to find, and we are glad.

Within a few pages, we will have taken leave of convenience. The words will have been held responsible for their concepts: the ambiguity of wealth *presenting itself as* an accumulation of commodities could be glossed over in the first blush of familiar signification, but not in the later depiction of exchange-value as "presenting itself." Here, it "presents itself" only at first sight and, at that sight, as "a relation constantly changing with time and place." While this gives vague confirmation to the initial bias toward the usefulness of (capitalist) wealth (in the hope of a second sight), the complexity of a presentation that is only first and the dizzying extremism of that presentation's content hint at trouble ahead. So we immediately read: "Let us consider the matter a little more closely" (p. 36). An invitation to talk has been changed to an invitation to talk about talk.

The pleasure of easy speech can become guilt or embarrassment when we are obliged to account for what has been said. Such moods are registered for reading's consciousness as a sudden reflexivity of words. That is, what would have passed now will be figured. Phrases such as "presents itself," "may be looked at," "so far as it is a," "becomes a reality," "at first sight," and "appears to be something" now take their place within reading's accumulation. There, they breed mischief by giving to what would otherwise be idle or easy activity an aura of contradiction. This is made manifest by the sudden proliferation of exhausting extensions of initially harmless propositions:

1. "Exchange-value, at first sight, presents itself as a quantitative relation, as the proportion in which values in use of one sort are exchanged for those of another sort," [and then the phrase]
2. "a relation constantly changing with time and place." [Finally, and catastrophically]
3. "Hence exchange-value appears to be something accidental and purely relative, and consequently an intrinsic value, i.e., an exchange-value that is inseparably connected with, inherent in commodities, seems a contradiction in terms. Let us consider the matter a little more closely." (1967, p. 36; brackets mine)

Proposition 1 merely adds to the easy discourse on wealth, society, and needs, though, as we have seen, the "at first sight, presents" is ominous. But the soft elaborations of wealth introduced by the terms *use* and *exchange* have placed us in peril. One can hardly refuse to interrogate those terms without having to admit that we have been frivolous in their reading and that we have lacked commitment to their discourse.

So we find that exchange, which we know to be progressive and desirable as well as necessary (immense, satisfying, and the point of view of quantity), and which we already knew to be superior to gambling and barter, breeds a dangerous extreme. Proposition 2 is more than we had bargained for, a conclusion whose implication of irrationality is made explicit in proposition 3. Two threatens us with the arbitrariness of exchange-value and the impossibility of commerce. Three threatens us with the incoherence of commodities and therefore the rational impossibility of wealth. The "let us consider the matter a little more closely" acknowledges that we find ourselves breathless, in an attitude of waiting, caught by a crisis of accumulation. Reading is beginning to know itself and to feel the obligation to invest. But, since its own wealth is not yet secure, its way of feeling the obligation is to return to the optimism of words. "Let us consider" operates as the subject's relief. The material will speak for a while.

Yet, before we are done, we will have sacrificed "use-value" and with it our original notion of wealth (though that will only be apparent much later). We will find ourselves drawn into a discussion of value in the vain hope of repairing the damage wrought by accident, relativism, and contradiction. We will discover ourselves endorsing, as a matter of necessity, the exploitation of labor—if exchange, and hence economy, is to be rational; and we will have to admit, though we will not mind too much, that, "in the form of society we are about to consider," in "those societies in which the capitalist mode of production prevails" (both of these phrases now beyond being glossed over), somebody gives and somebody else gets, and wealth in capitalism is not the wealth of society. Along the way, and long before we see the mediation of economy by class struggle, we will have had to confront a crucial predicament, the possibility that we have been led to absurdity. *Capital* as a whole, for us making the distinction between analysis and reading, does not, of course, rest on the absurdity of its opponents' positions. It shows only that the expansion of capital occurs through power and that expansion must eventuate in chaos, the end of exploitation, or, and this is only hinted at, a political hegemony in which neither production nor distribution are subject to the "laws of value." But this is beyond the scope of *reading*. For that, it is necessary to describe what happens between "let us consider the matter a little more closely" and an absurdity that will not yet have brought itself into line with moral indignation and political strategy, the idea of universal exchange.

Once we enter the world of "value" (section 3), we have moved beyond cliché. But because entering this world offers a response to our crisis of accumulation through the flow of words and their concepts, we are again relatively at ease. The puzzle is working its way out. Section 3 has this property through and through, and our engagement with it once again breeds the confidence of righteousness. We define, make distinctions, and manipulate figures. We move from the single to the complex, from the "elementary or accidental form of value" to the "total or expanded form" and then to "the general form," and we end with a discussion of money that appears to encompass all that had gone before: "The simple commodity-form is therefore the germ of the money-form" (p. 70). The *therefore* uses the logical function to textualize what has been read. What is important for us is not its adequacy to the analysis of value, but the trick it turns within the course of reading. The discussion of value had begun with an uneasy recognition of extremes and the obligation to talk about talk. But it transpired like an episode, freed from the preceding moments and capable of self-fulfillment. The "therefore" represents that freedom and self-fulfillment. It brings rest to one whose labor was difficult but happy in its absorption of material.

Capital began with the ease of an external discourse to which it immediately paid homage. The reader relaxed only to discover guilt and embarrassment. Reading's desperation was relieved in section 3 by entering yet another easy discourse. This time, however, it was entirely internal to the course of reading, and reading was kept calm by the technicalities of its work. These technicalities operated in the same way as the earlier economic clichés, to pin the subject to its material. As in the first case, section 3 eventuates in what would have been unthinkable during the episode. We immediately discover that not only our words (as in the first case) but our technician's ease, the convenience of our labors, has become an issue. Where we thought we had come to a conclusion and had settled the issue of exchange, we discover that we can congratulate ourselves only if we are willing to look ridiculous. What is at stake is not the course of an argument. That, certainly, is settled.[6] It is, rather, that the reader wishes to know *that* certain success (the argument) is the accomplishment of reading, though that is clearly impossible. The reader, in other words, thinks he or she has done the analysis found in the course of reading, when that reader has, in fact, only read and therefore only been involved (in this case, totally).

This confusion is the key to the reader's vulnerability. It signifies an illusion of total and transcendent subjectivity, and it is that illusion that is so thoroughly punctured by the fourth section, on "the fetishism of commodities." Yet, section 4 is not an assault on the reader, since if it were, reading would have failed as an event and become instead either a drama of author and victim or the correction of past error by the punishment of humiliation. Our obligation is to show how reading succeeds *as an event*, how it invests in its own continuation, sustains the dialectic of reader/reading/material, and prevents itself from being replaced by an analytically objective relation of text and author. As we will see, the puncturing of the illusion of total subjectivity is part of reading's self-discipline: It operates as memory *for* the event and its progress. To show this, it is necessary to move back a few steps to the point at which exchange becomes entirely explicit rather than simply conceptual. Then and only then is it possible to appreciate the reader's predicament and its influence upon the further course of reading. Moreover, then and only then is it possible to appreciate—and this comment is at odds with the methodology of this chapter but perhaps helpful nevertheless—the pedagogical force of Marx's writing.

Three things invite memory to do its work: (1) the accumulation of sus-picious phrases (e.g., "presents itself") and suspect passages (e.g., "let us consider the matter . . .") among the otherwise easy flow of words; (2) the gathering of extremes from otherwise simple and tolerable propositions, as reading reluctantly takes up its obligation to demonstrate that it is serious; and (3) the sudden relaxation provided by the game-like atmosphere of sec-tion 3's autonomous technical discourse—the suddenness of that relaxation leaves prior troubles dangling and portends, for the moment of completion, a resolution that will take advantage of that sense of relief, of having played the game. The moment of completion is false in its own palpable vulnera-bility, and section 4 turns that to reading's advantage.

The upshot of section 3 is that once commodities are seen as necessar-ily equivalent, having an identity that cannot be accounted for by use, and once this equivalence is seen as depending wholly upon an abstraction of labor and an abstraction of use, we see that exchange-value is *superior* to use-value: The fact that people create things is less important than the fact that they expend energy, and the fact that they need concrete things is less important than the fact that they have the power and will to purchase anything.

A thing can be useful, and the product of human labour, without being a commodity. Whoever directly satisfies his wants with the produce of his own labour, creates, indeed, use-values, but not commodities. In order to produce the latter, he must not only produce use-values, but use-values for others, social use-values.

Unlike needs, these "social use-values" have no necessary connection to a concrete producer's consumers. The "utility" of the commodity becomes no more than a formal property of the ideal aggregation of consumption, as the "labor" of humans becomes a formal property of ideally aggregated pro-duction. In the midst of all of this form, the only content that remains is the *constancy* of exchange. That is all that economy can witness.

One finds, then, that "value" and "wealth" have nothing to do with hu-man needs and their satisfaction, that the exchangeability of commodities depends upon the abstraction of labor and cannot be sustained by itself (as by "the market"),[7] and that every commodity is and must be "directly ex-changeable with other commodities." If value depends upon abstracted la-bor, and wealth is the accumulation of value, the real accumulation must be that of labor as a facility and not goods that satisfy needs. The wealth of page 1 and the society that cannot do without it have, by the end of section 3, ceased to exist.

Up to this point, reading has been driven by the interrogation of words. The movement of chapter 1 is not simply the order of an argument or a demonstration. It is the movement of transformation in which speech ad-dresses itself by worrying over its own accumulation. One can trace this as well through the succession of ideas, as one can trace a journey by referring to a map. At first wealth, then value; at first use-value, then exchange-value; at first human need, then the supervening reality of the thing; at first the concrete, then the abstract; at first the work of people, then abstracted labor; at first the unitary commodity, then the universe of exchange. In each case, one has lived through the decay of the veritable, the exhaustion of certainty's energy, the dispossession of convenience. One has not witnessed the demonstration of theorems or the induction of laws from facts.

This theater of decay reaches its denouement at the point at which the objects of exchange are instances of abstraction (if they are to be objective), and exchange is the state of the universe (if there is to be exchange). The addition of money to this scheme, at the end of section 3, merely seals that fate: "The universal equivalent form is a form of value in general. It can, therefore, be assumed by any commodity," though the commodity that actually assumes it is "excluded from the rest of all other commodities as their equivalent, *and that by their own act*" (p. 69, my italics). In fact, to recognize universal exchange within the limits of chapter 1—within the limits and self-transformations of the easy economics of society, wealth, commodities, needs, quality, and quantity—is to recognize without hesitation or inference that only commodities can act and that only among them can "society" be constituted. This is the basis for section 4's move against the success of section 3's total subject. *It is the irony that characterizes chapter 1 and demonstrates that it is a chapter for reading rather than for analysis.*

Section 4, "The Fetishism of Commodities and the Secret Thereof," makes explicit, and thereby creates a parody of self, the implicit subjectivity of the world of exchange. The subject is not the reader of economics; nor is it the one who played section 3's game, and that section's last sentence represents those illusions as *having been* implicit. The "real" subject, to whose side the reader has been driven, even to the extent of having identified with its reality, is the society of things:

> A commodity is therefore a mysterious thing, simply because in it the social character of men's labour appears to them as an objective character stamped upon the product of that labour; because the relation of the producers to the sum total of their own labour is presented to them as a social relation, existing not between themselves, but between the products of their labour. (p. 72)

But this is not simply an appearance to *those who labor*, but to those who had begun within the discourse of society, wealth, commodities, needs, quality, and quantity, who had found in their first speech a certain loyalty to and pleasure in economy, and who had undertaken to play with the concept of value as a distraction from the extremes to which their obligation to be serious had carried them.

That is clear in the first sentence of section 4: "A commodity appears, at first sight, a very trivial thing, and easily understood" (p. 71). The first chapter of *Capital* only intimates, but does not establish within reading itself, that the capitalist mode of production and the struggle of classes *found* the opposition of bourgeois and communist economics. Therefore, one must, in order to understand reading, take the first sentence of section 4 as an appeal to the critique of appearance rather than to the theory of economy. The positive statements of that section (statements about what producers do for each other, and the extension of exchange, for example) can only be, at this point, ambiguous for the sake of further reading and responsive to the difficulties in which reading had placed itself. For the latter, there is no ambiguity. The first sentence clearly marks the onset of a self-critique that is also an investment in a reading that will soon discover the human agency that had been lost: Chapter 2 is entitled "Exchange," and begins in the same temper as section 4—soon to change.

It is plain that commodities cannot go to market and make exchanges of their own account. We must, therefore, have recourse to their guardians, who are also their owners. Commodities are things, and therefore without power of resistance against man. (p. 84)

The self-parody of reading is even more obvious at the end of section 4, when commodities begin to talk to the reader:

Could commodities themselves speak, they would say: Our use-value may be a thing that interests men. It is no part of us as objects. What, however, does belong to us as objects, is our value. Our natural intercourse as commodities proves it. In the eyes of each other we are nothing but exchange-values. (p. 83)

Immediately following this passage, the commodities are enjoined to "speak through the mouth of the economist." But, so far, few economists have made their appearance. In fact, "the economist" is none other than the reader who began with, one can now say, a certain outlook. If society is no more than "based upon the production of commodities," then the society of things is its consciousness. But so far, all that is at stake is the discourse in which commodities are the units of societal wealth, and all these statements are directed toward that discourse and its microhistory within the reading of chapter 1. This is why we must not, if we are to maintain the sense of *reading*, give positive interpretation to the statement:

The religious world is but the reflex of the real world. And for a society based upon the production of commodities, in which the producers in general enter into social relations with one another by treating their products as commodities and values, whereby they reduce their individual private labour to the standard of homogenous human labour—for such a society, Christianity, with its *cultus* of abstract man, more especially in its bourgeois developments, Protestantism, Deism, etc., is the most fitting form of religion. (p. 79)

So far, society is based upon the production of commodities solely because it can be said to be; and the "reflex" of that "real world" is the absurdity to which saying/reading has found itself to have been committed even at the point of its greatest faith in its own activity.

Religion and the economists are not the targets of section 4, nor are the illusions of the producer. The target is reading's aspect of accumulation. Religion and the rest are there only to defuse some of the tension of the reader's self-parody. At this point, they deserve no particular hostility or derision. Their putative otherness to the reader merely marks the reader's development from an unconscious beginning, much as the image of infantile perversity is not intended to discredit childhood so much as to display growth.

Section 4 is *a mnemonic operation for the sake of reading as an event.* It protects the reader's reading by rendering it unrepeatable as an aspect of an appropriation. Section 4's banter and tease represents the political determination of the reflection it accomplishes. It demarcates a vital turn in the course of reading. It constitutes memory in the dialectic of consciousness, and therefore it can be said to be reading teaching itself. But the parody, banter, and tease do not constitute an assault on self-righteousness or ignorance, nor on the idle chatter of theology and metaphysics, though these are mentioned derisively with the economists and the illusions of the producer. If they did, the reader's first moments would have been impossible; or, if not impossible, beyond the reason of a humanity that could be one with that of the reader. In either case, reading could not have developed from its original engagement with the book. But then its present enlightenment, registered by the parody, could have no history, and no capacity to imagine any further movement.

On the other hand, there is no doubt that section 4 is derisive and meanly ironical. There is no doubt that it ridicules the naive, the smug, the idle, and the self-deceiving. But the derision and meanness, and their ostensible targets, are, as I have tried to show, neither centered nor grounded. They are not centered because they represent no voice within reading or the reader's materials. They are not grounded because there had been no preparation to which reading had had to respond. They cannot authorize the temper they seem to require, and they do not provide a space within reading for the ostensible objects to breathe. Nor would derision and meanness do the trick, since memory must preserve rather than reject if it is to make the present a historic possibility. The real target, reading's aspect of accumulation, must be treated with the respect a self deserves and one's self requires. That the reader has been led by commodities into a world that only they can inhabit shows the necessity of a new beginning. But it is a beginning made possible by an earlier faith, the significance of which cannot be denied. Parenthetically, analysts of *Capital* often approach section 4, "The Fetishism of Commodities and the Secret Thereof," without remarking on its humor and by treating it as a disquisition on the social psychology of capitalism. This approach necessarily divorces the section from the reading that discovers it. The result has been that variety of culture study that attempts to prove the "hypothesis," or to show the validity of the insight, that commodity production distorts consciousness by giving things the appearance of people and people the appearance of things. The rub is that this is an insight from which the study itself must be somehow exempt.

This is, I believe, part of the confusion generated by the appealingly intuitive works on "technology and ideology" and "the bureaucratic society of controlled consumption" (Habermas 1970; Lefebvre 1971), and a lot of the research that goes under the label "hegemony." One consequence of this confusion is a failure of theory to envision opposition and, if it does, to formulate its possibility. From there to "the end of political economy" and "the crisis of historical materialism" is a short step that includes the presumption that Marxism was, in its rigorous formulation, merely political economy. This, in turn, provides the ticket to a transportation beyond the world of capitalist production, accumulation, classes, and class struggle, precisely the world on which even the move to the study of culture depended. What began as a social psychology of capitalist production, centered upon the fetishism of commodities, becomes a sociology of fetishism in general, with one eye focused on the overwhelming domination of individuals by structures of unnamable hegemonies and the other left wandering loose over the terrain of an ungovernable and unchallengeable semiosis.

But it is the beginning and not the end that is at fault. Even as text, the section on fetishism must refer to what precedes it. It is, from that point of view, a comment on the paradoxical world of exchange posited by capital (in its own words) as what capital must bring about if it is to have economy. It is an initial observation on the impossibility of knowing economy through the eyes and mechanisms of capital.

But this is analysis' problem and not ours. How does section 4 operate as a mnemonic device? What are the elements of its operation? The turn itself is signaled by the fact that the tone of volume I changes abruptly and cataclysmically at the very beginning of "The Fetishism of Commodities":

A commodity appears, at first sight, a very trivial thing, and easily understood. Its analysis shows that it is, in reality, a very queer thing, abounding in metaphysical subtleties and theological niceties. . . . It is as clear as noon-day, that man, by his industry, changes the forms of the materials furnished by Nature, in such a way as to make them useful to him. The form of wood, for instance, is altered, by making a table out of it. Yet, for all that, the table continues to be that common, every-day thing, wood. But so soon as it steps forth as a commodity, it is changed into something transcendent. It not only stands with its feet on the ground, but, in relation to all other commodities, it stands on its head, and evolves out of its wooden brain grotesque ideas, far more wonderful than "table-turning" ever was. (p. 71)

A commodity is therefore a mysterious thing, simply because in it the social character of men's labour appears to them as an objective character stamped upon the product of that labour; because the relation of the producers to the sum total of their own labour is presented to them as a social relation, existing not between themselves, but between the products of their labour. (p. 72)

[T]he existence of the things *qua* commodities, and the value-relation between the products of labour which stamps them as commodities, have absolutely no connexion with their physical properties and with the material relations arising therefrom. There it is a definite social relation between men, that assumes, in their eyes, the fantastic form of a relation between things. In order, therefore, to find an analogy, we must have recourse to the mist-enveloped regions of the religious world. In that world the productions of the human brain appear as independent beings endowed with life, and entering into relation both with one another and the human race. So it is in the world of commodities with the products of men's hands. This I call the Fetishism which attaches itself to the products of labour, so soon as they are produced as commodities, and which is therefore inseparable from the production of commodities. (p. 72)

Between trivia and fantasy, Pinocchio and idol, clarity and mist, lies the gentle reminiscence of the second passage, its alteration of tone both a relief and an intimation of respect. The whole cycle, its twin peaks and valley, has the look of the parental strategy of reproof punctuated by reason for the sake of reflection without shame or regret.

The section moves on to several points of textualization that consolidate this mood of reflection: (1) that the objective character of commodities (objective for capitalism) mystifies the social character of the labor upon which the commodity presumes; (2) that the objectivity of the commodity lies in its capacity to be exchanged; (3) that the mystification occurs for those "producers" totally absorbed in the processes of exchange (and for the reader who had mistaken production for exchange for all socially useful labor); (4) that the "ultimate money-form of the world of commodities . . . actually conceals, instead of disclosing, the social character of private labour, and the social relations between the individual producers"—the "actually conceals" indicating the failure of the concept and hence the failure of the reader's first moments of certainty; (5) that it is *for the bourgeois project as such* that all these tricks are turned, rather than that they represent the tragedy of any production that could be said to be modern:

The categories of bourgeois economy . . . are forms of thought expressing with social validity the conditions and relations of a definite, historically determined mode of production, viz., the production of commodities. The whole mystery of commodities, all the magic and necromancy that surrounds the products of labour as long as they take the form of commodities, vanishes therefore, so soon as we come to other forms of production. (p. 76)

· This definition and historical determination of commodity production does not refer to an objective existence beyond a human project, but a definite project tied to class. Yet, class has not made its interest known to this point. What this passage does, however, is to establish a set of images, vaguely related to the presumptions of class, by means of which the sense of the reader's initial innocence might be dispelled. We have, in chapter 1, lived through "the categories of bourgeois economy" even as we had thought of ourselves as merely living in the world. The categories, and the magic and necromancy, mix an accusation of bias with compassion for someone who got into trouble unwittingly and without bad intent. If there were only accusation (of class bias), then reading would be discredited as the source of the present sophistication; if there were only compassion, the reflection would be dulled.

The case is strengthened by referring to the passages that immediately precede this one, passages that give the mnemonic operation over to the reader and make what would otherwise be a reflection on someone else's problem a consciousness of one's own history:

Man's reflection on the forms of social life, and consequently, also, his scientific analysis of those forms, take a course directly opposite to that of their actual historical development. He begins, post festum, with the results of the process of development ready to hand before him. The characters that stamp products as commodities, and whose establishment is a necessary preliminary to the circulation of commodities, have already acquired the stability of natural, self-understood forms of social life, before man seeks to decipher, not their historical character, for in his eyes they are immutable, but their meaning. Consequently it was the analysis of the prices of commodities that alone led to the determination of the magnitude of value, and it was the common expression of all commodities in money that alone led to the establishment of their characters as values. It is, however, just this ultimate money-form of the world of commodities that actually conceals, instead of disclosing, the social character of private labour, and the social relations between the individual producers.

When I state that coats or boots stand in a relation to linen, because it is the universal incarnation of abstract human labour, the absurdity of the statement is self-evident. Nevertheless, when the producers of coats and boots compare those articles with linen, or, what is the same thing, with gold or silver, as the universal equivalent, they express the relation between their own private labour and the collective labour of society in the same absurd form. (pp. 75–76)

By itself, this passage is too instructive, too analytical for reading to get a grip on *itself*. As part of the cycle of reproof and reason, it brings reading back to its first moment of self-deception with the sense that there could have been no other beginning and the recognition that one has accomplished a genuine self-transformation: One has, in phenomenological terms, produced the brackets rather than simply *found* them as the mind's logical option.

The fact that the images of the reader's innocence evoke as well the sense of a guilty party (the bourgeoisie, theology, metaphysics, the economists) allows the reader to use reading's own past, without disavowing it, against any evidence of a return to the ungoverned pleasure of and loyalty to the capitalist mode of production. Reading has become vigilant against the possibility of regression. The fact that that innocence was the reader's beginning, and the condition of the critical development, transfers the old pleasure and loyalty to reading itself. We might say, at this point, that this is the first stage of Marx's pedagogy, and it works not because of the quality of the argument—though the argument has quality—but because of the poetics of Marx's prose, because of what the written material does within the reading.

What have been discussed so far are still not sufficient to complete the case. We need to pay some attention to material that analysis would have taken as irrelevant, but which reading's play cannot avoid, the footnoted "comments" and the polemical references to the economists, their friends, and their illusions. More, certainly, can be said about the provocations that range through the quoted passages—the references to trivia, subtleties and niceties, the transcendent, the grotesque and wonderful, fantasy and mist, fetishism, magic and necromancy, and their ironical formulations. But the comments and polemics will at least complete the establishment of the ground for this critique. I will focus on the contribution they make to the specific constitution of reading's memory.

It is only after the tone has been set and reading made reflective, only after the initial eruption and its consolidation within the history that is reading's self-consciousness, that the economists make their clown appearance:

1. Even Ricardo has stories a la Robinson. "He makes the primitive hunter and the primitive fisher straightaway, as owners of commodities, exchange fish and game in proportion in which labour-time is incorporated in these exchange-values. On this occasion

he commits the anachronism of making these men apply to the calculation, so far as their implements have to be taken into account, the annuity tables in current use on the London Exchange in the year 1817." (p. 76n)

2. Ricardo himself pays so little attention to the two-fold character of the labour which has a two-fold embodiment, that he devotes the whole of this chapter on "Value and Riches, Their Distinctive Properties," to a laborious examination of the trivialities of a J. B. Say. And at the finish he is quite astonished to find that Destutt on the one hand agrees with him as to labour being the source of value, and on the other hand with J. B. Say as to the notion of value. (p. 80n)

3. Truly comical is M. Bastiat, who imagines that the ancient Greeks and Romans lived by plunder alone. But when people plunder for centuries, there must always be something at hand for them to seize, the objects of plunder must be continually reproduced. (p. 82n)

4. [W]hy should a dwarf economist like Bastiat be right in his appreciation of wage-labour? (p. 82n)

5. To what extent some economists are misled by the Fetishism inherent in commodities, or by the objective appearance of the social characteristics of labour, is shown, amongst other ways, by the dull and tedious quarrel over the part played by Nature in the formation of exchange-value. (p. 82)

6. And modern economy, which looks down with such disdain on the monetary system, does not its superstition come out as clear as noon-day, whenever it treats of capital? How long is it since economy discarded the physiocratic illusion, that rents grow out of the soil and not out of society? (pp. 82–83)

7. Now listen how those commodities speak through the mouth of the economist. (p. 83)

Aside from the expressions of impatience ("clear as noon-day," "how long . . .") and sheer invective ("dwarf economist," "truly comical"), these passages present some familiar comic figures: (1) the confusion of one set of circumstances for another; (2) uncritical devotion; (3) double-take; (4) dopiness; (5) pomposity; (6) self-righteousness; and (7) the encrustation of the mechanical upon the organic. The moralism of these comedies does not belong to Marx, but to the reader as an inevitable concomitant of reflection in the service of self-consciousness. Even then, it is only moralism for us who witness that reflection. That particular heaviness indicates, for reading, the pleasure of self-discovery.

Moreover, in each case, the comic figure participates in the same innocence that reading finds at its own beginning. But innocence made comic is not necessarily rejected. That transformation, as reading's work, is the mnemonic operation. The irony of section 4 reflects on the reader's point of embarkation, but it does not deny the validity of that move. It makes of it a true embarkation, a leaving that cannot be undone. The beginning (first page of chapter 1; 1967, p. 35) is no longer possible, through its present impossibility, and the present itself—as a new beginning—depends on its having occurred.

The irony in Marx's writing, visible only as a matter of reading, registers a reader's accomplishment rather than other intellectuals' failure. It registers that accomplishment in such a way that we would be embarrassed to begin again but are not embarrassed to have begun. This, I take it, is radical humor, reflective within a dialectic of consciousness, respectful of its target as it is of the self for which it is humor, responsive to the historical aspect of subjectivity, and constructive, so far as the continuation of subjectivity is concerned. The humor of reading, unlike the writer constructed by analysis as author and the foundation of the text, is the pedagogy of self. It is an intervention the subject can know as its own, rather than a disruption, a didacticism, or a demand that the subject be absolutely other than what it is. The memory that it constitutes provides a sense of reading's having taken a turn beyond a critical point. In this particular totalization of what has been predominantly accumulation, it is an investment in a present pregnant with a greater history.

It should now be apparent in what sense the reading of *Capital* is more and other than analysis. It is more because it is educative; it is other because it is historical. It does not attempt to identify the false text of "ideology" and superimpose on it the result of analysis. It glorifies neither superimposition nor content. And this indicates, as well, a difference in political design. Reading was taken as an instance of history. To that extent, its place is within the politics of class struggle. The revolution in its own course, the mnemonic act, spoke not from above and beyond but from within the course of its own struggle. The enemy of radical politics is not merely an external agency that has temporarily dispossessed radicals from centers of power and authority—it is that politics itself, and then only because it is in process and its acts are constitutive rather than simply instrumental. In *Capital*, the enemy is not yet the bourgeois; it is the reader's first confident engagement with materials. Radical consciousness must at least, as Thompson almost said, make itself. But this cannot be done with the same tactics that serve against the external enemy, the tactics of power politics. One cannot find oneself by obliterating one's moments.

Still, consciousness is neither the property nor the obligation of individuals, for if it were, the discipline of subordination would be both necessary and sufficient for its full development. If the individual is anywhere to be found in reading, as in political action, he or she is only on the verge. But if consciousness is, in some sense, itself a history, then it must proceed through the dialectic of subjectivity/objectivity. It must involve an engagement with materials through a succession of transformations in relation to which an individual identity is little more than an epi- or sub-phenomenon. In either case, though it may flicker from time to time, it is of little significance, and the loyalties, pleasures, shocks, and reconstructions are those of a subject that is freed of psychology. The use of terms such as "event" and "discourse" is intended to suggest, without doing much more, that history and society do not reduce to individually psychical moments, and that individuality is always refractory to development and the spontaneity of involvement of people by which society registers itself. In my account of reading, though the "individual" may, at any given time, be the beneficiary of development, the development itself can only be traced through the subjectivity of reading, and for that the "individual" is replaceable. This is the key to gauging the significance of this study to the pedagogy of Marxism and, I believe, to its politics as well.

I am not denying that power is a decisive element in radical political encounters or that it may be part of radical discipline on occasion. I am merely trying to resuscitate pedagogy within the context of Left theory and practice, to show that it is not separate from politics, and to suggest that the terms by which we clarify teaching as a self-education agitated by materials and already socialized to radical settings and discourses are precisely those by which we also know the development of political agency. If I have been able to distinguish reading from analysis, then we can see how analysis fits into the complex of a content metaphysics and its methodology of containment. It is part of a privileged exercise the ideological import of which is its paradox. Therefore, its truth can claim no generality beyond its own historical setting. To demonstrate that limitation, it was necessary to make explicit the opposition of analysis to reading. The former presumed upon the latter; therefore, their opposition was seen to be on the order of a contradiction. This, in turn, clarified both the historical limitation of analysis and the danger inherent in the transgression of those limits. The phenomenology of reading reestablished the perspective of history in the development of subjectivity without, at the same time, introducing an unacceptable idealism. At that point, it became possible to speculate about the degree to which that perspective could be inclusive, that is, the degree to which it provides a basis for a Marxian "theory" of politics, the focus of which is on the radical development itself rather than on the implementation of powers that presuppose that development.

What I am suggesting is not subversive of Left practice. Marxism has always taught and been taught; radicals have never disavowed critique; the Left has never, for all its perception of the dangers of elitism and intellectualism, burned its books; the issue of subjectivity continues to be a constant in the encyclopedia of Left issues; finally, there is no socialist movement "in history" that has not made itself known and come to know itself by writing and reading. What this chapter contributes is a distinction within all of this and a rehabilitation of the subjectivity that had been kept crippled by the politics of textualization and the textualization of politics.

The question now is what are possible ramifications of this historicism of the book? I will argue, essentially, that ideology is not a proper phenomenon for Marxism if the term refers to false contents, cognitive structures, influential messages, hegemonic formations, bad ideas, the expression of interest, or the negative of science. I will not deny that these are all possible; the point is, however, that they can only account for the course of class struggle and bourgeois control if struggle and control are conceived nondialectically. But then, one term of the class struggle vanishes and it ceases to be struggle altogether.

Instead, I will argue that the key phenomenon is constituted by the mnemonic operation, the sense of a turn (embodied within a discourse or any historical subjectivity), that divides a movement into what it had been but no longer can be and what it is for the sake of moving further. This allows one to conceive of a "class" for example and, as Thompson says, a class making itself. The study of "ideology" becomes, in this light, the study of the development of a certain consciousness or subjectivity that includes an awareness of its own historical possibility and therefore an awareness of the essential otherness of imposed "structure" and permanent "presence."

Ideology and Culture

One begins, after all, in the middle of discourse, not with an originating intention or idea. Reading involves an accumulation and a decay; and it involves investment. The initial position, founded as it is beyond the immediate encounter with the book, is not "ideological" in the conventional sense and on its own account. One can use the term only to bring the prior discourse into focus, and therefore to mark the reader's point of embarkation. Or, if the term is to be used in the sense not of critique but of criticism, it can name the reader's beginning as a possibly permanent state, that is from the standpoint of either a lapse in memory or a possible absence of any reflection. But the latter is merely heuristic, since if there were to be such a lapse or such an absence, the seeing of words would not be thought of as reading. At that point, one would have to admit that the term merely signifies the subject's loss to a world of easy and fluid signification. Reading would be analogous to a dumb chant, its content merely a distraction of the subject.

That this is a possible condition cannot be doubted. That it can reflect the political aim of an elite that wishes only to suppress the subjectivity of "its constituencies" can easily be imagined. Chatter can, after all, have a life of its own. But, then, I would claim that much of the research that chases after "hegemony" deals with the proliferation of chatter. What is underneath that, however, still needs to be disclosed, and research leaves it entirely untouched. While it is worthwhile to witness the proliferation, it is essential for Marxism to recognize it for what it is, and therefore to recognize the subjectivity that it leaves inexpressible within the total society.

Yet, the indication of a lapse in memory or an absence of reflection can be understood as a reflection on intervention itself. To imagine chatter is analogous to perceiving clutter or mess at the point at which intervention confronts accumulation. That is, imagining chatter need not be prior to the "decision" to intervene or reflect but may be the latter's accompanying reflex. The danger is, of course, that the imagination of chatter can arise outside of the subject's own development, as analysis. In that case, it can only add to the cynicism of the external position. If it arises within, as in reading, it simply marks the moment that a turn is recognized.

More generally, to recognize ideology in either case—the point of embarkation or chatter—is to have gone beyond it. Recognition is either constituted in the mnemonic operation or reflects a position outside of reading altogether. If it is the latter, what follows if cynicism is to be avoided is the teacher's move, to join what has been observed and therefore to speak with, rather than speak at, the subject. In that case, the subject, too, is invited into reading. It is only the false teacher that determines to install a proper text, only the master who has not yet realized its dependence on the slave.

The temptation of the false teacher is, however, not to be seen as merely an error in motivation and reason. It has its own informing setting. Like reading itself, false teaching arises within the context that establishes the necessity of reading and the significance of the particular book. To yield to the temptation is to yield to the futility of utopia, result without process. The yielding itself can only be cured by the exhaustion of its own beginnings, as in reading. It too has a pedagogy. But its pedagogy is misunderstood if it is thought to be directed at the target it names, just as reading is not simply about the world but about itself. On the other hand, a given setting may pose reading against false teaching. This generates its own development, the thrust of which is to restore the former and remove the latter from the scene. For our purposes, however, this is to have gone too far. The discussion of false teaching is intended only to highlight the ramifications of recognizing reading.

To study ideology by textualizing discourse is to remain at the beginning of the development of consciousness, which is why, I suppose, so many Marxists have become wearied, without being able to account for their weariness, of ideology critique even in its most sophisticated forms. The "key" question of ideology posed at the beginning of this chapter, the effect of content on individuals, or groups, is less a real question than the indication of a commitment to remain at the point of the reader's embarkation and to divorce that point—and it is only that, not a state or a condition—from reading as history. It is to intend a holding action that is doomed from the start since the real subject will have faded away before any work is done. It is to hold the bag and to mistake one's own filling of it for an intemperance of the subject.

The study of content cannot, then, be used to verify a theory of domination. In fact, that theory, as presently formulated in the literature of neo-Marxism, presupposes a world of contents and containers; or, if it does not, it presupposes a world sprayed with the chatter of slaves. This would preclude much of what has been done under the rubric of culture research. Raymond Williams has shown how overdetermined "culture" is for us, and even his own attempt to rehabilitate the study reflects that overdetermination. Somehow, and this is difficult to formulate, the study of culture must involve a move within a developing subjectivity. Within that, it must both notice and provoke further movement either by its own mnemonic articulation (Thompson's *Making of the English Working Class* reads that "making" as turns) or by joining the material (e.g., the material that is being read) in the demands it makes upon readers (as Deleuze and Guattari and Foucault have done at times). This might be called critical activity in contrast with the construction of critical texts or "texts of critique." But this means that culture studies would have to be activist rather than, as Williams seems to suggest, merely more perceptive (and from where?), and its activism might well emerge on two fronts: one, on the front of the internal development; and two, on the front where reading notes its context—class struggle.

One practical consequence of this shift might involve challenging the strategic assumption that capitalism's tricks with media must be countered by Left tricks—images with images, slogans with slogans, points with points, representations with representations, frames with frames, mythic constructions with mythic constructions, utopias with utopias. But this is to reiterate the analyst's, and capital's, mistake, that of confirming by one's own procedures what one has rejected, the idealization of content and of subjectivity. Too many moves of this sort have failed by virtue of the fact that they operate on a terrain that is already fully occupied. The metaphysics of content ultimately leads to a relativism of contents, to a skepticism that is the bourgeois' stock in trade. One cannot offer to unsettle what is taken for a *status quo* with mere ideas, "relative" contents. Only the bourgeois need not be serious on such terrain. No text can be more than a relative content, something to be replaced, merely to be evaluated. This is why analysis produces endless debate that rapidly moves to the side as the world moves on. Teaching, and culture study as teaching, must discover its position within an inclusive struggle before it can do its work; but this is true only if one agrees that *Capital* teaches before it is a text and that all activity gathers the commitment of its subject(s) through an analogous historical movement, through experience.

This play with *Capital*'s classicism represents an internal move to the development of which the insistence on classics was a part. We have arrived at a point of departure, and at the phenomenology of action we call the relation of theory and practice.

6
"Society Against the State"
The Fullness of the Primitive

It is clear that modern anthropology is a knowledge-constituting field, and in that sense is scientific whether or not it is classified as a science. Yet, its very subject—the study of "Others"—has nonetheless remained a source of embarrassment coloring the writings of the most important ethnologists (see Geertz 2000, chapter 5). In *Tristes Tropiques*, for instance, Claude Lévi-Strauss is anxious to dissociate himself from that agent of an untroubled, a merely curious, interest in the Other: the tourist. And though his first sentence begins with denunciation: "Travel and travellers are two things I loathe," it ends with an admission of complicity: "and yet here I am, all set to tell the story of my expeditions. But at least I've taken a long while to make up my mind to it."

Lévi-Strauss acknowledges his identity as traveler. *Tristes Tropiques* begins with a section entitled "destinations," and ends with one called "the return." It is from the dread of this complicity, of a discipline somehow compromised in advance, by more, as we shall see, than just the necessary act of travel that the moralizing tone of anthropology arises. *Tristes Tropiques* is not simply the story of this particular author's adventure. Though it is written in the first person, the *I* is transcendental; it stands beyond the relations of struggle that the narrative recounts. It proceeds in the force of its denunciation from impression to point and from point to lesson. The book is, like so much of the literature of ethnology, didactic and hence suspicious—suspicious of both the reader and of other works the reader might encounter. It does not simply embrace the reader, but assumes him to be committed to a view that

must be corrected, purged. The reader is not assumed innocent, like the beginning student or the child, but as already immersed in error.
Tristes Tropiques attempts to correct beliefs about Indians, Brazil, and the primitive. The opening confession about travel prepares the reader for the administration of a lesson. It does so by arguing a possibly common origin, and by displaying a certain ambivalence toward the reader as any reader. One can be the traveler who is not the tourist. One can begin with open eyes, waiting for what will appear rather than pouncing, like a photographic journalist, upon a prey whose photogenic properties are already known in advance. And while this is all promised, it is the tourist, the false scientist, that is the possibility in the reader that Lévi-Strauss addresses.

Yet it is not only the reader who is assumed to be in error. The suspicion displayed by works of anthropology is ultimately collegial. Even Stanley Diamond, whose opening sentence in *In Search of the Primitive* is "Civilization originates in conquest abroad and repression at home," begins his field report with a false confession: "From the beginning it was a star-crossed field trip. In August of 1959, accompanied by my wife and daughters." Here again is a new beginning that denies that another's is a real beginning:

> Lévi-Strauss admits to the relative poverty of his own ethnographic experience. His field work has been episodic and can be counted in months, rather than years; he has never lived in any primitive or archaic society for an extended period of time.

Thus, though Diamond's work constantly indicates its origin in the internal critique of Western capitalism, it nevertheless reproduces the pathos and suspicion that is the anthropologist's lot and method. Not Lévi-Strauss, but the poverty of experience, the lack of contact, is Diamond's target in this passage. Here, time is the dimension along which Lévi-Strauss suddenly appears with the false traveler and outside of society. It might just as well be presence of mind, depth of appreciation, interest, or space.

This method and the specific distrust it aims to clarify may stem from the anthropologist's special situation. It is not that the ethnologist deals with the concrete and so must constantly guard against empirical error, nor is it that he or she addresses the most complex concerns of social science. Rather, the discipline has always been the province of adventurers, missionaries, conquerors, and others whose work blends the political and the aesthetic within the continually invented traditions of the false society of the nation-state. And because it is taught among the sciences, and like them must be concerned for its reputation, the fact that it has always borne the home country's self-righteousness becomes an additional burden.

The anthropological field report (and this is, as always, the military sense of "field" and the businessman's sense of "report") aims at the completeness of texts, at both singularity and repeatability. It presumes to know an Other. Like all self-conscious pedagogic acts, it aims to conquer.

In this intention, the field report appears as Legend. Unlike Myth, which lives only in new and collective tellings, Legend is external to the social. It is something to be written, preserved, stored; it aspires to a perfection intolerable to praxis.

The innocence displayed in the field report, the Legend that confronts the reader with the discoverer's confidence, and the collegiality of the polemic that insists upon the relation of the report to a more general commentary on civilization itself form the basis for the surprise that is the reader's inevitable predicament. Together, they turn what is obvious into a topic, thereby establishing debate as the medium of knowledge. It is obvious that the traveler carries a flag and that the possibility of travel has exploitation as its theme. The topic that surprises is the temptation this traveler has to know others as less. The contemporary field report reckons with this temptation. To that extent, it reckons within a political discourse the terms of whose application and final direction can be displayed but not controlled.

Power and nature have always been the primal figures of anthropology. Therefore, its study begins with the fundamental distinction it finally and self-consciously demonstrates, that between the higher and lower. The reality to which the work testifies is not the concrete society studied but the territorial boundary that segregates "civil society" from the nature, human and otherwise, that lies beyond. With regard to boundary, a fundamental, informing fact that can only be challenged or obliterated by the laws that maps summarize, theory is essentially the knowledge of the Other, of a difference that is utterly secure and must serve as both beginning and end.

Thus, anthropology begins with a certainty of Otherness, a beyond to which one can point, a difference that can, in principle, be charted. This difference, which is enacted in the practice of citizenship before it is the object of the specialist's discourse, leaves the scientist with a choice: Either the display of difference invites reconciliation or it entails the calculation, manipulation, or management of unbridgeable distance. Either the quality of the Other, and hence one's self, is at stake or one is engaged in quantification and technical analysis. But the control of distance is, in the order of knowledge, subsidiary to judgment and possible reconciliation. Analysis must already have decided, in its application, that the "we" and the "they" can be brought into line, that difference can be overcome or at least overlooked. And it is territory that dictates the parameters of this decision. Crossing the boundary already places the burden upon the Other. Consequently, field reports either tell how others are like us such that some mediation of the conflict becomes necessary—learning their language, publishing their literature, exchanging personnel and goods, engaging in negotiations—or they display difference for the sake of the home society's self-justification.

In the case of the former, politics is implicated as a matter of state. In the case of the latter, politics is strictly internal and the text constitutes an apology for the home country's sociopolitical and economic order. Such an apology is, however, covert and usually appears as general theory illustrated with facts. This deception is not founded in the self-consciousness of the author, but in the structure of the object itself. The field report deals with specific others as instances of Otherness constituted by boundary, by all that is beyond the territorial bounds of the home country. It therefore provides an account that assumes but does not demonstrate the home country's contemporary order. This apology does not, then, appear as ideology. It might even appear as self-criticism or self-reproach. The Other's world may provide a glimpse of what civilization could be but for historical contaminations of writing, work, and organization. In such a case one learns of the nobility of the Other, but only in the abstract, as a pure praxis. The Other need not be cultivated or acknowledged—worked with—or even permitted to live.

In a world in which capital has denied the permanence of boundary, and labor is no longer the individuated productive effort of persons, territory has become an issue for the contemporary theory of society. Likewise, in a world in which conquest has shifted to the realm of economy, and where both knowledge and power are increasingly registered as technique, it has become necessary to distinguish the nation-state from society. And because of these shifts, the tension between the factual reference of anthropological writing and the writing itself has become overpowering. This tension goes back to that first recognition of the primitive with which both anthropology and the clarification of modern capitalism began.

Anthropology, particularly political anthropology, operates within the strategies and obligations of the contemporary discourses of power. Its truth lies in the trouble it makes rather than in the new facts it discloses. Criticizing civilization's total movement into the archaic world of the savage, anthropology intends to complete the critique of capitalist industrialization that begins in labor's struggle. It thereby reproduces, however, the very image of total community at home that was suspect before the anthropologist bought a ticket, assembled equipment and personnel, and raised pen to paper. The original suspicion, preceding anthropology, existing within the public discourse that science joins but does not initiate, is the suspicion of the nation-state itself. It is the suspicion that the home country is not a society but a division in which rule is external and participation compulsory: It is the suspicion that there are classes. And it is only with the acknowledgment of this suspicion, and the division that "society" hides, that we can begin to understand the origin of the fundamental categories of the science. In other words, *one already knows to look for the Savage before one discovers it.* One knows to look before one finds not because there is always someone beyond one's own world, but because the perfection of an already familiar type is always readily available. Anything, any cue, can indicate the image so long as that which bears the cue can be read outside the observer's own context: The perfection of aging appears in the small shifts of the flesh, that of the criminal in the single deed.

What, then, establishes the familiarity of the Savage? What distinction must already have been made before the representation of others becomes sufficiently unproblematic to allow for the simple recording of visits to strange places to constitute discoveries?

One can begin to answer this question by noticing the distinction, fundamental to Western philosophy and political and social economy, between purpose and activity, plan and execution, knowledge and application, work and interest, labor and capital. It is with regard to this distinction—at once ideological, theoretical, and practical—that Western social science finds the axis along which it locates all instances of the human for purposes of comparison and socialization. This axis is defined by the poles "rationality" (the idealization of decision in the interest of the private accumulation of wealth) and "primitive" (the idealization of activity without purpose, predictable only with regard to external factors—rules, orders, etc.). The primitive includes all those elements of human association that neoclassical economics found dangerous to the market because they were not determined by monetary interest: family and regional loyalties, religion, interest in one's work rather than the sale of one's labor power, affection for those with whom one must bargain. The primitive marks the limits of the ideal market and the ideal state, and it establishes for theory a category of the human that is absolutely unassimilable, absolutely beyond the evolution of society in the direction of increased rationality, and absolutely before and against the state. In the early nineteenth century, this primitive referred to "the dangerous classes." In the twentieth, it came to refer to noninstitutional behavior, informal organization, particularism, collective behavior, and deviance.

The Savage is, then, an adequate representation of a primitive already familiar in the West. It represents those who are beneath society, before the state, those whose activity is without purpose and are therefore obsessed, compelled, or simply instrumental. The exoticism of the native is an illusion, exotic goods a distraction. Costume, artifact, attitude, and behavior are the marks borne by the native, which draw attention away from the fact that the observer is bound to find indices of strangeness in order that the category *Savage* be applied without implicating its political origins. The marks called exotic draw attention beyond the bounds of territory, just as does travel itself. The credibility of the field report lies, to a large extent, in its deployment of such marks so that this travel appears to be unlike any other travel, so that it is an event in the political economy of discovery.

The search for the primitive is the transformation of a domestic category into a wild one. The Other is domesticated in terms of its very wildness, while the domestic category is suppressed in its very appropriation as the knowledge of the utterly Other, against whom can be asserted, with a security assured by memory's failure, the societal unity that the state has always proclaimed. The contradictions are cast out as one feature of the mystification of exploitation that is the culture of the West.

Still, within this anthropological critique of Western civilization, so limited by its foundations, suspicion eventually turns more clearly against itself.

To have begun with the dominance of capital and the state is not necessarily to end with it. Moreover, the mystification of exploitation upon which the distinction between rationality and the primitive is predicated is no longer secure. As the nation-state and its sociopolitical forms give way to world economy, the Savage loses its representational force. On the one hand, the construction of new nations through anticolonial struggle and the increasing compartmentalization and territorial specialization of economic operations—interdependence within a world capitalist market—have reduced the distinctiveness of the exotic's marks. The political force of the Other supersedes its zoological and anthropological curiosity. But so does its commercial force. What had been found is now manufactured and takes its place among the other indices of the pluralism of cultures that have been tentatively reconstituted as a world society by the rules of the world market. On the other hand, the search for cheap and weakly organized labor has given rise to a new consciousness of race and a new racial politics aware of literature's role in the justification of exploitation and oppression.

It is within these practices that Otherness, which remains the distinctive object of anthropology, and the suspicion of knowing Otherness, which remains the core of anthropological methodology, are transformed. And it is within these practices that knowledge is turned back upon itself, and hence upon its setting; it is in this way that the anticritique that poses a challenge by wrestling with its own security becomes critique.

A 1977 book by Pierre Clastres, *Society Against the State*, affords a glimpse of this ambivalently radical possibility for an anthropology that would still insist on its distinctiveness as a field of study. The title itself brings into critical juxtaposition the notion of human association and its history and the restrictive notion of rationalized domination. Clastres wishes to show the reason and creativity of the Brazilian Indians, at what he calls "the level of the group," as no less, and perhaps more, than the reason and creativity of the societies of the industrial West. He treats the orders of the Indian societies as the realization of a project, namely, the negation of precisely that which the West takes for granted: the state against the society it constitutes, the location of the political within a coercively sustained relation of command and obedience. In this way, Clastres not only condemns the modern understanding and use of the Savage, but shows the historical specificity and tension of the Western state. Such is his dual answer to the question with which his book begins: "Can serious questions regarding power be asked?" It is not the Indians who are the issue, but we who know them as our primitive.

Clastres grants that "the social cannot be conceived without the political. In other words, there are no societies without power" (p. 15). But that power need not be based upon coercion. The Indian societies demonstrate this by insisting, as a matter of societal practice, on a power founded in the association of equals rather than applied to society. From this, Clastres concludes that "the political can be conceived apart from violence." That all societies are political whether or not they are state societies, that the model of political life that requires coercion reflects Western ethnocentrism rather than science. This model can therefore have no privileged application in political anthropology and cannot be used as a standard for grading societies according to degree of "development." The political is "at the heart of the social," and this is where one must begin in order to define power.

Clastres interrogates the world not from the standpoint of its possible manageability, but from that of a critical interest in self-understanding within the more general critique of domination. It is in the light of this project that one must interpret his initial claim that anthropology has substituted opinion for science. At face value, he seems to say that political anthropology has expressed bias and distorted fact, in contrast with science, which is beyond bias and protected from distortion through the application of scientific method. However, the overall thrust of his book, its exhaustion of various types of argument, its continual return to themes that arise from the critique of conquest and domination, and the very selection of topics, testify to the irony with which he uses the term *scientific*. When he speaks of the scientific failures of anthropology, he is not advocating positive science, but attacking, on its own terrain, the terms of anthropology's self-deception. The Indians exist for Clastres primarily because the Western comprehension and treatment of them has so clearly revealed that deception. The Indians are not *first*. Clastres indicates, however ambivalently, that to know Others (otherness) is always to make representations. It is, he says, the order of the savage "against which looms the shape of political power in our own culture" (p. 3).

What is accomplished by knowing Others as primitive and hence subject to mechanism? What is accomplished by knowing Others as creative and hence acting in reason? It is, at the least, to know one's own world as an undertaking, as a possible Other. To ask a serious question about power is, ultimately, to show the reason for power as we know it, practice it, and are constituted by it. Clastres formulates this project, but he fails to go beyond the clarification and elaboration of its statement.

Nevertheless, he has intervened in a familiar political discourse by challenging one of its most fundamental recommendations, namely, that the state is "a compulsory association with a territorial basis. . . . The claim of the modern state to monopolize the use of force is as essential to it as its character of compulsory jurisdiction and of continuous organization"[1] (Weber 1947, 156). The force of Clastres's argument lies in his refusal to accept that the absence of this state is identical with the prehistory of society, that it is the primary condition of the failure of primitive communities to develop an internal principle of historical development. Clastres's method differs from that of *Tristes Tropiques*, where the falsely innocent was already trapped and the truly innocent displayed at all turns. For Clastres, innocence is not the issue. He begins within the categories he wishes to challenge, as Marx began within the category of the commodity, and undermines them in their very use. In the process, he systematically reconstructs Indian society in such a way that reason, rather than need and rule, appears as its foundation. From categories "in complete accord with the objectives of white colonization" (p. 38), he moves to categories that challenge the basis of the colonizing societies.

One can agree with Clastres only if one acknowledges that the political does not necessarily rest upon a relation of command and obedience. Then one must be able to locate power even where it appears to be absent. In the particular case in point, one must show that the lack of powers of enforcement in the Brazilian societies does not imply a lack of power in the institution of chieftainship, that the absence of hierarchy is not the absence of coordination. On the other hand, equality does not, in itself, allow us to speak of society, the political, or history. One must find difference. Thus, Clastres's reconstruction of Indian society, his replacement of need and rule by reason, insists upon difference as that society's foundation. But that difference is not internal to the society itself, a difference of control or rank; rather, it is the difference between society and the state. The history of the Indian societies is that of their struggle against a state upon which their capacity to struggle, and therefore to be a society, nevertheless depends. Kinship and work—divisions of lineage and labor—are two of the constitutive divisions that haunt this project. For the Indians, the cooperative work in the rejection of authority never forgets its origins; it is self-conscious, reflexive. It preserves one difference—that found in working together—against another—the externality of the state. Clastres attempts to show that the relationship between the social and the political is a relationship between subject and mediation, is constructed by collective work, is produced rather than simply realized—is creative rather than mechanical, is constantly chosen, and is constituted against the possibility of the external state.

Two procedures are involved in this. First, it must be shown that several peculiar features of chieftainship—the existence of certain chiefly advantages and disadvantages, the lack of sanctioning authority, and the obligation of the chief to speak without the right to be heard or the power to demand a hearing—are founded in reason rather than domination, custom, or mechanism. Second, it must appear that the relation of the political to the social represents a commitment and a history.

Clastres proposes to implement these procedures by taking the Indians seriously. This is the way in which he finds reason in action. This intention to appreciate is what separates his book from the literature in which the Indian societies appear as less. His first task is, then, to treat that literature as having proposed to take the Indians seriously and failed. This he does on the basis of evidence and the analysis of data that show the inapplicability of the classical conception of the primitive to the Brazilian societies, in particular those features of the primitive that leave no room for reason: subsistence economy, simple organization, isolation, predictable superstructure.[1] The image that these features rationalize is life governed by need and rule.

It is an image coordinate with the classical images of the child, the Jew, the woman, and the schizophrenic.

But even if one successfully argues against the justifications for classifying the Indians as primitive, it is necessary to establish the reason and the creativity of the concrete practices of those societies. In beginning with chieftainship, Clastres again establishes his problem in its most immediately accessible form and in terms of the categories and expectations that he wishes to displace. One begins with the chief because he is higher. The paradox of the chief who lacks power is predicated, then, upon an uncritical expectation. To find reason in this is not only to resolve the paradox but to challenge the expectation upon which it is based.

The chief arbitrates. He disposes of his goods. He speaks. He is polygamous. Taken simultaneously, what do these features of chieftainship reveal about power? First, they indicate that the chief is in a paradoxical relation with the institutions of society, in particular with the fundamental "exchanges of goods, women, and words." For example, the chief is the orator; he must speak, but no one need listen. He speaks beyond the exchange of words. "The chief's discourse recalls, by its solitude, the speech of a poet for whom words are values before they are signs" (p. 37). The chief must also give of his goods until they are gone. This obligation, again, marks a lack of reciprocity at the level of material economy, for his gifts elicit no response. Nor are his wives the result of an exchange. The gift of women does not repay the chief's words or goods. Clastres concludes that it is "meant to sanction the social status of the holder of a responsibility established for the purpose of not being exercised" (p. 31). Two things follow from this: Power is not an event in time, an accomplishment, but a feature of structure. And, based as it is "on the good will of the group" (p. 28), power enjoys a singular relation with the elements of social exchange, with society. In fact, "the one called chief is the man in whom the exchange of women, words, and goods shatters" (p. 35). The political negates the social by denying exchange at the level of the group, and the social negates the political by isolating it and depriving it of authority.

But why is there power at all? Clastres acknowledges that the chief performs certain functions, but power is not the result of the need for coordination as such. Power, like nature, is prior to society. It expresses difference but does not resolve it. Society thus "apprehends power as the very resurgence of nature" (p. 31) and therefore nullifies it in its exercise. The chief is "the group's prisoner" (p. 36). The exchange of signs becomes the holding of pure values, making difference visible at the heart of the social.

The Indian societies are residential communities composed of a number of extended families. The chief intervenes as the level of their interaction and with regard to the terms by which they assert their identity. But he makes peace by persuasion only.

Thus the social structure of the group and the structure of its power are seen to ratify, attract, and complete one another; . . . it is because there is a central institution, a principal leader expressing the real existence of the community ... that the community can permit itself ... a certain *quantum* of centrifugal force that is actualized in each group's tendency to preserve its individuality. (p. 47)

Equilibrium is a constant accomplishment rather than a state or an adaptation to nature. It is societies at work, reasoning together. "In the last analysis, the forces 'working' on these primitive societies aim, directly or indirectly, at securing an equilibrium that is constantly endangered" (p. 58) by the existence of components whose identity must nevertheless be maintained. It is in this sense that the Indian societies are not without history.

Because power displays a tension between society as a whole and difference, the problematic of power is reproduced at the level of the group in institutions other than chieftainship. And it is language and representation that disclose the tension. Torture, the technology of initiation, marks the body of each individual with the law. "Primitive law, cruelly taught, is a prohibition of inequality that each person will remember. Being the very substance of the group, primitive law becomes the substance of the individual, a personal willingness to fulfill all the law" (p. 156). The law is, therefore, not external to society, but the cruelly taught injunction shows that it might be.

Similarly, Clastres finds that "what makes the Indians laugh" is the tale of power gone wrong. The Shaman, feared in life, appears in the tale as determined and incompetent. His missions go awry; his desires contaminate his duty. Here, in speech, is the refusal of a difference that life enforces. And so it is, with the terms reversed, for song. The Guayaki hunter sings at night of his exploits, his courage, his accomplishments. But this hymn to the self is a denial of the interdependence that in fact exists among the hunters. No hunter may eat of his own kill; rather, all are united in consumption. In this union the sexes, distinct in their practices and signs, are brought together. The women, those of the basket, and the men, those of the bow, conjoin in the difference between consumption and production. There is, in this complex of song, practice, and representation the continual confrontation of difference with unity, and unity is always achieved against the possibility of difference. One lives only through the mediation of others, yet that mediation is refused in language. This desire to escape destiny is an opposition to society, but not in the interest of a state. The refusal of society is the refusal of state. It is a rejection of the dialectic of society and state from within the dialectic of individual and society.

The relation of power to speech is common to societies both with and without a state. But "if in societies with a State speech is power's right, in societies without a State speech is power's duty" (p. 130). For the Indians, the chief's power is not *what* he says but *that* he speaks. And similarly, the "power" of the individual appears only in speech. Clastres concludes that "primitive society is the place where separate power is refused, because the society itself, and not the chief, is the real locus of power" (p. 131).

Clastres, then, establishes the concrete historicity of the Western polity and its discourse of power. But in so doing he also shows that the extreme difference presented by the archaic does not indicate that there is nothing there. The Indian societies are not primitive in the sense that term has come to have for us. The Indians are not full with need and rule; nor are their collectivities immature, prehistoric, mechanical. "The history of peoples without history is the history of their struggle against the State" (pp. 185–6). This is their reason. "What the Savages exhibit is the continual effort to prevent chiefs from being chiefs, the refusal of unification, the endeavor to exorcise the One, the State" (p. 185).

The fundamental problem of this analysis is that in criticizing the notion of the primitive for the sake of a basic critique of Western capitalism, in establishing for political anthropology a relationship between knowledge and interest, Clastres has inadvertently reconstituted the primitive and thus lost the critical force of his inquiry. But this is not simply his *error*. *Society Against the State* reflects, as a whole, upon the presumed originality and independence of anthropology itself. It is no surprise that, having begun with boundaries and Otherness, Clastres's text returns to them in the end. Indian societies are not what we had thought them to be, but they are still Other. And moreover, we—the West as a totality—face the Indians, cruelly, graciously, or academically, but still as *we*. It does not matter that Clastres's primitive now appears as the better. Though it has taken on a moral character, the distance between us and them remains.

There is, on the other hand, no doubt that Clastres has, in his critique of political anthropology, placed the Western polity in historical perspective. Nor is his model of socialism, although not constructed in relation to the history of capitalism, simply a romance with the archaic, an idealization of the Savage. He has shown how it is possible to have society without the oppressive externalities of the state but nevertheless founded in reason.

Clastres has not, however, abolished the fundamental distinction between the rational and the primitive that, as we have seen, marks Western social science as ethnocentric at its core. He has simply reversed the order of value and used the distinction for a critical rather than an ideological purpose. The Indians reproach the West's ethnocentrism, its coercion, its exploitation. But they do so from the vast distance constituted by boundaries. But how have the Indians come to be selected for study? How have they come to fit so nicely into the category of the primitive? How has the problem of the Other come about? These are the decisive questions, and it is only by raising them that Clastres can deliver on the promise of critique. The Indians constructed by Clastres are still incomprehensible to us. Their reason is beyond us; indeed his critique implies that reason in general is beyond us. This externalization of reason leaves the problem of unreason in the home country untouched, and the origin of the primitive remains entirely problematic. In fact reason, being external, assumes the status of the state that Clastres had hoped to call into question. It is Clastres himself who affirms the external, the difference, the standpoint of the judge beyond society and the law.

What, then, is this category of the primitive that Clastres has constructed behind his own back? What does it conceal? He proposed to displace the image of the isolated, desperate, illiterate, autistic Savage, particularly the traces of that image that abide within contemporary anthropology. This he did by answering each claim with evidence: The conditions normally thought to restrict reason do not apply; the range of Indian thought is considerable; Indian societies produce surplus; their linguistic practices indicate societal memory; their chief's lack of power does not constitute the lack of a certain authority. Still, one could answer that the image remains intact. What his evidence has shown is only that the "primitives" are more complex than one had thought, just as the study of non-human species has shown that their lives are more social than had been presumed.

Clastres has addressed indices of the primitive, but not the image or even the concept. What is this image beyond its indices? It is the utterly full, the complete. The primitive is that which is full of impulse and rule, that which lacks room for creative work. The subsidiary images of this fullness abound, and they are, as Foucault has said, consistently found in connection with discipline, control, and the possibility of disorder. The primitive consumes, is gratified or not, acts always in the midst of obsession or need, and repeats itself again and again. Here is the dance that is utterly expressive, that pushes energy to the limits of the skin, the ritual that compels a total accord, the work that lacks all but a glimmer of reflection, the artifact that has its precise place in the totalizing tabular order of the primitive's world. This primitive is not simply the reduced, the urgent, the restricted—all categories of data. It is, rather, the utterly full, and it is that which remains when the evidence is finally debated.

Clastres has reconstituted the primitive as the very fullness of reason. In taking the Indians seriously, he has made them utterly serious. No element is problematic; no moment unaccountable. There is no release from sense. Consequently, one cannot find one's self among them. They remain unimaginable, or merely imaginable. In the opening passage of the book, Clastres points out that to find power everywhere is not to find it at all. But the same can be said for reason: To find it in every moment of action is to leave no room for its identification and hence its value. He has provided us with a scenario, with a reproducible coherence; but it is itself mechanical, beyond practice.

It is not that Clastres has written in the form of Legend—he has, instead, written about a Legend: His Indians are strictly Legendary. They are reasonable both in fact and in principle. In this they are not the old traveler's primitives. But they are still replete with a definite fullness. What now becomes exotic is dignity, seriousness, rather than habit and artifact. The strangeness of the Indian remains, not as the strangeness of the foreign, which allows for learning, but as the strangeness of another order of being. This radical disconnection that Clastres displays is at the level of daily life, where action is not simply reasonable but problematic. As a result, one does not learn about reason but about the Indians. One does not learn how reason is a problem in the home country, how it is connected with interest, what bearing it has on comprehending society from the standpoint of class struggle, how it relates to domination. One learns nothing of one's self.

But this had to be the case. Clastres began with anthropology, with the objectivity of the boundary and the Other. To achieve the radicalism of his aims, he would first have had to draw attention to the weakness of this own categories. However, that would have reduced the practical force of his argument, of its capacity to challenge beliefs about the primitive that serve the interests of conquest and domination. Clastres's method requires the construction of types, and thus the exaggeration of boundaries, identities, and names. Religion, family, production, consumption are not simply analytic terms for Clastres. They locate the real.

Finally, Clastres adopted an unnecessarily restrictive definition of "taking the Indians seriously," one that could not but have reproduced the very image he had hoped to displace. As a result, his method can only produce an appreciation for the plight of the Indians and their mission. But it cannot produce an appreciation of them so that knowing them is a condition of knowing ourselves. Knowing others is an act of appropriation. This does not mean that we should not know others as Clastres does. It simply means that we cannot know them both in this way and, at the same time, know them in their spontaneity, creativity, and internal incomprehensibility, as we know ourselves. It means that we cannot truly appreciate them, which is what Clastres wants us to do and what we must do if we are to find in his analysis the kernel of a genuine critique of Western capitalism.[2]

The apparent primitive originates what the class-dominated society knows as its distinctive danger. It is the representation of all those features of life that the market cannot tolerate. It refers to those who are wild in the face of discipline, beneath administration, governed by the crowd, given to unbridled affections for concrete others or objects, and concentrated in need. It refers to the negation of "free labor" and therefore of the market itself. But it is a danger that theory and conquest have displaced beyond capitalism's boundaries. In the very externality of its sign—the Savage—the concept suppresses its origin and its significance for critique. In falling prey to this suppression, Clastres has left us with the sense of an error discovered and corrected, and with a model that abstractly demonstrates the possibility of communism. This is a real contribution, but it leaves us too far from history and ourselves.

7

Left Futures

(with Randy Martin)

If it is at all reasonable to speak of "moments" in history, the breakup of the Soviet Union is certainly one if only because its immediate effect was catastrophic for so many nations and so many millions of people. Less dramatically, the breakup has become a force in the critical consciousness of the American Left, and to such a degree that it is almost impossible today to discuss the prospects of progressive social change without appealing to an idea of democracy that excludes all reference to socialism and previous movements implicated in the Socialist vision of progress.

There is no clear sense of what happened and why. Yet, the breakup now operates both as a foundational image in many recent texts of critical historiography and a systematically potent referent in virtually all Left political discourse. What we find odd is that so monumental and significant an event was not greeted in the United States with at least some dismay from more quarters of the Left than just the Communist Party. Instead, the most common reaction to "the collapse of communism" was relief.

For liberals, part of this had to do with the hope that the "end of the Cold War" would ease fiscal constraints on reform, opening the way for a recovery of what had, perhaps necessarily, been deferred—America's progress toward a mixed economy and toward civility. For the greater population, there seemed to be no doubt that the end of the Cold War eliminated the threat of nuclear destruction and that the United States was now in a position to lead the world's peoples from the brink to a "new world order." From either point of view, the "collapse of communism" seemed to validate the general outlines if not all the specifics of American foreign policy since 1947.

For many on the Left, relief expressed something quite different, namely a sense of freedom—not merely from the fear of war and the social distortions of the military economy, but from the immense burden of the history of communism, which for so long had cast a pall on their best efforts. Leftists would no longer have to debate questions about the direction, content, and agency of social progress on the inhospitable terrain of Cold War anticommunism and in regard to its most visible object, the Soviet Union. Nor would they any longer have to account for why their own criticisms of Soviet communism and Stalinism had seemed so weak, that is, why they had not been led by those criticisms to the same conclusion arrived at by those Theodore Draper once approvingly called the professional anti-Communists—rejection of everything that the latter associated with socialism. Perhaps most importantly, Leftists no longer had to think of themselves as bound to the history of social revolution. At last, an indigenous postindustrial, possibly even postcapitalist, American Left could be left to its own devices, its own ability to work within rather than against American institutions and the democratic promise of the United States Constitution.

For intellectual work, this meant that it was sufficient to return to a traditional philosophy of individual rights, the history of which—not the history of class struggle—would now serve to orient and justify progressive social policies. This renewed appeal to the universalistic reason identified with "the Enlightenment" would distinguish the struggle to reinstate a socially responsible liberalism from that of the dogmatic old Left of the Comintern and the sentimental anti-intellectualism of the 1960s. Given this, it would be possible to distinguish the positive impulse of a newer, truer Left from the divisive ideologies, rationalized organizations, and militant strategies of what had once been identified as all the Left there could be—and especially from the Marxian critique of capital with its unsettling implications for the relation of theory to practice.

The fact that it was now possible to separate activism from the Communist movement and its history meant that organizational work would no longer have to appeal to the disquieting idea of class struggle. Ideological work could focus on the prospects of a more gradualist and research-oriented approach to "structural reform" than had previously been conceivable. In this regard, the Left could finally be what it should have been all along. All that was necessary was to construct a vehicle for the reorientation of Left politics toward a new and more modest sense of what is possible, including a thematic principle of unity in terms of which goals could be legitimately chosen and pursued. Given the "collapse" and this rediscovery of the *reason* of civility, one could, in good conscience, be optimistic.

In this state, one could imagine how the use of reason itself would allow Leftists to avoid the more serious obstacles to the formation of a credible Left, in particular those posed by unreasoned and unreasonable political dispositions. The obstacles that remained, primarily reactionary authoritarianism and the unassimilated remnants of earlier Leftist "experiments," could either be effectively disregarded—as in the case of an apparently marginal neo-Fascist right—or considered educable—as in the case of the masses of people increasingly disenchanted with government, big business, and the state.

Consistent with this optimism, there seemed to be good reason to oppose or at least reconsider the earlier claim that the electronic media had become effective instruments for total and monological cultural domination by the "power elite." Rather, television and radio now seemed sufficiently susceptible to ideological and moral contest to provide fertile soil for counterhegemonic expressions of formerly suppressed needs and identities. From this point of view, though the power elite may have been able to determine generally the content of what was broadcast, it could not control the substance and ramifications of audience responses.

Specifically, several audience-based social processes were said to remain relatively free, in the sense of operating under influences quite different from those associated with the transmission of specific messages. These influences have to do with the conditions under which viewers and listeners receive message material and transform it into (1) currency of conversation, (2) means of participating in public affairs, and (3) principles of reference objectively able to validate acts of self-definition.

While each of these might remain subject to manipulation from above, it was thought that this was not presently the most important factor in determining the responses of audiences to the media. Instead, television and radio messages, for example, were said to be "received" in the contexts of lives riven with unsettling contradictions and subject to social forces that could not be reduced to hierarchical control. It followed that audiences are not *created* as objects by the media but "found" as subjects. Audience members are not merely passive recipients but morally involved in activities that profoundly influence the effects of the media on the groups, organizations, and communities in which messages are interpreted and entered into social praxis. This growing emphasis on the *agency* aspect of audiences provided support for the idea that "late capitalism" had given rise as much to "resistance" as to domination, reinforcing the new optimism and the politics authorized by it.

Despite the optimism, and despite the hopefulness implicit in the proliferation of a literature of this conjuncture, the expected development of a new and finally true "new Left" has yet to occur. Activism is even more identified today with issue-based politics than it had been during the 1970s, and theory and analysis are no longer thought of as the work of organic intellectuals, much less as oriented by the idea of an association of interest aimed at ending exploitation. The desire for a unity of practice seems for many writing on the Left to have given way to a more reflective and philosophical mood appropriate to a unity of theory. In this vein, "democracy" is again idealized in terms of interconnected notions of individual rights, public goods and values, and the dependency of social justice on reason, and reason on a realist generalization of science.

On the other hand, the prospects of social reform are evaluated in the context of an expansive and intensifying market, which is itself considered intractable and therefore no longer a proper object of political action, at least in the foreseeable future. This limits the range of conceivable reform to social life taken apart from the materiality of life, implying that the relationship between the development of society and the development of capital is contingent rather than constitutive.

The speculative aspects of the market, previously thought of as exacerbating the difficulties capital has in reproducing the social labor on which its economy depends, have encouraged what might be called a post-postmodernist attention to gaps opening in the otherwise seamless universe of exchange—e.g., consumer demands for more information about processes and products, citizen demands for greater access to media and greater accountability of officials. Thus, arguments have been made in support of emphasizing instrumentally rational attempts to mobilize resources in the interest of a newly vital and at least potentially socially conscious consumer culture.

At one extreme, taking the market for granted once again has led to an endorsement of "civil society" as the appropriate vehicle for the promotion of "democracy." Though its principle remains to be defined, a totalizing image of democracy is deployed as a beacon, redirecting disappointment with the revolutions, labor organizations, and parties toward an expansive political and social renewal. In that light, the classical critique of civil society as mystifying power and exploitation seems to have been either misguided or an exercise in bad faith. At the other extreme, a revitalized interest in "the people" posits the latter as both the decisively social medium of a cultural politics and a category that overwhelms and supersedes class and the relations that constitute the concept of class. Such a politics had once been thought capable only of ratifying the essentialist boundaries by which capital divided its global workforce into competing categories of ethnicity, gender, nationality, and local community. Now, according to this abstraction of the social, the assumption of a popular base for society apart from economy implies that the politics of "the people" is intrinsically progressive though not, perhaps because it is conceived of as primarily cultural, necessarily oriented by practical considerations.

From this point of view, that capacity of the people to engage in political practice can only be realized through a metapolitics. But politics can only come from the *idea* of politics if the latter already exists, and therefore if it exists aside from or beyond the body politic whose mobilization is at issue. Therefore, this notion, that popular politics requires a prior metapolitics, implies a nonpopular practice, a subjectivity conceived of as external to the popular, something altogether different from "the people," which had initially been identified as the natural site and manifestation of critical practice. If this politics is *to be* Socialist, it must not *already be* Socialist. If it is to be progressive, it can only be so as a potential the actuality of which can, in turn, only be realized through an untheorized agency capable of the essential metapolitics of popular politics.

To be sure, these attempts to marginalize or mystify socialism in favor of either a thematic realignment of progressive forces, a substitution of metapolitics for politics, or a redefinition of "the Left" leave some ground for discussing whether we are still dealing with the dynamics of capitalism or merely trying to keep pace with what are so often said to be postindustrial, postcapitalist, postmodern developments in society. Not unexpectedly, even those who defend the Marxian critique of capital—with its implication that an internally generated Socialist impulse provides the starting point for progressive politics—occasionally find themselves tempted to work toward an altogether new North American Left, thereby either taking the market economy for granted or ignoring their own historical understanding of social change in terms of the immanence of Socialist movement to the development of capital.

It goes almost without saying that the logic of the Cold War still infects our literature on the "collapse" (cf. Wallerstein 1994). The sense of what it is to be *Left* is thereby still mediated by the main stream of political discourse for which "Left" and "Right" are equally irrational and illegitimate extremes of this discourse's primary dimension of political reference. However, equally important is what every instance of anticommunism reinforces beyond its incessant broadening of its own discursive categories, namely a concomitant idealization of what Karl Polanyi called "the price-making money market." This is significant to political thought primarily for its ideological constitution of an ostensible civil society. In this, an abstract and ahistorical idea of the "civility" of exchange is imposed on the concrete historicity of a social praxis that can only exist as such, whatever other qualities it must have, in opposition to the universalization of exchange.

We understand the perspective of socialism to refer to the critique of capital in terms of its inability to reproduce the productive society of cooperative labor on which it depends. The theory of this contradiction has provided the foundation for a century and a half of research on the impact of capitalist development on the vitalities, needs, and conditions of life of national populations. What embarrasses this theory today is not that the dynamics have changed or that the condition of humanity has improved. It is, rather, that one can no longer identify any instance of class domination with a national population, much less with a population presumed to co-here as a "society." In this case, it appears as if the working class has dis-appeared or become neutralized beyond redemption. In fact, what have changed are the scale and dimensions of the practical interdependencies that define labor both as an operation of the capitalist mode of production and as the latter's "society of producers."

Thus, equally embarrassing to the Marxist Left's traditional focus on the labor pool of national capitals is the realization, forced upon contempo-rary historical materialism by its own attempts to come to terms with glob- ɣ alization, that it is not possible, indeed should never have been thought possible, to identify socialism as such with specific national formations. In any case, all national states—Socialist, Social Democratic, Capitalist Re-publican, etc.—seem to be if not withering at least wilting in the face of a globally mobile capital, increasingly de-territorialized peoples, and the growing currency of "fictitious capital," which fuels and exacerbates that mobility (cf. Sweezy 1994).

Given that dynamism, the perspective of socialism can only be sustained on the *denationed* terrain of whatever renewed class struggle is constituted by the global mobilization of capital at the end of the twentieth century.[1] But it is by no means clear how that perspective can guide the struggle with-out yielding to the same temptations as its putative liberal alternative—to assume the market, to remove democracy from its historical context, and to identify the prospects of reform accordingly. Nor is it clear how that per-spective can even define the terms by which desocializing exploitation on a world scale can and should be confronted. If Socialists are to act according to their own understanding of globalization, their appeal to renew the struggle for socialism must not beg the vexing questions posed by the transnational dispersion of populations—the capitalist diaspora and its "popular multiplicities."

Without that sense of the relevance of material conditions to Left poli-tics, without the perspective of historical materialism, the revival of the cri-tique of denationalization (formerly tied to theories of imperialism based on national models of capitalist development) has been as one-sided in its at-tention to the cultural and demographic diasporic consequences of capital's mobility as the anticommunism of the Cold War had been one-dimensional in its obsession with the dangers of collectivization, particularly the eco-nomic threat posed by the possibility that national models of Socialist econ-omy might have been able to succeed.[2]

It is obviously important to analyze both cultural and demographic as-pects of the global capitalist diaspora, as current scholarship demonstrates. But we believe that analyzing effects and theorizing dynamics have to be con-sidered, for the moment, in quite different terms. It is theory that seems to have suffered a lapse. This is evident, in part, in the way events in the for-mer Communist nations have been interpreted and incorporated into pro-posals for a new unifying departure for the Left. To be sure, the emphasis on

culture exposes once again the social, psychologically oppressive, and geno-
cidal aspects of capitalist postmodernity. But its chief problems arise because
of its bearing on theories of resistance to oppression and genocide—as
against the modernist residues of violence within postmodernity rather than
as against the remorseless expansiveness and relentless intensities of capitalism. Given this implication of the emphasis on culture, it is easy to understand
why oppression appears to be a product of depersonalized and ostensibly rational forms of absolutist power rather than a byproduct of the relativizing
contradictions of production and circulation, value and price, economy and
society.

This certainly highlights the centrality of domination and, with that,
brings to light concomitant forms of resistance otherwise unaccountable except by reference to heroic acts of will. But culturalist theory underempha-
sizes the exploitation of what is societally generative about the cooperation
on which capital relies, that is, social labor. It therefore tends to deny that
what it sees as "older," archaic forms of struggle are relevant to Left politics. That the re-emergence of those forms often has nationalist or even sectarian overtones is certainly true. But, then, the same must be admitted
about many of the struggles of waged laborers in the shops and factories of
the early nineteenth century. To ignore this type of struggle, or to declare its
irrelevance under the new conditions posed by globalization, is to ignore the
way in which precisely such conditions have been part of the development
of "the society of the producers" over the past two-and-one-half centuries.
Capitalist expansion always puts labor's gains at peril, requiring a constant
rethinking of the prospects of Left politics. This is no less true today than it
was two hundred years ago. The lesson, therefore, is not that history is at an
end, but that the present situation is itself historical.

Thus, given an overemphasis on culture and the politics of culture, it is
easy to exclude the struggle against exploitation from any authentic politics of resistance. The latter, in turn, is seen as drawing its impulse from
something altogether different from exploitation—e.g., the oppressiveness
of abstract power in the form of "statism." It follows that the only legitimate politics for the Left is whatever remains when the despised forms of
the past and their content (exploitation) are eliminated. Conceived of in
this way, legitimate politics excludes whatever processes and organizations attempt to engage the agencies of exploitation in their own terms
and according to their own contexts. Here, however, the baby is thrown
out with the bath. A focus on exploitation is, ipso facto, denied legitimacy; or exploitation is recast as a moral or social problem (e.g., inequality) rather than understood as a fundamental historical feature of the
capitalist development of society.

In any case, for culturalism or historical materialism, it is one thing
to identify a conjuncture—globalization, the collapse of communism, or
what have you—and another to define the political significance (therefore
prospects) of that conjuncture. The more complex the analysis, presumably

according to the greater complexity and urgency of events, the less it is possible to imagine a politics that makes a difference—that is, which covers and is competent to the conjuncture itself, which subjects the "balance of forces" *as a whole* directly to the agency of society however conceived. What makes this problem yet more poignant today is that one cost of exulting in the "collapse of communism" has been the loss of continuity within critical practice across the diverse, multidimensional, extravagantly mediated, and often self-weakening history of the Left.

Two related consequences of the attempt to devise an utterly "new Left," thematically united against all that the Left had been, are (1) the loss of interest in the historiographical validity of the claims on which that attempt is based and (2) a corresponding inability to account for the historical significance attributed at the outset to those formations that are presumably to be unified. Given this lapse of historical imagination, it is difficult to conceive of whatever struggle is now to be taken as the core of Left politics (e.g., in regard to self-management, multiculturalism, participatory democracy) as part of the greater struggle against exploitation throughout the ages of class society. It is also difficult to conceive of how such a "new" thematically unified politics can participate in the diversity of current struggles, and themes of struggle, operating across the diasporic universe contrived by capital as its final solution to the myriad problems engendered by its dependence on the socialized production of unsocialized wealth.

How is this lapse of historical imagination incorporated into the North American Left's understanding of itself, specifically in the ways in which debates on the Left contribute to or detract from a critical and forward looking process of learning, teaching, and self-reflection? When issues (themes) are taken out of their historical context for the sake of a formal unity, that unity in turn loses its own capacity to refer to a coherent context. On the other hand, the tendency to decontextualize issues, and therefore to idealize politics, doubtless reflects desperate conditions— e.g., the erosion of the Social Democratic social and legal foundation, such as it is, on which progressive activism once reluctantly relied and which it often took for granted.

There is a practical problem related to the elision of context. The attempt to unify a Left based on separating a unifying theme from the context in which it is possible to conceive of a historically significant Left (e.g., the critique of capital) can itself cause disunity. This is so because the attempt to unite diverse tendencies in this way (the unaccountably elevated subject position from which the diversity of activism inevitably appears as "fragmented") is bound to appear disruptive to those already engaged, for good and well-formed reasons, in concretely situated political action. Thus, the very attempt to create unity on the Left, in the terms by which this is presently being defended, seems most likely to exacerbate the condition its proponents had hoped to cure.

Anticipating this dilemma, more than a few writers seem to advocate organizational forms that are more similar to the "old" and "old new" Lefts than they are willing to admit. In this case, the terms by which they have defined their idea of a new Left (e.g., "new social movements") need to be reconsidered. More commonly, however, programmatic suggestions for thematic unity typically arouse opposition from those said to be dividing the Left—perhaps because what appears to be a fragment from one point of view is, from another, based on its own principle of unification. In this case, those advocating unity need to reconsider their diagnosis of the "crisis" that they attribute to the Left. If that crisis is not that of an internally generated negative disunity, as it is usually said to be, then it is necessary to reconsider the issue of "difference" on the Left, its causes, implications, and the perspective from which difference is perceived and interpreted.

Not only differences among specific political projects, but the significance attributed to the difference between the putatively legitimate "new social movements" and the putatively illegitimate "old Left," would have to be given altogether different readings from, for example, Stanley Aronowitz's brief for a new unity around the several themes that he identifies with "radical democracy" (1993, 1996).

Independently of but related to these criticisms, there remains a crucial gap in the argument for thematic unity. It is not possible both to claim that progressive politics is oriented by the social base of capitalism ("the people") and to claim that the traditionally organized politics of that base (unions, parties, revolutions) are antidemocratic, totalitarian, or otherwise intrinsically sectarian. Or, if it is possible, then the social base must be conceived of as distinct from politics, and politics must be conceived of as essentially without a base. In that case, political agency can only be conceived of in idealist and antihistorical terms, as something arising unaccountably from outside the population to be mobilized, therefore capable of appealing to that population only apart from and against whatever forms of subjectivity are generated from within it as matters of social praxis or "will-formation." Thus, it does not seem possible, without reifying "civil society" or idealizing a political subjectivity (agency, reason, neutrality, etc.) beyond politics as such, to reconcile rejecting the Left's past with an option of an autonomous population whose mobilization as a constituency (or capacity for such mobilization) is said to be a necessary condition of progressive movement (see Cohen and Arato, 1992, for an example of an analysis that begs the questions raised by this dilemma).

The most important implication of this version of unity is, then, an elitist and potentially reactionary politics. It offers guidance to people (as constituency) whose concerns are defined thematically, as "moral values" rather than as features of an interest. But the proposal of so abstract a unity can only represent the practical imperatives of a subject position that defines itself as radically distinct from the popular body politic it purports to unite. Therefore, its political project can only operate outside of those processes that were supposed to have generated the need for and possibility of unity in the first place—if unity is to be "of the people," therefore presumably "radically democratic."

Some writers on the Left have confronted the dilemma directly, as a problem within the Marxian critique of capital. Discussions of unification along these lines focus on conditions presented by the contradictions inherent in the dependency of capitalist accumulation on the reproducibility of social labor. From this point of view, it can be and has been argued that (1) the idea of democracy (popular sovereignty) is implicit in the more general idea of socialism (universal voluntary cooperation), and (2) politics must be seen as a constitutive feature of capitalism and, within the vicissitudes of the capitalist political economy, contingent in its organization and manifest content. Among the most important social historical implications of these propositions are: People are not absolutely free to choose the terms of their struggles; they must often confront organization with organization and power with power; and political action has its own dilemmas that cannot be avoided in advance.

This characterization of political action avoids some of the problems involved in attempting to separate the history of people (society) from the history of politics. However, even for its proponents, it remains tempting to imagine an altogether new form of political organization that could, at least in the short run, supersede the older forms. To that extent, Marxism becomes eclectic when applied to the political question, thereby presenting itself, metatheoretically, as a de facto defense of the principle of eclecticism. Then, there is little choice but to favor insight and assertion over critique, making it impossible to distinguish between what is and what is not valid in political action and to clarify how validity is in any case to be determined.

Non-Marxian attempts to establish a foundation for Left unity have, with few exceptions, relied on the empirical methods of the social sciences to demonstrate that a non-divisive politics of unity can be generated from within society if the latter is conceived of as a system. This typically implies an interaction of system functions that can only be defined as superordinate to and fundamentally different from what is said in that light to be everyday life. The latter neither constitutes society (which is exhaustively defined by its own functions and their institutional forms) nor is otherwise positively generative—because all social change that proceeds from the rationality of action is, according to this view, a function of the self-regulating interaction of institutions. All instances of popular mobilization are, by definition, non-rational symptomatic expressions (e.g., of "system strain"), historically significant only to the extent to which they disrupt normal equilibrating processes. Such a view, with its occasional appeal to a microtheory of "rational choice," tends to support a politics consistent with the operations of institutional formations—educational, economic, communicative, religious, and political—that have been for decades consistently criticized for their mystification of power and exploitation.

The upshot of all of this is that if it is reasonable to see the Left as in crisis, a large part of that crisis certainly consists of a failure to make theoretically coherent the distinction between those social and societal formations that should be understood as resistance (the putative Left) and those that should be understood as manifesting little more than an interest in power. More generally, the largest part of it lies in the failure to recognize that every instance of criticism (e.g., attempts to unify the Left against a history of fragmentation, or to construct a new Left against the Left's past) is itself a proper object of criticism.

Intolerance for history is also at the heart of basing the idea of a new Left on the claim that the record of traditional Left thought and politics presents little more than elitism, dogmatism, and subservience to the Soviet Union. The unaccountable abstractness of such a claim and the dispositionalism that it presupposes are inconsistent with the critique of positivism that generates and supports critical thinking in general. To that extent, the claim invokes a model for understanding the history of the Left that even its advocates agree is invalid when applied to the history of capitalist modernization. It involves understanding events as symptoms of relatively fixed structures, intentions, and dispositions revealed conclusively by the behavior and statements of putatively significant actors.

This is a different way of understanding history than what is in critical thought referred to as dialectics. The latter analyzes events as instances of learning and, in that regard, as both relational and reflexive. Events involving decision and the mobilization of effort are, for dialectics, intrinsically variable political features of a process. It should be noted that "process" does not refer here to a series of behaviors or to motions of some body, actor, or collectivity, but to what might loosely be called a social dynamics, therefore a politics, of self-transformation. Such a process, in turn, is conceived of in terms of a fundamental paradox, which is the tragic feature of all political action to the extent to which politics is conceived of as a practice involving learning rather than an instance of administration, an application of rules, or a project. The implications of this paradox have been widely discussed in the activist literature and by many writers associated with the tradition of "critical social theory," or what Sartre more precisely calls "dialectical reason," though almost never in mainstream political science, economics, or sociology.

The paradox consists of the following. For there to be politics at all, at least beyond the constraints of the institutional apparatuses of the state, decisions can only be arrived at through a deliberation that is conspicuously multifarious, discursive, and contentious. Yet, for *an act* to take place, the process must be brought to a decisive conclusion regardless of ambiguity, ambivalence, doubt, and residual differences of opinion. It is the *decisiveness* of the conclusion more than its content that, if action is to proceed, must ultimately become the focus of at least some degree of consensus. The momentarily final conclusion, therefore, can only be *logically* provisional, which is to say provisional and subject to doubt only *after* the fact and from the standpoint of renewed deliberation (often called in this context *theory* in contrast with practice) momentarily apart from the act itself (often called in this context *practice*).

For this moment of action to occur, ambiguities and uncertainties must be taken by the parties to have been resolved, though they nevertheless remain latent to the political process and, therefore, a covert feature of the subsequent history of events and their agents. Such decisions can only have an effect, thereby becoming part of learning, if they are then acted on with sufficient rigor and determination—*as if* those resolutions were finally beyond doubt. This is so despite the fact that it is not possible in advance to foresee the significance of particular consequences or to predict unequivocally, or with a specific order of probabilities, the ways in which such consequences might interact with one another producing yet another situation in which self-reflection and political action are unavoidable. Only from the perspective of self-critical reflection can one begin to appreciate the significance of the regression of self-criticism to an idealized rationalization of Left politics and a moralistic and dangerously self-serving re-reading of history consistent with it.

One of the more dramatic casualties of seeing the history of the Left undialectically—exclusively in terms of failures that reflect dispositions built into Socialist and Communist politics—was a weakening of support on the part of many Democratic Socialists for the Cuban and Nicaraguan Revolutions, on the grounds that neither government was "democratic." The principle of this rejection was indefinable as typically stated, and in no case was it or could it have been generalized rationally to other more favored nations. The judgment was, in that form, antihistorical and inconsistent with any notion of politics as a self-reflective and complexly mediated development of organization, consciousness, direction, definition, and power.

When we refer to this as a casualty, then, we mean that it is a casualty *for* the North American Left's understanding of itself: in particular for attempts to reconcile prescriptions for reforming that Left with descriptions and analyses of what is happening elsewhere in the world. We are not claiming that particular cases should never be evaluated and criticized, but only that being judgmental in so categorical a way is inconsistent with respecting the types of noninstitutional political processes that are inevitable as such under conditions which generate a political Left (including the Left attempting to reform itself). Such a categorical attitude assumes as well that referring to historical conditions of those instances of social/political action that make it necessary and possible to reflect on further prospects of action is merely incidental to such reflections and, indeed, can only be disruptive of them.

This is analogous to someone attempting to come to terms with his or her self by doing so as a radically-other-deliberative-self against which the object-self (of such rational deliberation) can only be seen as inferior, poorly formed, irrational, symptomatic, or otherwise incapable of reflection and self-knowledge. If this were so, one could not have been anything like what one had become, nor could one ever tolerate what one had been. Self-reflection and practice would be utterly divided and opposed, as the master and the slave. The former would know and decide, while the latter would do. Knowing would be altogether incompatible with doing, if only because detachment is sullied by interest and pleasure, and engagement is endangered by the relativism of perspective and choice. As G.W.F. Hegel showed for the phenomenology of self-consciousness, the subjectivity of master can only reenter the realm of practice by rediscovering the subjectivity of slave (the actor in the world) *within the self*, thereby rejecting the dualism of an *activity* altogether external to and other than *thought*.

The contradiction inherent in the relationship between conclusiveness and doubt, described above, presents quite a different sort of "crisis" from the notion of failure currently diagnosed by those who find it both necessary and convenient to take an absolute distance from their own Leftist past. It requires that it be admitted at the outset that the Left is always in crisis, that crisis is, in a sense, the Left's mode of being—if only because it is explicitly burdened with the obligation continually to reconsider whatever relationship of theory and practice had been taken for granted and, in the process, to reflect critically on its own experience of the activity of reconsideration. Otherwise, one is too easily led to agree that the fragmentation of the Left and the failure of at least some Leftists to deny that their own history is significant to their project are symptoms of a totalizing disease that must be cured and for which a cure can only be found from a perspective outside of the disease and the diseased body.

In another perhaps more important sense, whatever can be said for a crisis of the Left beyond that fundamental crisis that is intrinsic to any self-reflective critical activity, it should not be thought of as a specific state arising uniquely from uncured defects, inherently antiprogressive dispositions, or bad faith. Certainly, internally generated problems must be taken into account in any attempt to revisit the history of the Left in regard to prospects for the future. But it is necessary to place such problems within a yet greater frame of reference, one which avoids treating the problems the Left has had in remaining afloat as reasons for abandoning the ship.

The "crisis," thought of then as a set of problems rather than as a condition requiring radical surgery, can be understood in somewhat the same ways in which critically minded intellectuals and activists understand other events. Above all, this means, logically, that if "the crisis of the Left" must be considered as a whole, it should be seen as reflecting the inclusive situation for which it is legitimate to define the Left as a whole. We believe that the two most relevant features of this situation are the radicalization of capital's project of socially unimpeded (global) mobility and the correlative attack on all political boundaries, formations, and ideas that have anything whatsoever to do with the viability of the community of strangers commonly called "society." This perspective reintegrates the crisis of the Left, such as it is, with other problems, needs, and crises. Therefore, it precludes situating that crisis in the context (and its greater supporting contexts) of a pure self-generating subjectivity able to complete itself (make itself whole), voluntaristically, through the application of a type of reason that can operate beyond crisis and independently of politics.

Deriving the "crisis of the Left" from intrinsic flaws and dispositions of past Leftisms implies a corresponding analysis of the greater society in which those Leftisms emerged and suffered their special fates. When we consider these two analyses together, as we must if the methodology and conclusions of either are to be defended, it is possible to see how thoroughly and problematically revisionist each position becomes when allowed to develop independently of its relationship with the other. In regard to the greater society, instead of a contradictory interest-based formation comprised of the various struggles associated with capitalist expansionism, the North American state—as the background against which the Left's failure to achieve unity (and democracy) is understood as a lost opportunity that could have been taken—now appears quite different from the sort of thing against which an authentic Left might mobilize or might ever have mobilized. It appears to be open to the very pluralism that generations of Left thinkers and researchers had shown to be impossible without decidedly and oppressively unpluralistic qualifications of the principle of distributive justice. It is that renewed but covert idealization of the American body politic that must be taken into account in evaluating calls for a thematic and organizational unification of the Left (excluding virtually all that the Left had been), therefore, implicitly, for a more institutionally oriented Left politics.

The theory, or diagnosis, that sees "the crisis of the Left" as a result of failures and dispositions, a disease of the ostensible concrete totality, thus yields a revised history of the greater context, which makes it relatively easy to imagine a concretely total cure. But this, in turn, requires a view of the context (American institutions, capitalism, etc.) as able to sustain in its own terms the prospective health of a newly crisis-resistant Left politics. Thus, a Left unified thematically and identified in opposition to its past can only be one dependent on the very structures and projects the critique of which has been the basis for defining what it has meant and continues to mean to be "of the Left." Moreover, such a context itself requires a theory, since pluralism must now be described in regard to a previously unexpected capacity to include among representative interests those critical ideas and practices that it has never been able to tolerate. At a minimum, pluralism would have to be driven somehow by an underlying culture of mutual recognition and reciprocity. This is possible only if supported by the fair and socially rational distribution of resources and systematically reliable and socially responsible relations of authority. But, if these values can be achieved only by a change in the material order itself, and if pluralism can only be sustained by preventing those "structural" issues from being raised in the forms in which their effects are experienced, then the cost of Left participation in a pluralist institutional order (implicit in any issue-based notion of thematic unity) is a rejection of the very issues and constituencies that have always made and continue to make a Left necessary.

Such a new Left that cannot be recognizably Left, such a putative post-pluralist moment of pluralism, would have to be organized along the politically expressive dimension from which pluralism derives its claim exhaustively to represent the field of legitimate interests. This dimension ranges from left to right, and defines all legitimate positions as variations of a basic liberalism of equality before the law, tolerance, and civility. This determination of which interests can legitimately be represented is presumed able, uniquely, to provide for a type of interaction that allows progressive programs to be achieved without struggle. More generally, it is assumed that this type of interaction composes itself as an organic solidarity that supports a politics of negotiation among putative representatives of putatively represented constituencies prepared endlessly to endure whatever conditions (including the lack of political agency) made them constituencies of the Left in the first place.

Despite the problems it poses for the very idea of a Left, this turn in theory and practice has doubtless helped to reinvigorate the critique of neoimperialism. But it has done so at considerable expense: by deemphasizing the capitalist dynamics of globalization in favor of the generalization and intensification of exploitation as a direct product of modernity. Thus, the mobility of capital is often personalized, hence trivialized, by focusing on the various conspiracies that facilitate it. Similarly, emphasis on the continual and escalating violations of regional, national, and local populations by agencies of the global market tends to moralize such events, to depoliticize them. In that way it neutralizes them as political referents, though the fact of such violations remains as at least a haunting presence, indicating that the call for a new unified Left around the themes of "radical democracy"—participatory democracy, self-management, and the like—may be so parochial as to be more part of the problem than a legitimate solution. By itself, however, the neutralization within political discourse of the varied oppressions associated with globalization easily reinforces the tendency, as we have seen vividly displayed in so much of current Left self-criticism, to reject anything remotely resembling instruments of counterhegemonic power.

To that extent, the moralization, and concomitant abstraction, of those oppressions ends by depriving them of their human significance as well as their significance for defining a Left politics adequate, as Theodor Adorno might have said, to the concept of a "Left." What is missing, and what tends to be thrown out when the history of the Left is itself denied validity, is the sort of historical materialism of globalization that is so aptly and succinctly presented in one of its versions by Paul Sweezy (1994). For Sweezy, this involves a critique of globalization in terms of the dynamics of capitalist development: The circulation of fictitious capital ("market") has become incapable, apparently incurably so, of responding to the needs of both productive capital and its socialized system of production (what is often called "infrastructure"). To the extent to which this appears as an intelligible extension of the relationship between the socialization of labor (on the basis of which capitalist wealth is possible and class struggle necessary) and circulation ("the price-making money market"), it is tied to concepts (value, class, exploitation) that at least provide for the possibility of considering what types of politics might correspond to the historical situation we now share and, more generally, might express the need of all humanity to sustain the "society of the producers."

Considerable effort has been expended toward re-examining the social implications of the globalization of the capitalist market and its transnational political agencies, especially the diasporic compulsions introduced by the increasingly rapid movements of currency, people, and capital (see Aronowitz and Gautney 2003; Hardt and Negri 2000). However, there has been a significant linguistic change from the terms and metaphors of the canonical materialist account to a language that reflects the implications of a fundamental opposition between power and culture for critical thought. The exploitative and desocializing character of capitalist accumulation now begins to appear, to those most eager to abandon the Socialist project, to be more the totalizing impulse of statism than anything having to do with the transformation of the capitalist political economy according to the self-contradictory logic of what Marx called, variously, "universal exchange" and "circulation." Even some of the most provocative of the new models of economic and cultural imperialism problematically remain tied to images of national power, despite the fact that the discussion of national polities is increasingly focused on the "destabilizing" effects of powers beyond the control of governments or states. To the extent to which the latter has been framed by images of national power, the emphasis has been increasingly on violations of culture and identity rather than on the material violations of everyday life, which we believe remain at the heart of the matter. From this point of view, all acts of "resistance" appear to express the authentic Left side of a dialectic of totalizing power and absolute emancipation. Any project short of universal emancipation is thereby disqualified; and since all concrete examples of struggle display the ambiguities and ambivalent undertakings of such concreteness, practice can do little more than disqualify itself. The same is true for all concrete manifestations of opposition to the historically limited form of domination we refer to as capitalism.

It almost goes without saying that one of the truly divisive and, it must be admitted, intellectually unresolved issues in the history of the U.S. Left has been how to relate to those countries formerly or still governed by Communist parties. While the most intense debates originally took place within and around the parties, the issue was given its publicly most significant expression during the Cold War, when no discourse was free of the rhetoric, propaganda, and terroristic aspects of anticommunism. This is still a mighty legacy of "distorted communication" from which none of us is yet free.

Like racism, hegemonic anticommunism has found adequate guises for its occult and apocalyptic logic, particularly in its identification of new enemies and its suspicions of old friends. The Russians may no longer be coming, but what they *really* were might be here already in the familiar forms of secular humanism, welfare, collectivism, multiculturalism, feminism, internationalism, and, ironically, liberalism. Subtler versions of this list can be found among the more respectably authoritarian neoconservatives, as the range of what they see as virtue's antagonists enlarges day by day and social liberalism is forced into narrower and narrower ideological frames of reference.

For example, in a typical burst of enthusiasm for the suppression of ideas with which he either does not agree or of which he lacks knowledge, President John Silber of Boston University constructed a bizarre list of enemies, similar in principle to those of his associates in the Right-wing National Association of Scholars. It includes, among other things, ethnomethodology, postmodernism, dance therapy, structuralism, critical theory, Marxism, and virtually all of what the human sciences have produced in the past several decades. It is obviously important to try and discover the deep structure of such a list if reaction is at all to become comprehensible. At present, however, there seems to be only an invocation of the principle of reaction to all instances of self-critical reason. This new wave of authoritarianism is at least part of the context faced by any attempt to define a Left and evaluate its prospects, as well as to try and find ways of speaking publicly in a critically emancipatory way.

This persistence of the expansive reactionary logic—though not necessarily the original substance—of anticommunism within the public confluences of discourses in which all of us in one way or another participate, still infects discussions of political principle. On the other hand, any attempt to summarize history, to textualize it, is by now well known to resolve ambiguities in ways that cannot be justified merely by reference to information or "sources," to depend on modes of representation that cannot be shown to correspond unequivocally to what is supposedly represented (e.g., processes, structures, events, practices), and to attribute a direction or directions to the past according to present interests. In regard to this, the Left needs to show the same intellectual modesty that it correctly requires of reactionary claims. By themselves, the persistence of anticommunism and the radical skepticism that should always accompany the writing or reading of history, should be enough to justify caution in appealing to "the past" to justify instituting a "new" Left project. This is even more so given the desperation with which one can hardly avoid viewing current events. At least it should temper if not unsettle the enthusiasm, especially of those for whom power and resistance had come to represent the only viable dialectic of change, for what once appeared to be popular mobilizations in the former Soviet Union and Eastern and Central Europe.

Assuming that it is and was possible to examine such events free of the discourses of the Cold War, and simultaneously and in the same terms to reconsider the history of the Left, it must still be admitted that we are in no better position today to evaluate what portion of the problem posed by those events and that history reflects intractable internally destructive dispositions of communism (or socialism), and what portion reflects the complex and uncertain contexts in which decisions were made and implemented and loyalties became explicit. Even if it is reasonable to define complex events by simple formulae, it was and is no more reasonable to assume that whatever happened in and around the former "Communist world" was due to the nature of the beast than that it was due to conditions beyond the beast's control.

The most influential American literature on socialism prior to 1991 was, with some exceptions, produced by one of the most clearly definable apparatuses of the foreign policy establishment, its academic branch. As Stephen Cohen argued in an early issue of *Socialism and Democracy*, scholarly studies of the Soviet Union were riven with methodological and conceptual defects that could only be considered insignificant from the overall point of view which informed that research (1986). The studies, above all, were intended to reinforce the propaganda of the Cold War. It is clear that had this literature been oriented to any other topic but communism, the mainstream field of "Soviet studies" would have been an academic scandal.

Since the "end of the Cold War," the situation is not much improved, though the referents used in analyses of world affairs have changed in significant ways. The Communist icon of the Cold War is now the negative ideal type against which an absolutely idealized capitalist market is both taken to be real and deemed the only sustainable paradigm for universal human organization. Perhaps for this reason, it has become morally imperative—no longer merely a matter of national security but one of virtue itself—to destroy Cuba and to enforce the antisocial standards of finance capital on nations and populations without regard to their social ramifications, in particular the immensity of human suffering the global "free market" has caused and continues to cause—though recent events in Latin America may have momentarily disrupted the hegemonic project.

But it was not merely propaganda that constituted the core of this literature. It would have been difficult in any case to tell what of communism's problems, defects, and fate were inherent in it and what were the results of pressures and problems engendered by a context common to all nations and peoples. There was no available theory of social development within the mainstream disciplines that could have distinguished clearly enough between what about a society derives from intrinsic features and what derives from factors external to it. That was left to the inferential strictures of ideology. Speculation about essence and appearance has, as is well known, always been rife within the social sciences. But, unfortunately, the theoretical coherence of attempts to distinguish between internal and external determinants has been attained only by idealizing capitalist modernity and treating communism as something altogether *sui generis*.

The literature on the Soviet system, with its negatively idealist eccentricity, has failed for the most part to provide any conceptually defensible evaluation, even when the system was intact (cf., however, Kerblay 1983 and Lane 1978). No wonder that the aftermath of the Cold War has seen little improvement in the public discussion of "actually existing socialism" much less in discussions of the history of which it is part. Moreover, while there have been a number of fine studies by more critically inclined scholars, these typically rely on "class" and "state" models more suitable for a sociology of capitalism than for the analysis of social economies such as Soviet socialism. The controversy over "communism" and its role in the history of the Left thus remains as impassioned and undecidable today as ever. It is important, as we have argued, to appreciate how much the defects of that controversy still influence the content and rhetoric of debates on the Left, particularly about prospects for a politically vital future.

After the Second World War, in the context of McCarthyism and the Cold War, the so-called North American old Left was identified exclusively with Soviet communism.[3] Within its ranks, however, there were strong differences of opinion. For some, the Soviet Union was not the center of the Socialist movement, but only one form socialism might take among nation states. In that case, it was argued, the only socialism that could be valid in the national context of the United States would have to be one tied to the history of the American version of the class struggle and its historical mediations within the international division of labor and the global extensions of the multinational corporate economy and the North American state. The anti-Communist's test of political and ideological virtue, however, was not what one believed about the USSR, but whether or not one repudiated it altogether.

While the "new Left" of the 1960s began with a specific repudiation of the old parties, its leaders, for the most part, initially refused to take a definite stand against the Soviet Union, preferring instead to focus on the relationship between the democratic potential of popular mobilizations and the obstacles posed by the state and its institutions to "participatory democracy." For polemicists like Theodore Draper and Irving Howe, both Leftisms were equal, and both had to be condemned, though what could then be advocated as socially progressive could hardly be clear. Interestingly enough, all those positions reflected certain features of Cold War ideology, regardless of disagreements and no matter how acerbic their expressions. Thus, all accepted as a fact that the United States and the Soviet Union were two equally dominant superpowers operating in two independent and fully organized worlds, though the Soviet sphere of influence was referred to as a "bloc" and that of the United States as "the free world" of "the democracies." While the two might vie for influence in or control of the third world, and build arsenals for possible use against one another, they were thought to embody two distinct and complete formations, beyond any history but that of a conflict between the obsessively fixed and totalitarian disposition of one and the inherently progressive entrepreneurship, humanism, and democracy of the other.

The dilemma that this state of affairs presented for the U.S. Left was how to imagine its own political project without first having to account for the USSR as something any Left was either destined to become or had absolutely to avoid. A dualistic strategy was adopted by the public Left outside of the Communist Party. On the one hand, the Soviet system was described by a vocabulary of interchangeable labels that, regardless of pedigree, evaded the theoretical and historical issues altogether: state capitalism, state socialism, bureaucracy, party rule, totalitarianism, etc. On the other hand, it was argued on the basis of this denotational evasion that it is possible to ignore the Soviet Union in the interest of mobilizing popular opposition to the capitalist state. For that, the significance of international communism lay primarily in the justification it provided for the U.S. government's decision in the late 1970s to shift investment from society to the expansion of its military machinery.

From the point of view of international relations, this encouraged many on the Left to adopt the principle of national self-determination, in opposition to U.S. militarism, and to focus on popular movements within the third world as models for the struggle at home. In this regard, the ideas and practices associated with socialism became increasingly irrelevant. To the extent that the irrelevance of socialism was accepted as a foundation for critical intellectual work, theories about the prospects of progressive politics were likely to be compatible with the Left rejectionism of the Cold War ideological formation—at least to the degree to which they refused to recognize any form of resistance and opposition but the most simplistic and exclusionary versions of "dissent."

That is part of the context in which political practice, whatever its appropriateness to its own situation, became disconnected from what had been a theoretically elaborate sense of a historically defensible project. This, we believe, has opened the way for present speculations on the possibility of unifying the Left around the themes and principles of an as yet undefined "radical democracy" identified for the moment with equally inchoate principles of self-management, localism, and, most problematically, the radically anti-organizational constituencies referred to both as "new social movements" and as the most legitimate expression of "civil society."

This tendency was doubtless reinforced by the momentous events of 1989. The fall of the Berlin wall and the apparent collapse of the Communist parties seemed to signal a final break with the past and with the burdens it had imposed on the Left. However, rather than settling the matter once and for all, this global reformation inspired yet another division. On the one hand, the "collapse," and with it the loss of historical connection with the social revolutions, seemed to open the way for a truly democratic socialism of the people. In that case, the very experience in terms of which the Left had come to formulate the possibility of socially progressive politics is eradicated by the act of denying that revolutionary practice did or could play any progressive role whatsoever in history. In the most extreme cases, reentering the "order" of global capital has itself been cast as progressive and as an instance of positive revolution.

On the other hand, it seemed as likely that socialism itself had been eclipsed or somehow transcended by the putative return of "civil society." Given this way of understanding the events of the late 1980s, it seemed sufficient merely to form the notion of radical democracy. It was apparently not necessary to account either for its historical conditions or the contradictions inherent in the new geopolitical context in which radical democracy would have to make its way in intentions, projects, and formations as far removed from its ideals as the "old Left" was said to have been from its ideal of universal cooperation. Whatever the complications introduced by the "collapse of communism," it seems clear that the most prominent ideas on the Left still depend on structures of meaning derived from an insufficiently examined past, in particular the same *spectres* and binaries that had so thoroughly limited the frame of reference within which Leftists had tried to define themselves prior to 1989 and, for that matter, earlier as well. Thus, it may not be practical, whether or not it is desirable on other grounds, to consider the present as a turn both in the fortunes and the constitution of the North American Left. At least this seems to be so in regard to the sort of self-critical discussion we believe is necessary if the prospects of the Left are to be fairly assessed in the light of the urgency that now motivates Left thinking and activism, and where it must be admitted that such self-reflections are bound to be limited by the very discourses from which they still draw their vitality.

The ostensible newness of the various "new Lefts" now apparently on the agenda may be less important than the possibility that there is a way of coming to terms with the past and the present different from that of defining the latter against the former and different from recognizing only those tendencies that qualify for admission to a new non- or anti-Socialist Left by virtue of accepting precisely this role of self-negation—in whatever terms are now used to justify it. Specifically, it is necessary to try and free our discourse from the counterproductive Cold War polarity of socialism and democracy by which Leftists find themselves divided without a coherent account of the division. That polarity has bred a concept of socialism tied to the imagination of a totalitarianism unable to support the idea of any process but the Communist cell's own self-elaboration. It has given rise to an idealization of democracy so practically and conceptually impoverished that it is scarcely credible in its own terms, and so implicated in anti-collectivist discussions of individual rights that it has lost any clear relevance to the overwhelming facts of interdependency and collective life.

This obviously entails a more cautious approach to the development of the American Left than we are used to. Above all, it involves reexamining the various ways in which the idea of socialism has been simplified and distorted, and thereby been placed beyond examination. Contrary to the notion that the Socialist countries constituted a distinct and fixed system outside of capitalism, we need to think of socialism, and all its manifestations, in the critical terms by which it was first theorized by Marx, namely as the suppressed internally self-critical principle of capital itself. From this point of view, the Socialist nations were merely sites in which the possibility of a self-reproducing "society of producers" was expressed, with whatever limitations, defects, confusions, and contradictions that inevitably characterized those expressions.

Socialist movements, then, were and are movements within capitalism, expressions of the latter's own contradictory project—the asocial accumulation of wealth on the basis of social labor and the attempt to mitigate the general costs to capital of the society of that labor. Such movements must be understood at least as much in terms of the mediations of their own settings as in terms of their internal dynamics. Whatever the American Left might be, it will to some extent be what it was, and that is at least one source of its strength however it otherwise manifests itself. In the context of the globalization of finance, there is a greater need for the tolerance of precisely the diversity that had been identified as fragmentation and, through that, as part of the Left's crisis rather than a feature of its strength.

Self-recognition by the Left requires recognition of its history, therefore of the problems involved in trying to organize against that history and the possibilities inherent in organizing in terms of it. It means re-evaluating the extent to which globalization should be seen fundamentally in its capitalist aspect or in some other aspect however defined—as postmodern, postcapitalist, post-Socialist, or post-Marxist. For the U.S. Left this means connecting its inexplicitly Socialist elements with those that have been and are explicitly Socialist.

The efforts to generate socialism within and against the global dominance of capital are recognizable along two dimensions. The first includes attempts, however fitful, deformed, or immature, to struggle for a social economy, for which the production of social life in general has priority over production for profit. The second includes all organizations in which the forms of participation—and their mediations—are conceivably consistent with the interdependence and forms of association that Marx referred to as the *society* of the producers beyond the *producers* of society. It follows that socialism and democracy are two aspects of the same politics as they are of the same theoretical problematic even when their expressions are historically compromised. It also follows that any process by which the Left can be said to develop will be one that is as internally critical as it is externally articulate.

From this point of view, the Left's future is, as always, now; and "now" is a distinctly historical present, both in its need to incorporate a past it nevertheless must transcend and in its need to recognize the activist, ideological, and theoretical elements that continue to constitute it despite the momentary desire of so many to redefine it beyond recognition and, apparently, beyond hope.

But this "now" is also a process of self-reflection and learning. For whether part of a distant and glorious past or an as yet unachieved future, an idealized conception of socialism—negative or positive—makes the future utterly obscure if only because practice, infinitely mediated as it can only be, is never perfectible. Therefore the idealist prospect of practical perfection can never be a basis from which to cross the utopian divide into a perfectly progressive state of being. Indeed, it can only render all present efforts as in perfect error. It is, as we hope we have shown, just such an implicitly negative utopian perspective that yields the current self-defeating desire for a yet newer, true Left.

If the history of socialism continues to operate, as we believe it does, as the shadow of contemporary progressive thought and action, no matter what the latter makes momentarily explicit and appealing, this has as much to do with what has produced the Left as with the general context in which it operates. That is to say, socialism persists because it continues to be the creatively negative condition of a globally mobile capital, and the latter's fundamental contradiction.

Even in the war now being waged globally by capital against all society, there are echoes of socialism in the directions that are actively excluded and the metapolicies by which that exclusion is implemented. The diverse movements that comprise today's Left, those that struggle against "the market" and its agencies in favor of a social economy and for the possibility of such a socially valid practice may or may not admit to the socialism of their efforts. But capital continues to constitute that socialism as its base. Thus, those movements remain part of the same context that breeds the desperation that brought us to the point of denying what we must not deny, that if we are to compose a progressive movement we must first agree that we are all Socialists together.

8
Rethinking the Crisis
of Socialism
(with Randy Martin)

Introduction

This chapter is one of a series of papers originally published in *Socialism and Democracy* that attempt to rethink the terms by which it has become possible to speak of a "crisis of socialism." It addresses several features of what has become a complex debate over the significance of the political decline of the Communist parties to the prospects of the North American Left.

Strategically, we have tried to provide some intellectual resources for disentangling different but conflated meanings of the word *socialism*. We argue that this conflation combines otherwise unrelated characterizations of different things in a total characterization of what, by virtue of the combination, appears to be a single and unambiguously identifiable thing. The totality constructed in this way supports a radical critique of socialism far too broad and polemical to allow for a self-critical reflection on the social nature, one might say the socialism, of the activity of critique itself.

Among the most important of these different meanings are process, project, site, and formation. The first has to do with the socialization of productive activity as an irreducible feature of the capitalist accumulation of wealth. The second refers to a historical practice that expresses a radical sociality both intrinsic to capitalist production and in contradiction with the dynamics of the price-making money market, that is with the project of universalizing exchange. The third, socialism as the site of certain practices (e.g., planning, coordinating), refers to the possibility of identifying boundaries—territorial, juridical, ethnic, etc.—within which one might speak meaningfully of "the Socialist world," "actually existing socialism," "communism," and "Communist nations or societies." Finally, "Socialist formation" refers to something relatively fixed as a structure and contained within boundaries, a kind of content presumed, on the basis of selected features, to be unmistakably Socialist. Each meaning has its own discourse. The confusion of meanings brings the various discourses together in a debate that only appears to have found a singular object, socialism, and to have achieved the status of dialogue.

As the debate developed after 1989, the focus of some participants changed from the empirical question of what actually happened in Eastern Europe and the USSR to yet more deeply controversial questions having to do with conceptualization and methodology. We believe that the reason for this is, in part, that the facts available are either hopelessly ambiguous or of an otherwise suspicious nature—because of their sources, because of their lack of representativeness in regard to what all have come to believe is a far greater picture, or because they seem often to have been taken out of a context that itself has never been satisfactorily comprehended.

Whatever the case, it has become necessary at least for those studying this debate to situate its competing evaluations within more inclusive frames of reference—moral, political, or theoretical. This has raised a variety of disturbing but unavoidable issues. We believe that some of the most important of these have to do with (1) the types of theory that are appropriate for arriving at evaluations of events believed to be momentous, (2) problems that accompany attempts to identify events in contexts that are thought to be constitutive of those events but are themselves relatively undefined, (3) difficulties involved in attempting to disentangle those aspects of the debate that seem overly encumbered with the discourses of media and politics in which the events have found their most vivid and perhaps most compelling representations, (4) and the difficulty of regulating the use of available theoretical terms, analogies, and metaphors to avoid exporting meanings from one context where they are appropriate to others where they are not.

This chapter is organized according to four topics. First, it discusses the relationship between critical studies in social science and our understanding of socialism as a theoretical concept. Second, it addresses and provides a critique of the types of language we have come to use in speaking of "the" crisis of socialism. Third, it examines theories of crisis in order to clarify the distinction between "conjunctural" and "historical" analyses. Finally, it attempts to give some terminological and conceptual focus to the discussion of the historical aspects of socialism from the point of view of the relationship between its national forms and global presence. We conclude with some remarks intended to explore some of the more controversial implications of our argument for further discussions of the relationship between socialism and democracy.

Socialism and Social Science

Whatever its moral and practical effects, the decade of the 1960s brought to a crashing conclusion the long attempt to theorize social life as a tendency toward a structured and durable "integration" of effort sustained in its autonomy as "system" by a functionally tuned self-regulation of interactive performances. Conditions had failed to sustain the sense of social reality on which a particular language of modernization, namely "structural functionalism," depended. It was no longer possible to think of societies as what Talcott Parsons called "boundary maintaining systems," in other words, as if the oppositional aspects of wealth, power, and class interest were merely "externalities" of the equilibrating relation of collective problem solving to confirmations of shared identity (1951).

A more skeptical sociology was influenced at first by C. Wright Mills and later by the more rigorous and philosophically based literatures of "Western Marxism," especially the Frankfurt School. Its fundamental point was that the study of society is effective and disciplined only to the degree to which it acknowledges in the formation of its basic concepts both the historical and practical aspects of sociality. That is, sociology could only justify its claim to provide knowledge if it became an essentially critical discipline. In effect, this challenged the validity of two dominant research strategies as general models for social analysis.

The first, what might be called the descriptive/analytical approach, was directed positively toward (a) the apparently immediate unities of social phenomena—what seemed both naturally arranged (e.g., groups) and in some sense morally compelling (e.g., norms, roles, institutions), and (b) concretely specifiable behaviors that seemed either paradigmatic of "social action" (e.g., decision-making) or probable, simplified in their characterization as "types" of action in normative relation to other "types" (e.g., the socialization of new members in relation to the performance of instrumental role obligations). In each case, the observer/theoretician was considered to be of an order radically different from that of the observed, sociology thus presupposing that it was exempt from the society it studied.

This, in turn, was acceptable only if knowledge was essentially free of material interests and uncompromised by moral and cultural commitments. Both conditions were undermined in the late 1960s and 1970s when sociologists attempted to account for social change (dissent and opposition) by the application of concepts originally formed to explain the enduring rather than the vital and generative aspects of society (see Brown and Goldin, 1973, for an early review; see Parsons, 1965, originally published in *Daedalus*, 1961, for an example).

The discovery that theory and ideology were not so easily separated made it impossible to assume any longer that the position of the observer is radically external to the behaviors in question. Comprehensive propositions about paradigms and types inevitably became suspect. The behaviors that had been thought capable of observation independently of their being lived, that is ostensibly objective, could no longer be taken for granted as indicating preexisting paradigms or types but had to be seen as features of social relations in active process of self-definition and redefinition. There was, then, a turn toward examining social life from the standpoint of a decidedly critical frame of reference and a suitably critical methodology, that is, from the standpoint of "practice" and the differences and conflicts by which the sociopractical is constituted as, one might say, an instance of reason (Garfinkel 1967; Habermas 1971).

The second research strategy, what might be called the constructionist approach, was directed toward what appeared to be the most durable and consensually valid, evidently legitimate, features of society. The collapse of the conditions under which it might have been claimed that general consensus existed about basic values, the pressure of previously unrepresented interests (e.g., minorities, women, the poor) and the impossibility of justifying accounts of social action by reference to the principled neutrality of the observer made it necessary for sociologists to focus on "durability" and "legitimacy" as projects and representations rather than properties of society, as socially practical activities rather than attributes. This required a redefinition of the subject matter of social science according to an internal relationship of order and change. In particular, politics, power, and conflict emerged as the more fundamental phenomena to durability and consensus. The latter were now seen, for the moment, as merely apparent and as interest-based claims (ideology) disguised as objective facts.

It was through the critique of both strategies that "history" finally worked its way into the social sciences; and it was, if not Marxist, a neo-Marxist history comprised dialectically of tensions, interests, power, conflicts, and contradictions. This emphasis on internal dynamics, self-transformation, and the unrepeatability of events was radically different from the positive notions of successions, accumulations, spreads, growths, progress, and cycles. That is, it differed from notions that substantiated theories by allowing for reference to an idealized objective nature, therefore to events treated as externally related to one another and to whatever subjectivity might inexplicably have taken them as its objects.

Above all, the newly skeptical turn had to demonstrate for every ostensible instance of unity the conflicts by which it was achieved and the interested socially reflexive practices against which it had to be defended. This reemphasis on power, ideology, and the political/economic differences that underlay the public relations of "civil society" inevitably invoked literatures alternative to those of a more reactionary cast of thought. These refocused attention on the dynamics of social life, the ways in which those dynamics are disguised by representations and representational practices suited to particular interests, and the conjunctures or crises that they effect as "moments."

In contrast, attempts to salvage the "system frame of reference" and its structural-functionalist paradigm—i.e., by emphasizing particular features of it such as collectively "rational choice"—denied in effect that these literatures offered anything new beyond an elaboration of the notion of context. This, it seemed, was already implicit though admittedly underdeveloped in the established sociological frames of reference. For these, "context" referred to the environment of an otherwise independent "system of action" that operates on that system in two ways: (1) it subjects the system to problems that challenge its capacity to remain adaptive, and (2) it contributes, through the ways in which context is represented within the system as a condition of rational action, to some system-level outcome or system-level decision.

But what was new was in fact quite different from the requirement that actions, events, and objects be understood in relation to a qualifying context conceived of as an external environment and thus, presumably, as a "system" of a different order from that of society. This sort of reference to context was used to qualify propositions about phenomena rather than as part of their identification and analysis. Seen in that light, it represented a theoretical move geared to strictly managerial practices, namely estimating influences and evaluating effects from and in regard to a relatively fixed perspective, almost always that of an official centralizing administration. That identification presupposed, then, an uncritical acceptance of standards oriented by what Jurgen Habermas referred to as an "interest" in control.[1]

Instead, and in order that a theory of society be able to account for itself as a feature of society, that is as self-critical as well as critical, its basic concepts were reformulated according to an irreducible dynamics of change. Formerly, social bodies (e.g., groups, societies) were relatively still or univocal in orientation, subject to what Parsons had once spoken of metaphorically as "inertia," until motivated by an external force. Now, social life was to be conceived of as already mobile, in motion, disturbed always by constant realizations of its internal divisions; and such disturbance was to be understood as operating from within and effecting a transformation (that might appear as a divergence or cessation) rather than acting as an unaccountably external cause of motion.

It should be mentioned that with this move came a shift in the use of the term "internal." It had qualified as a technical term on intellectual conditions that could no longer be sustained. It continued to be used in regard to the reformulated problematic of social change, but only as a provisional metaphor, a bridge between what was now being subjected to critique and the point of view from which that critique was generated. The term could no longer serve to signify spatial division, boundaries, and the kind of autonomy attributed to sociality when process and site are conflated. "Internality," rather than signifying circumscription and realms, was now indicative, of features identifiable with the dynamics of certain relations of difference. That is, it indicated, regardless of site, the self-reflective opposition of complements (e.g., practices, operations, etc.).

Not "social order" but social change, or movement, became the focus of theory; and with that, emphasis on "mediations" replaced the ostensibly fixed referents identified uniquely by points at which spatial and temporal dimensions intersect (for a current version, see Latour 2005). Not change, but instances of stability were now problematic and therefore obvious topics for research. "Social problems," formerly identified with popular movements, everyday life outside of institutional settings, "deviance," and all unofficial disturbances of the steady state, were redefined as antisocietal excesses of various official and officially sponsored consolidations—e.g., of power and wealth. What had once been so identified now reappeared as the practical matter of sociality itself. Society, in this "turning of the tables," was now thought of as always in a fluxion of multiple and provisional directions and self-definitions; and that motion or constant (noninstrumental, noncomprehensive) mobilization could only be specified by identifying society with mutually constitutive but essentially oppositional differences.

For example, conflicts around the issue of race had once been thought to enter sociality from outside of the spatially limited functional ordering of its relations—as prejudice, the results of agitation, a lack of "contact," misunderstanding, etc.—and introduced like a virus into an otherwise stable body politic. Later, it was seen as the surfacing of a contradiction already present in the form of a conflict on which social organization depended rather than one it merely had to endure.[2]

From this it followed that to understand racism was to see it as an opposition at the core of a dominant project, but one on which that project was, inadmissibly, dependent. If the dominant project was, for the sake of illustration, taken to be the capitalist accumulation of wealth, then racism had to be described in part as a feature of that project, and the maintenance of racism with or without reforms had in some sense to be relevant to the process of accumulation.[3]

Thus, change was to be considered intrinsic to the definition of all actions, events, and objects at the very point at which they were most concretely identifiable. More than just a problem of explanation, "social change," thought of in terms of a dynamics or dialectic of opposition, became a constitutive feature of all subject matter, a matter of analysis rather than merely an "external" factor accounting for variations along dimensions of act and organization. Under the ambiguous auspices of renewed critical energies directed at (and problematically from within) neocolonialism, patriarchy, racism, and the relatively newly pervasive and extraterritorial "systems of empire" often referred to as "hegemonic," and despite considerable resistance, the discourse of social change became the language of all the "human sciences."

In this way, the point of reference shifted fitfully from presumptively national societies (an orthodox reference to the sort of social life identified with place or territory, such as nation, and therefore seen as essentially rule-governed, static, and "cultural") to social practices arising amidst processes that could in no sense be adequately identified territorially, as what this or that national society does, and therefore as design features of independent cultures within the boundary-dependent logic of "comparative analysis."

The newly evident critical disposition, despite having a certain affinity with relativism, particularly in its critique of ethnocentrism, did not share the relativists' assumptions about the autonomy of populations, the uniqueness and self-determination of social formations, and the univocality of collective references to self in territorially defined societies. Instead, it offered a historical relativism in which the significance of what people do depends upon the various mobilizations, accumulations of wealth and power, and contradictory operations (e.g., labor and capital, production and circulation) in which arise their activities and the principles of those activities.

It is clear then that this move against territorial conceptions and toward a deterritorializing global idea of society—seen as an indissoluble mix of projects, processes, and movements—represented more a critique then an endorsement of relativism. On the other hand, critics often conflated the challenge posed by the deterritorializing idea of social life to the idea of fixed and tradition-based standards (Deleuze and Guattari 1983, 1987), with a relativism so extreme that it suggested, by association, that the former is as nihilistic as the latter is held to be. Apart from the fact that such a conflation ignored the important differences between historical and cultural "relativism," it justified, as the only reasonable response to the "nihilism" attributed indifferently to both, a return to various moral and intellectual absolutisms and an epistemology of finality altogether hostile to critical and self-critical reason, therefore no doubt to democracy as well as socialism. This, we take it, describes the current rightist attack, occasionally joined by some on the Left, on critical language and critical theory, as if what is at stake in any attempt to redress injustice is little more than the sort of "political correctness" demanded by "totalitarianism." This rehash of anticommunism comes with a new and even more mean-spirited twist. It is now directed with consciously reactionary satire at minorities, women, and various other groups whose opposition to intolerance and oppression has finally created at least the possibility of a greater concern for egalitarianism.[4]

Philosophically, this emphasis on social change invoked a point of view rarely if ever before taken as fundamental to conceptualizing much less describing the world: the perspective of what is constituted by projects of domination as "the other" upon which such projects depend but in regard to which they can only remain obdurately silent, and in that silence oppressive. The most immediate theoretical consequence was that even those intellectuals and activists living ambivalently under the auspices (and protection) of institutions of domination had no choice but either to allow themselves to be subjected to that point of view or to confront the limitations of their own self-understanding, hence of any claim of objectivity they might otherwise make. Therefore, it became necessary, if there was to be a science(s) of humanity(ies), not only to identify the forms and processes by which those global majorities, previously shunted to the margins of "society," articulate self and other on their own behalf, but to find those in the light of which social theory could be freed of the finality implicit in the desire for fixed rules of "civility" or complete and consistent standards of evaluation ("excellence").[5]

The moral imperative of this radical critique of official institutions, ethnology, and ethnocentrism was not merely to understand or tolerate "the other" but to recognize the subject-power, authority, of that other by confronting and reflecting upon the limits of the critic's own privileged "understanding" in the historical conditions of domination, oppression, and exploitation. It was, in other words, to recognize the creativity and political "will formation" that constituted the active culture of what was otherwise only "the oppressed." This must be admitted in any case if domination, oppression, and exploitation are to be seen as an attack on life (lives) rather than merely on certain unfortunates or on people taken mechanically, and inhumanly, as instances of statistical categories in the light of which populations are identified and managed for interests not strictly their own.[6]

The Bias of Prophetic Language

In this recognition of culture as active rather than merely passive, the oppressed (and what has come to be known more generally as subaltern) reappears not as abject and unself-motivated, as if without significant subjectivity, but as subjectively vital. Those intellectuals who had taken their own practical auspices for granted within the institutions of domination, and with that, paradoxically and inadmissibly, their own subjection, could now claim with greater legitimacy than before to bear witness to all manner of domination and resistance. But though this witnessing of the relation of oppressor to oppressed within the observing self was an advance over perceptions of each as a separate category or sphere (the poor, business, war, suffering), it could only be partially satisfactory. Despite opening to a more self-critical criticism, this position remained objectivist, oriented rather than engaged. Its own subjectivity was not yet implicated in the politics of the relation to which it had hoped to bear witness. It could not yet provide the sort of subjectively open or vulnerable comprehensiveness of vision and practical reversal of power intended in the first place by politics and ideology much less by theory.

As unsatisfactory as it might have been merely to claim a capacity to bear such witness without in turn being recognized by those whose lives were presumably witnessed, it was even more unsatisfactory to have as a result no choice but to accept the complicity implied in the freedom assumed for itself by such witness. Under those circumstances, one also had no choice but to acknowledge a certain unfreedom within that ostensibly free act, namely the impossibility of curing oneself of complicity on one's own.

However, this was at least the beginning of a renewed reflection upon the content and conditions of "bad faith." It was certainly an improvement over self-righteousness to be able credibly to deny that politics is adequate to its social value when (1) it mollifies those in power (by, e.g., a politics of "moderation" that aims merely to temper the disposition to dominate) or (2) it attempts to subject power to the sort of gradualist programmatics, what might be called regressively distributive reformism, that tolerates the suffering, experience, and claims of "present generations" in favor of vague and even casual promises (the conditions of fulfillment of which are rarely considered or, when considered, even more rarely taken seriously) to those who might come later.[7]

There have been severe reversals since the early 1980s, partly because critical discourse had not yet made itself explicit in a disciplinary way as a mediated relation of theory and practice. In any case, bearing witness was inadequate to the self-critical subjectivity that recognition—in contrast with acknowledgment, sympathy, representation—of "the Other" required; and many of us were not yet prepared for the dizzying experience of seeing ourselves from others' eyes. Perhaps these are some of the reasons why, despite itself, the language of social change has taken on an increasingly elevated, absolutist, and concomitantly self-righteous tone.

Events are once again considered indiscriminately and epochally momentous (the collapse of socialism marked by the emergence of what Hardt and Negri call "Empire"), polarized moralistically by totalizing definitions of planning and market (East-West relations), taken as evidence of foibles rather than decisions (e.g., Islamist politics), or seen to indicate savage dispositions or tendencies (anything hostile to the absolute market). As in the past, for example during the early heady days of "the Cold War," naming is more likely to precede and ultimately consume analysis, and assertions of conclusions are more important than doubt, questioning, deliberation, or dialogue.

Whether this is a decline or business as usual is difficult to say; though it is tempting to believe that there have been more democratic periods in the history of the U.S. public polity. Whatever the case, it is difficult to attend to the news pertaining to the former Socialist economies, much less those of capital, without finding such reports framed by the discourse of an anticritical, self-congratulatory, national celebration of market society (what Marx called "the society of things") and the peculiar "freedoms" of its ostensible democracy.

The celebratory discourse is as common to liberals as conservatives, academics as well as journalists, and for a certain segment of the Left as well as, though with a different intention, for reactionaries. It is especially prevalent when what is being discussed is the fate of socialism, the prospects of privatization and marketization, the apparent resistance of various nations and groups to the latter, the ambiguous and multifaceted mobilizations of populations in the countries of what had once more confidently been called "the East," and what George H. Bush named, disturbingly, "The New

World Order." Even the widely acknowledged horrors of the G. W. Bush regime have not found a language adequate to them and adequate to the class war against the society of the producers to which those horrors correspond and which they were certainly intended to facilitate.

But the temptation to celebrate need not be understood as something deliberately chosen by specific individuals or groups. It has proven difficult at best for most of us to avoid over-moralizing politics, and it is worthwhile to speculate a moment about what might be the cause of this lack of vitality in our discourse on public affairs, assuming not that the speculation is free of it but that the conversation, in itself, can extend and intensify doubt beyond the complicit doubt that motivates what today is called "moderation."

Certainly, the context of contemporary discussions of world affairs has become, as Max Weber might have said, re-enchanted. It now appears littered with references to all manner of ancient attributions of identity and their putative loyalties and hatreds. These clichés had once been sources of embarrassment to moderate constituents who might have expected their politicians to at least mute their militaristic and nationalistic superstitions, to be able to temper their desire for power, and to avoid publicly embracing socially regressive movements whose favor they must, in any case, seek. To be sure, events have magnified our sense of urgency; and this, influenced by the penchant of the established media for mystifyingly terse and undiscussably concise reportage, has itself tended to enforce a simplification of ideas, if only by way of reducing ambiguity and ambivalence in favor of official discourse—at, one must add, whatever the cost.

But independent of momentous events, there has been one development so remarkable and so taken for granted that it has yet to register even its own significance on our capacity to speak and think critically. That is the emergence and pervasiveness of Rightist language—beyond words, frame, or ideology—in connection with a polity so extremely and dangerously skewed toward reaction, often in the name of "culture," "values," or "civilization," that one feels pressed to deny its significance altogether.

The result has been a virtually unopposed proliferation of reactionary propaganda of all sorts, with its specialized jargon of contempt—for the poor, minorities, the weak, the different, and for the very idea of society— and its tendency to substitute the certainty of prejudice for deliberation, sectarianism for universalism, and the interests of the powerful for those of humanity itself. Within all of this, the Right has been able to set the public agenda for virtually every topic of geopolitical significance, and it has been able to deny, at least for the moment, the need for a socially responsible domestic polity in favor of a geopolitics of global imperial power.

Moreover, the struggle within the American Left to salvage progressive principles has quite often added to this predicament an unfortunate temptation, tied to world events, and seen by some as a unique opportunity to achieve respectability. The changes in Eastern Europe and the Soviet Union, so far as they can be characterized at all, have made it tempting for many

Left intellectuals finally to take their leave of the burdens of their own history, though the recent turn to the Left in Latin America may, at least momentarily, challenge that temptation.

By denouncing what the Right was already adept at denouncing, by declaring an end to the attempt to define a Left through the endorsement of conclusive diagnoses about the end of all that once stood for the Left, by joining those very agendas of which they had once been victim, some progressives no doubt sought to find greater public presence, and through that greater influence, as well as a greater measure of self-criticism aimed at the construction of yet another Left, untarnished by the history of its predecessor, and in that sense antihistorical.[8] And who would not wish them, indeed all of us, well in such a quest? And who would not feel at least tempted to adopt such a strategy under the present circumstances? In this, it may not be too much to say that the declaratory and conclusionist tendencies of this more officially respectful discourse have something in common with the mixture of apocalyptic vision and preaching from the perspective of an acute crisis typical of the poetics of prophecy.

There are two particularly important abstract objects these reconstructed antihistorical Left discourses have recognized and then, for different reasons and in different ways, neutralized. First is the Rightist confluence of antidemocratic, anticollectivist, and racialist associations. This had seemed not so long ago to be only a weak tendency finally consigned by the defeat of the "Axis" in the Second World War to the phantom zone of failed and forgotten fascisms, beyond the horizon of history but for a few eccentric and therefore manageable disturbances in political culture.

As of the 1980s, it seemed of sufficient potency to some to warrant an alarm great enough to suspend or render mute loyalty to the poor and others variously exploited and oppressed, and to diminish significantly most criticism of "civil society," "capitalist democracy," and "the market." Threatening to overwhelm critical consciousness has been a desperate renewal of a liberalism quite tolerant of "privatization" and marketization, apparently indifferent to its own ambivalent history as state ideology, and equally indifferent to the reasons why it had been, for more than a century and a half, subject to so thorough and searching a criticism from that democratic and collectivist Left concerned with the social interest economically as well as politically (see Wallerstein, 1995, on "the collapse of liberalism").

This has been implemented in part by a tendency to reject or neutralize what is theoretically systematic and critical in Marxism and Socialist thought: on the one hand by simplification ("analytic Marxism's" reduction of Marxism to a technocratic interest in the problem of inequality) and on the other by caricature (Marxism understood as a "master narrative" or as the theory of socialism's inevitability). The attitude of this disposition has been correspondingly suspicious, particularly of those popular politics that are difficult to thematize and of those groups it still finds to its own Left.

This is one reason why its proponents have had little to offer politically except pleas for more responsible leadership, the futile prospects of a third party, or the complicity of affiliating with a Democratic Party that had already sacrificed most of the interests in socially progressive policies for which liberalism itself had once claimed to stand. In any case, they have had little to teach about what is as a matter of practice possible for humankind, little to say about democracy beyond endorsing elections and counter-organizational social movements ("new social movements"), and little of consequence to say, apart simply from admission, about the sources of capital's depredations and the miseries caused around the world by the accelerating attempt of capital to consolidate itself on a global scale. Other post-Marxists have rediscovered progressive politics in movements that reach beyond the nation and expand the tradition of nonviolent militancy. Emblematic of these movements are the World Social Forums and the demonstration on July 21, 2001, against the Group of Eight summit in Genoa. The global reach of these and other movements against corporate globalization may yet prove the optimists among those who reject the traditional Left to have been correct. But even if such movements do succeed in disturbing the consolidation of Empire and contributing to a more generalized challenge to its hegemony, it will have been in the context of traditional Left activism, especially in countries where some measure of socialism is still considered an option.

In that regard, another object of those discourses is socialism. But it is a new socialism qualified altogether by an identification with particular nations rather than oriented as an immanent critique of capital. What prompted this new object with an old name was the swiftness with which Socialist civil society in its variety seemed to erupt in a veritable marketplace of voices democratically disposed against all things Socialist. Consequently, it has more in common with social democracy than democratic socialism.

To those who minimized the global context within which all nations found themselves confronted by a highly mobile, extremely speculative, and determined capital, it seemed as if Socialist civility suddenly became over-ripened by the heat of seventy years of attempting to reconcile particular and local interests with universalistic concerns, of confronting the inevitably uneven and disturbing efforts of the state simultaneously to institute equality and rationalize loyalty and expertise, and of having had to accommodate to an incessant politicization of affairs not obviously intrinsically political. It was as if the various mobilizations within formerly Socialist nations represented the final, utopian, coming together of a revolution against a totalitarianism tied inextricably to socialism itself and in favor of a democratic ideal paradoxically freed at last from all social, therefore moral, content. From this perspective, reactionary nationalisms as well as those reflecting the historically unresolved problems of social division, stratum-based interests in marketization and privatization, the desire for greater democracy, discontent with labor policies, unrest over scarcities of goods, and all manner of political, social, and moral impulses, were taken to be equivalent in their desire but not in their origins. The Rightist confluence was cast until 2000 as of minor significance so far as the prospects of the U.S. polity were concerned. This did not mean that antidemocratic or, in its modernist guise, Fascist thought, was simply ignored, but that it was with few exceptions addressed as aberrant rather than as well rooted and capable of even partly capturing the political culture. The election of Reagan took place during a period very much like that which David Abraham described in his account of the collapse of the Weimar Republic, in which representative government (parliament, parties) had all but failed to meet the needs of the represented and national wealth had been squandered by war and speculation. This combination of a political vacuum (an opening for a leader capable of bypassing ineffective legislatures) and an ideological collapse (an opening for an antidemocratic and punitive authoritarianism) once again raised the specter of an authoritarian regime organized around an essentially reactionary populist appeal to a growing and otherwise hopeless and cynical constituency. This made it necessary and even possible to think about the dangers of fascism once again.

But the prevalent response in the Left press, especially at first, was to retreat several positions from the critique of capital to an endorsement of what the Left critics of the 1960s and 1970s had shown to be in the U.S. only a semblance of social democracy, namely "the welfare state." To be sure, some, like the editors of *Monthly Review*, put this in the more radical perspective of the prospects for a "New Deal" type of mobilization of labor. But another response on the Left, understandable in the light of what had happened, was to defend a history of capitalist state policy as if there had once been a true historic compromise, a socially transforming "contract," between labor and capital in the interest of the welfare of society itself.

Suddenly, a considerable number of people on the Left began to think, for the most part ambivalently but occasionally with a grandiosity born of desperation, of an "alliance" with the Democratic Party, or of somehow combining single issue movements in an inclusive, or "umbrella," organization, or of operating through the official political institutions and media that generations of Left scholars had shown to be in important ways corrupt and incapable of socially significant reformation. The result in any case was a growing sense that the authoritarian Right had escaped from its "phantom zone" and gotten, by virtue of having attained vast power, out of control. This apparently unprecedented event seemed to justify abandoning radical politics in favor of an almost apocalyptic resignation and the utopian politics of complicity that so often goes along with it.

This does not mean that there was less activism than before. Indeed, during the 1970s and 1980s, there may have been even more sustained political action than in the 1960s, and probably across a broader front—around issues pertaining to race, gender, poverty, housing, health, education, language, police violence, cultural repression, and community. It only points to the fact that a large portion of the public Left, ordinarily concerned with understanding the overall significance of these efforts beyond their particular sites, seemed to wilt and fade in the face of an altogether reactionary and obviously dangerous Right: not that people withdrew from politics so much as they withdrew from what had identified them as distinctively, and instructively, Left.

This was a sufficiently general phenomenon to have had serious consequences for social thought. One was an apparent lapse of theory as critique, and therefore of the capacity to sustain a sense of the historical and political significance of the roles and rationality of activism, militancy, and organization in socially oriented change. Another was a tendency to focus with increasing abstractness, as a matter of methodological principle, on an idealized universalistic politics polarized by the inexplicable images of utopian democracy and totalitarian "statism" (cf. Mouffe and Laclau 1985; see Cohen and Arate 1992). This prophetic turn could only either have ignored the experiences of those who suffered exploitation, oppression, and the denial of the opportunity to re-create society, or, what amounts to the same thing, combined all those predicaments in an index that begged by its unself-reflective abstractness the question of historical and material conditions and therefore political possibilities.

No matter what its reason and occasion, however, prophetic language has always drawn on the most immediately convenient expressions to inculcate a sense of sudden collapse and imminent reward or retribution commensurate with its overall antisecular task of reducing and then moralizing human affairs. In times past, it no doubt helped victimized people to achieve a certain commonality and purposefulness against the otherwise irrepressibly dehumanizing projects of the powerful. Its recent forms derive less from the needs of people and the corresponding utopian charismatics of its own discourse than from the self-interested clichés of politicians and the privileged simplifications by which the official media instate themselves above events and beyond even their own smaller history.

In either case, past or present, whatever is gained, the cost is significant. Prophetic discourse is intrinsically hostile to critical reason, therefore to self-criticism. This is not, however, to deny it what Hegel would call its moment of truth: i.e., when the enemy can be named, and is thereby clearly, if only momentarily, identifiable, and the people are gathered because that enemy has enforced their gathering—as in the early preindustrial riots against an imposed price-making market and the later industrial class struggles against the free marketing of labor. This moment of collective realization, struggle organized by prophetic agitation, may be all that is possible if dire circumstances are to be taken in hand, even though that condition of mobilization is not compatible with the need to sustain whatever results are achieved by the struggle.

But our model of life is predicated on the special modernization signified by industrialization, urbanization, and a delocalizing hence socializing mode of production for which class differentiation is a fundamental condition of authority, wealth, and societal (national) "development." Therefore, it is not possible from the point of view of that model to define a monolithic enemy, no longer so easy to identify what people have in common, and only possible to avoid the use of self-critically critical reason at the cost of any socially valid non-utopian project for improving society. It is then necessary to admit that the possibility of people informing themselves about themselves by means of such reason is predicated on the prior development, continually reaffirmed through struggle as a matter of practice, of vehicles by which critical thought and critical action are joined in a reflective movement of continual self-transformation. Such a movement must be referred to, whatever the ambiguity of the term, as "dialectical." This, in turn, requires something only hinted at by the expression "collective memory." Only hinted because that commonality of learning must, in any case, be sustained as a practical foundation for an active engagement of people with their situations, what might be called "popular institutions." Such arrangements are different from official "institutions" with their rules (projects) that occlude the interplay of fundamental interests, their insistence on absolute "values" in ways that deny that values are products of a history and therefore of interests, and their defense of operations intended to separate those who control from those who are controlled.

Rather, popular institutions, so conceived, consist of inherently collective self-critical practices more or less appropriate to the difficult task of responding to the historical situation with socially valid reflection. To acknowledge, to recognize, the self-critical aspect of these practices requires empathy with what "we" had been in the past (a problem-constituting relationship between identity and situation) as well as respect for the difficulty "we" or any group might have in engaging a present (a relationship between identity and problem thoroughly "situated" as a moment of the collective expenditure of effort). Above all, such recognition requires sympathy for what might have had to be tried and respect for the attempt whether or not it failed. But short of failure, it requires sympathy for the critical effort (as if for one's own) regardless of its limitations, on the one hand because no solution can be complete and incontrovertible, and on the other because all critical activity is, despite its aspirations, limited by the terms of whatever it challenges and by the conditions under which its challenges must be issued.

These self-critical practices can be seen, for example, in mobilizations otherwise difficult to identify, in theory employed, problematically to be sure, as mutually reflexive with practice, and in relations of sociality that are to some extent identifiable historically as collectively self-conscious relations of struggle. They cannot be understood, and therefore cannot be part of how a people teaches itself, if identified only through the sterilizing *ex post facto* projects of total judgment, unequivocal condemnation (that finally stands for unequivocality as much as for condemnation), or for that matter equally unequivocal support. Whether the results of such intellectual totalizations are positive or negative, they are always abstract in the specific sense of being ahistorical, anticritical, and without capacity to reflect on their own implications in the struggles they idealize.

The Discourse of Crisis

The resurgence of prophetic language provides a context in which we might read the continuing epochal discourses on the "collapse" of communism, the "final crisis" of socialism, and the "end" of Marxism. Thus, as a first observation, to rely on these discourses is at best to assume that official politics and journalism are sufficient to set the agenda for any attempt to connect theory and practice. A second preliminary observation is that the critique of these discourses can only be adequate if it is part of a greater recognition of the collective efforts of people to realize a democratically just society, that is, a society greater than the sum of individuals and more than what is established as the legitimate expression of the economic formation for which the achievement of society must be a continuing project and a continuing struggle.

Those phrases that refer to "collapse," "final crisis," and "end," by which so many now claim to know the history of "socialism," no doubt reflect various points of view. But their use tends in any case to summarize and elide an enormous complexity of conditions, situations, activities, accomplishments, and failures. The purposes of such summaries are themselves either unclear or suspicious. They invariably disorient the continuity of self-reference and self-respect necessary for collectivities to know what they do in the terms of what they have done, and to know the relation of present purposes to purposes that had been active before.

In one sense, as we have indicated, this recourse to prophecy is nothing new. Nor should it have been unexpected. Our political environment rarely lends itself to respect for its own historical complexity. In any case, we have never gotten used to thinking very soberly about affairs that challenge the familiar limits of nation, state, and organization, much less affairs that are historically global rather than tied to specific regimes or local settings.

Such a discourse of objectively absolute and absolutely objective crisis, with its abbreviated narratives of totalities and confessions, and rejections and rehabilitations, provides a constant tropism of modernist thought. It always signals a momentary surrender to the potentially repressive language of utopia, to the most convenient expressions of cynicism, to the unhappiness that admittedly accompanies any need to confront incommensurables, and to the inevitable lack of security raised by any attempt to identify facts and ascertain their significance. Above all, it signals an inability to tolerate the ambiguous memories of struggle that make it possible to understand what is historical about all human achievements, the failures and the successes. Insofar as we remain confident in our use of phrases that label things and that orient us to finalistic and therefore self-denying affirmations of self and to ahistorical judgments, we beg key questions. Not the least of these is how to reconcile our need to enhance self-criticism with the fact that self-criticism, enhanced or not, depends on acknowledging that human experience must be understood in terms of a historical dimension of struggle if there is to be any experience (theory) of experience itself.

We can simplify this by saying that such phrases—the collapse of communism, the crisis of socialism, the end of Marxism—beg the question of what might be their own realized and realizable objects. Each assumes the achievement of a totality internally immunized against any change but one that is total. Each assumes a position of observation beyond the conditions under which communism, socialism, and Marxism could have been thinkable and livable. Each summarizes a process—crisis, collapse, ending—reduced to a threshold at a point along an unmentioned and almost certainly unmentionable scale of measurement.

Together, they set a tone of final judgment rather than one of critical analysis. Each phrase risks displacing the very issues that may be most important for appreciating the social transformation it purports to represent. In other words, each denies the mutually constituting relationship between past and present and makes obscure, by begging the question of qualitative difference, the potentially self-correcting memory (learning) of situations, problems, and efforts to deal with common problems.

Together they reduce the enormous horizon-filling complexity of social transformation to vividly contained but simplifying, hence finally bewildering, images. The latter operate in effect to render communism, socialism, and Marxism as unchanging and unchangeable essences. This rendering is then protected by a second order trope in which each of the three completed and discredited entities is then declared guilty of the same critical reductionism and essentialism of which those entities had once accused bourgeois thought (see, e.g., Jean Cohen 1982). But if this ultimate critique of reductionism and essentialism is to hold (that Marxism et al., and not bourgeois theory, had been the guilty parties), it too must not reduce or typify. Its names and judgments must either be true (evidently so) or constitute an otherwise justifiable means to a defensible end. Moreover, it cannot simply identify its own reason negatively, as nonreductionist and antiessentialist, since it would thereby evade the force of one part of its own general critique—e.g., that Marxism was only a negation (of capitalism) in favor of a dream (liberation).

None of these counterclaims and self-identifications has the weight of either the argument or the evidence, nor by their terms could they. Therefore, this finalistic, judgmental, prophetic rhetoric has been unable to defend itself without using tactics it rejects or to claim a superior epistemology. The antihistorical declaration of finality thus completes its criticism, and rejection, of the historically identified Left (part of its own subjectivity) by denying, in its own moment of self-contradiction, that the impulse to criticize is anywhere to be found outside of the particular therefore momentarily desocialized minds of individual critics.

Having decided that there was nothing intrinsically self-critical in the first place in communism, socialism, or Marxism, antihistorical criticism can dismiss these practices as wrong-headed, inefficient, undemocratic, impractical, dogmatic, or disposed irrationally or in bad faith to "Stalinism." It can do so without asking how such a dismissal receives its social validation—how, in a word, it can be received by (rather than imposed upon) an audience that can learn about itself from that act of reception. But Marxism, communism, and socialism are too important to be left to such polemical devices: especially those of contemporary debates framed at the outset by a desire to deny shared history in favor of problem-solving and, by virtue of their rhetoric, far too relaxed in their obligation to defend those conclusive judgments.

Proclamations about the end of Marxism tend to substitute the monologue of a single putatively unifying voice for the intrinsically self-critical dialogue that has produced both the history of Marxism as the critique of capital and the history of its practice as the critique of the critique. Similarly, the claim that communism or socialism has collapsed—in the sense of the total failure of an idea and its critical practice—is predicated on a certain confusion. It conflates the fate of particular organizations (party, nation) with the entire, extra-organizational, historical effort to transform society by magnifying sociality against the desocializing project of creating a universe of exchange.

On the other hand, the answer to these claims and their assumptions would be insufficient if it merely insisted on the continuation of the same organizations, juridical arrangements, formations, and traditions that are hypostasized in those very claims. The answer must emphasize the volatile continuity of a certain situation, namely capital. It must emphasize the varieties of ways, or processes, in which that situation has been realized as a historic one through various forms of development as a project, and through equally various movements of opposition, conflicts at one or another site of capitalist development, and an uneven course of struggle that tends always, despite itself, to reach beyond the momentary confines of state, nation, and what is now called "tradition."

From this point of view, the fall of Communist parties, if it is that, does not signal an end to the process by which they once emerged as national organizations and regimes, though it does force us once again to consider that process on the expanded scale of global relations. The imposition of market relations in Eastern/Central Europe and the Soviet Union to whatever degree does not by itself decide the future of the struggle against the exploitation of labor, though it is no less important as one condition of that struggle, in the industrial East as it has been in the industrial West. The rejection of Marxist ideologies of older regimes by newer ones neither makes

Marxist theory—the critique of capital and the justification of that critique—obsolete, nor renders its application to the further history of capitalism either incompetent or irrelevant. Finally, the emergence of popular support for issues about which Marxism and socialism have had little to say or have provided no clear guidelines does not mean that they are out-of-date, otherwise unresponsive to crucial problems, or unable to add intelligence to the further formulation and politicization of those very issues.

Of course, not all reactions to Marxism, communism, and socialism are subject to this critique. But those that are not tend to be technical and not necessarily part of the larger debate. They also tend to be understandable only as active elements of arguments that are as yet inconclusive and still open, certainly not as findings driven to the point of conclusion by the force of logic or the weight of the evidence.

In any case, this chapter examines the rejective tendency as an attitude or basis for opinion. It assumes that the tendency influences even technical discussions of, for example, the labor theory of value, the modes of operation of various "regimes of accumulation," problems of "articulation," the relations of hegemony to counterhegemonies, and other theoretical issues connected with the dialectically constituted concepts of class, production, and what Marx called "the society of the producers," and with the generally critical categories of ideology, social control, regulation, law, state, revolution, organization, and political mobilization. The most important part of this tendency has to do with what it entails for discussions on the left about what the Left was, is, and should be; and this has more to do with the question of socialism than with the significance of the collapse of parties or even with opinions about, much less knowledge of, Marxism.

By "socialism," we mean more than opposition to capitalism and less than a fully democratic utopia of mutuality, equality, and justice. We mean a specific relation of capital to its own progressive moment, the socialization of production. Andrew Levine's "narrow" definition seems to capture what is most generally at stake when it attempts to address the sort of debate about the future of the Left in which we are now unfortunately engaged. Levine defines "socialism" negatively, as a certain relation of opposition to the "private ownership of society's principal means of production," and positively, as the socialization of those means of production (1984, p. 5).

This definition cannot satisfy the need for a full theoretical discussion of the material, social, cultural, historical, and methodological issues involved in identifying a Left oriented politically and epistemologically to the relationship between theory and practice. It merely states the principle difference that the idea of socialism makes in regard to the capitalism for which that idea provides the minimal, or most basic, internal, hence historical, critique.

Levine's book, *Arguing for Socialism*, discusses some of the subtler aspects of the definition in regard to a particular problem, namely the relative virtues and defects of socialism and capitalism taken in their simplest forms for the purpose of addressing contemporary attempts to defend capitalism against socialism. Our problem is somewhat different, namely how to address contemporary attacks on socialism that are not simultaneously defenses of capitalism. While Levine's definitions are sufficient for the discussion, any attempt to extend it beyond the topic of the tendency to reject socialism would require far more theoretical work. But, since the latter is possible only on condition that dialogue, self-critically critical discussion, replace rejection, it seems worthwhile to review what is involved in rejecting the relevance of socialism to what the Left ought now to say and do about itself.

The question of the fate of socialism is, then, of a different order of complexity than that of the legacy of the Communist parties or the significance of Marxism itself. The last two have to do with the Left's sense of its own history and what sort of theory is necessary for the critique of capital in its contemporary forms of concentration, mobility, and scale of exploitation, and in its indifference to its own past—in particular to levels of socialization already achieved.

However, the fate of socialism has to do with the most general orientation that could define a Left. While the party is one and only one determinate or conjunctural form of political expression, and Marxism is a practical dialogue that aims to substantiate, one might say materially, the principle of dialogue (sociality), socialism cannot be identified with any particular formation. Nor, it must be added, can its project, though focused on the "forces of production" (socialized labor understood in regard to the expanded and projectively autonomous circulation of wealth as the "society of the producers"), be specified independently of the capitalism that is at once its occasion, its context, and its object. To a certain extent, then, "socialism" is about a historical possibility—that is, the application of a principle: namely that of practical criticism in regard to the human conditions of capitalist accumulation, with specific reference to the social base of capitalist wealth that contemporary sociologists call "society."

Nevertheless, any discussion of socialism today, defined narrowly as above, must be in a certain sense empirical. That is, it must correspond to questions oriented to what E. P. Thompson calls "experience"—socially valid practical considerations—grounded in the relations of Socialist thought and practice to the various moments of capitalist production. Therefore, one must ask: How has it been possible to identify socialism in the midst of changes the scale and momentum of which seem far beyond any particular horizon of experience? From this point of view, the difficulty for a critically minded analysis is to identify the dynamics of socialism as they emerge within and against capitalist transformations of production (in the sense of the reproduction of the social relations of production that constitute "Value"). The perspective of the discussion that follows holds that Socialist dynamics are both an effect of and a limit upon capitalist development. This resituates the question of the crisis of socialism by engaging the problem of how particular moments of sociality, expressions of socialism, appear and are transformed under circumstances dominated by forces that need, yet cannot tolerate, social development.

In this sense, a crisis of socialism cannot be considered independently of the endemic critical relations of capitalism (forces and relations of production, production and circulation, sociality and contractually governed property). Against the claim that socialism could end as a consequence of its own manifest inadequacies as a complete and independent formation, emphasis on the internal relations of socialism and capitalism (the latter the occasion, the former the critique) sustains in principle the dynamics of opposition that form and reform the basis of politics, history, and a relation of theory to practice.

The challenge is two-fold. On the one hand, it is necessary to avoid identifying change with crisis and to remember that the conjunctural object of political reason (crisis in the sense of a rupture) is not an actual break but a momentary realization, from the standpoint of political decision, of a continuing historical dynamism. At the same time, it is necessary to consider how much of a departure from recognized socialism is possible within the categories of that recognition.[9] This requires a view of Socialist development as a conjunctural feature of any encounter between capitalist accumulation (the exploitation of labor, exchange, circulation) and its forces of production (at the level of analysis, reproduction). The term "crisis" has been typically used as if only territorially specifiable relations, internal in the sense of interior, could account for socialism's prospects, and as if any departure from a prior instance (e.g., the USSR) is sufficient to spell socialism's demise. Socialism is only as real (in the sense of being) as capitalism; but, as Marx showed, it is what is real (in the sense of becoming) about capitalism. It is not conceivable as a separate entity. To reconsider the question of crisis, it is therefore necessary to examine how socialism has been conceptualized with an eye toward how the prospects for socially progressive change have been framed, and with some reflection on the capitalist context from within and against which socialism can be said to emerge.

"Internal" Relations of Socialism

The quotation marks that bracket "really existing socialism," an expression commonly used in the 1980s, display a certain unease with respect to the formulation of what is at once an idea and a practice, but not uniquely a site. In a work that represents one major tendency in the literature on Socialist nation-states, Feher, Heller, and Markus identify their object of analysis as the "new societies of Eastern Europe, the societies of 'really existing socialism'" (1983, p. 1). However, they conclude, there is a crucial difference between what appears to be socialism and what socialism is and might be.

"Really existing socialism" is, therefore, definitively not true socialism, but instances of non-Socialist regimes displaying a Socialist facade (p. 295). The quotation marks are intended to convey this sense of a great deception. But deceptions of regimes are nothing new, nor are they uniquely products of "non-Western" nations. What is more important to Feher, Heller, and Markus is that "really existing socialisms" are only regimes, not only false to an ideal but false societies. Nevertheless they must be distinguished from capitalist social regimes. They ask:

in what sense can societies characterized by an absence in the means of production, by the far reaching reduction of market mechanism, . . . by a dissolution of the institutional separation between economy and state and by a general tendency to abolish the distinction between the public-political sphere and that of civil society—in what sense can such societies be considered capitalist at all? (pp. 23–25)

Here Feher, Heller, and Markus reject analogies between capitalism and "really existing socialism," for example, models like state capitalism (see Cliff 1974) for which the statist aspect of "really existing socialism" and relations of control within the productive system imply only a nominal shift in capitalist social relations. However, they accept the state as the point of reference for examining the social relations of ostensibly Socialist regimes.

Other accounts that share the state-centered perspective, such as those of Castoriadis (1973) and Nove (1986), differ in their willingness to see Socialist countries as autonomous from capitalism. Nove, for example, defines the USSR as a "new kind of social formation, or mode of production" (p. 39) based on the nomenklatura's "dominance of the political" (p. 43). There, "one is witnessing what could be called a 'crisis of system,' a degree of economic malfunctioning that the new generation of leaders is being called upon to remedy" (p. 51). Nove assumes that the only available agency for remedying the crisis is the party, there being no significant formations of civil society within which people might be motivated and have the capability for promoting social change.

This particular form of statism is, for Nove, exceptional. Most societies, even those dominated by strong state structures, are liable to assertions of popular will, presumably rooted in localizing tendencies of culture, inherent limitations of any system of regulation, and forms of solidarity tied to everyday life. However, the USSR is seen by Nove to be extreme in the weakness of its civil society. He asserts that

People do grumble, have many grievances no doubt, but hope to find remedies within the system, see no possibility to change it, and, more important, would probably oppose most proposals to reform it. (p. 48)

Accounts such as those of Nove and Feher et al. are notable coming on the eve of what were subsequently characterized as assertions of civil society in precisely those places where it was presumed to have been constitutionally weak or absent. Not that they should have been held responsible for predicting events, but the totalitarianist framework of their analysis of statism produced an account that precluded any recognition of the kinds of contribution made by nonstate-dominated elements, what might be called "critical publics," to the history of Soviet-type societies. That is, their analysis precluded in advance adequate reference to an even minimal relation of state and civil society that could generate social change (Martin 1988). If this were true, (1) the USSR would be an altogether unique historical case, and (2) the events of the late 1980s and early 1990s either could not have happened or, since they did occur, can only have represented total collapse, given the assumption that there had been no agency for order beyond the state.

Paradoxically, such accounts share a tendency to reduce Socialist societies to the forms of statist regimes with other perspectives that see "really existing socialism" as true socialism. Thus, there is an odd affinity between the Soviet Communist Party's identification of itself as the agency of the new society (see, e.g., Shakhnazarov 1974, p. 7) and the mainstream Western media identification of the party (or its leadership) with Soviet society as such. What is theoretically most important in all these perspectives is the denial of any creative tension between civil society and state in the Socialist countries. What is significant about the perspective represented by Feher, Heller, and Markus is the substitution of an absolute ideal for a historical model of socialism in evaluating the prospects of "really existing socialism."

Finally, what is historiographically most problematic about these accounts is their assumption, in our opinion indefensible, that countries such as the USSR were and would be sociologically unique in their inability to change, their lack of politically relevant popular sociality, and the mechanical way in which they fulfill the destinies of their original dispositions. The point is not that the assumption is indefensible because it is controverted by facts, but because it organizes the selection of facts in a way that is inconsistent with the general body of sociological and historical knowledge upon which the authors otherwise claim to draw.

On the other hand, this exceptionalist approach to socialism, and the corresponding reduction of Socialist society (and its civic realm of critical practice) to the apparatuses of the state, is common even in mainstream social scientific accounts, especially so in political science. This is evident, for example, in a volume intended to survey all national governments with Marxist-oriented leadership:

The regimes considered in this study are variously called People's Republic, People's Democratic Republic, Democratic Republic, or Socialist Republic. These designations in general terms denote the economic and political structures of the respective societies and indicate progression from one type of society to another. This progression relates to the stages in the revolutionary process, from bourgeois democratic revolution to socialist revolution, and consequently to the economic development of these societies, their state structure and the role of the state in the economy. (Szajkowski 1982, p. 2)

Like those discussed above, accounts of this sort that substitute state for society are unable to recognize, much less predict, change; and when change occurs, it can only appear from that point of view as a critical rupture of the national society as a whole, and as a total crisis of total socialism. There is no doubt that turns were taken in all the Socialist nations of the East. The transformations in the Soviet Union in the 1980s were institutionally and economically fundamental to be sure, and it must have seemed likely that whatever the final terms of confederation, the future would lie, and events bear this out, in directions very different from a Union of Soviet Republics. But if this constituted a total crisis, a rupture at the core of social life itself, it was clearly more one of analysis then of particular societies, though it may have been that; and it was not at all clearly one of socialism as such, though it may have been for many Socialists.

Indeed, the changes, while momentous, were not without precedent. As Stephen Cohen, Basile Kerblay, Moshe Lewin, and other Soviet specialists have pointed out, the post-revolutionary socialisms were always changing, more in some areas, less in others; the problem for Western analysts is that it has been difficult if not impossible to recognize and evaluate the changes that did take place, and the social forces involved, within the limitations of conventional Sovietology (cf. Cohen 1986; Kerblay 1983; Lewin 1985). Apart from the fact that federated systems are bound to be unstable (whether as the USSR or as the less politically and economically unified confederations now on the agenda), we suggest that the crisis of theory in the aftermath of *perestroika* was caused by the appearance of civil society where none had been thought to exist.[10]

Marx attempted to show how civil society emerged in the West with bourgeois relations of property and the self-development of the bourgeoisie, as a reflection of a conflict-driven formal (legal) separation of economy and polity. For such a society, the civil order could only be identified with the order and agencies of law. But, he held, it is in some sense a constitutive feature of all society.[11] In *The German Ideology*, civil society is defined as both the "whole material intercourse of individuals"—presupposing the separation—and the "true source and theatre of all history"—suggesting something more universal (Marx 1978, p. 163).

Thus, civil society is the "theatre" for the universal production of social life because it "transcends the State and the nation." In that sense, it is merely background. What gives it its positive historical force, its historical presence, are two imperatives of its formation, identifiable conceptually since Adam Smith: "it must assert itself in its foreign relations as nationality and inwardly must organize itself as State" (Marx 1978, p. 163). Both depend upon the prior (or concomitant) establishment of different (and self-differentiating) nationally bounded political economies.

This global division is the condition under which the civil society of the national state can be said to achieve its identity as one of a complex set of social relations that operate beyond the national boundaries with which they are nevertheless identified; and this identification can therefore only be understood as ideological, only apparently cultural. But, the development of bourgeois society is part of the development of capitalist production, hence of the socialization of production as, finally, "the society of the producers."

As a feature of that history, civil society must manifest in one way or another the aspect of socialization that is intrinsic to capitalist production. Since the latter is the practical force of socialism within the capitalist mode of production, what makes socialism not merely utopian, civil society must not now refer to the legally controlled, ostensibly normative, order of property relations with which it is often confused. Rather, it designates what sociologists call "informal organization," or popular culture taken as the practices of sociality. Thus, it must be thought of as a pervasive feature of any instance of socialism understood as the historically constituted (internal) negation of capitalist relations.

It is possible to analyze socialism without civil society only if one mystifies its history by denying that it is part of capitalist development, and therefore if one equally mystifies the history of capitalism itself. But Socialist civil society must, unlike the social order of private property in the means of socially necessary production, be seen as in a tense rather than definitive or complementary relation with the law. This has led some observers, committed to a Durkheimian equation of law and civility, (1) to see dissatisfaction with law and its agencies as evidence of a lack of civil society in the Socialist nations, and (2) to identify the problem of legitimation as the permanent foundation of the "crisis" of socialism.

Socialist civil society can be seen, then, as forming itself against the legal order that enables it to take form altogether. This is, indeed, the source of a problem, but it is so only because that tension is part of the historical constitution of socialism, its disposition to change regardless of (or even in opposition to) the operations of law and the state. In this sense, socialism is an example of what anthropologist Pierre Clastres wrote of as "society against the state," if this is taken to refer to a dialectical rather than an absolute opposition, and as a feature of modernity (Clastres 1977).

Without identifying the relations of state and civil society for socialism (and what those terms might mean in this different context of their use), the "theatre of all history" and Socialist history in particular, are lost to analysis. But, then, so is that crucial aspect of the history of capitalism that has to do with the practical self-realization of the society of the producers (cf. Thompson 1961). On the other hand, events since the mid-1980s provide an opening for an analysis of the "internal" relations of socialism—if and only if one acknowledges, as an intrinsic element of those relations, the legally undefined forms of sociality that constitute a civil society of people rather than one of property.[12]

Here, Marxism suggests that these relations can only be properly expressed from the point of view of their conditions, namely those determined by, made intelligible in regard to, the global context of capitalist production and accumulation. If socialism is to be seen now as at a critical juncture, it is necessary to appreciate the fact that it has not developed and does not develop freely. However, reference to "conditions," "relations," and matters that are "external" and "internal," raises an important methodological problem connected with our earlier discussion of the historical/theoretical conditions of socialism.

An analysis that focuses on such a critical moment is, strictly speaking, conjunctural. That is, it suspends, in effect, the relationship of historically significant opposition that made the idea of socialism conceivable in the first place. For a conjunctural analysis, and only for that, we can reduce the history of socialism to a relationship between formation and context: but just for the moment, which is after all a moment of a critical analysis that must find its way back in its own terms to the history/dialectic for which alone a conjuncture (and its analysis) can be conceived of as a momentary interruption of that history. We must constantly remind ourselves that the distinction implied thereby between internal and external relations is analytical, and only holds given the momentary suspension of the dialectic of capitalist accumulation (of which socialism is an aspect, a term at least partly of opposition). It is on this condition that we can examine modern socialism from the standpoint of its external relations.

External Relations of Socialism

The global dominance of capital is increasingly considered as providing absolute limits to social (hence Socialist) development, independent of those that might be inherent in any case of realizing society. Whatever the gains of this observation, and there are many, it can pose a serious problem in evaluating such limits. For example, revolutions against national bourgeois regimes (including regime change by election) may disturb a population's dependence on capitalist social relations, but they cannot establish in advance the specific forms of subsequent development. When situations produced by such revolutions are said to be "transitional" (Bettleheim 1975, p. 11), there is an insinuation of just such a final state.

Paul Sweezy's use of the term "post-revolutionary society" to designate social transformations in the "exploited periphery of the capitalist system" incorporates an even more subtle idealization. This derives from the assumption that the revolutionary polity can act independently, is in some sense free, of the relations of which the revolution itself can only have been an instance (Sweezy 1980, p. 148). That is, Sweezy's concept seems to assume that a revolution by its nature suspends the operation of all that it opposed, rather than is, as Poulantzas argued, constituted in its own history by the relations of that very opposition as part of (and not apart from) the latter's history. It is in the light of this implicit idealization that we can evaluate the significance of Sweezy's warning that the problems such societies confront are human and social, not technological. One might agree with the spirit of his conclusion that a policy emphasis on the latter can only lead to increasing dependence on capitalism and therefore, by standards appropriate to social progress, "to weakness rather than strength" (Sweezy 1980, p. 150), but only if we interpret it to mean that no revolution is ever complete.

Sweezy's conclusion cannot logically provide a basis for a retrospective evaluation of the specific policies of a revolutionary government since it itself is part of a conjunctural analysis that cannot be totally separated from the events that form its object. Such a conclusion can only be comprehensible as part of an argument (hypothetical or real) among differing positions at the time a decision must have been made. Unfortunately, too many scholars have seen in their own preference for one strategic position over another the basis for judgment *post hoc*, as if, but for what can now be seen as the correct decision, the revolution would have completed itself—as if revolution is an autonomous event with its own dispositions free from the history of which it is a part, and with its own capacity to serve as an object for another autonomous event, namely analysis.

It is important to remain cautious in estimating what revolutions can accomplish. But analysis becomes unacceptably ahistorical when this caution reflects a contextualization that fails to reinsert the conjunctural moment of revolution in the history of which it is constituted as an event. In that case, caution becomes a rule whereby analysis is made to seem separate from its object. In this way, the constraints of the global context are made to appear as conditions that operate to obstruct what otherwise would develop on its own relatively straight path toward perfect socialism.

To restate the general point, an event is distorted when what is posited as context is then taken to be nothing more than a set of absolutely external conditions. Such a conception of context in effect also idealizes that for which it is said to constitute conditions, namely the revolutionary formation whose putative independence is merely a property of the analytical abstraction, itself justified within the political situation for which conjunctural analysis has become necessary. It idealizes the formation by removing what is dynamic from it (e.g., the relations of conflict, the old and the new), and resituating that as the set of conditions comprising a permanent context of parameters.

The result, typically, is that the development of the event (e.g., revolution) is depicted as able to move in only one of two opposite directions: completion (of the ideal) or (total) deformation. This deprives revolution of its historical dimension; and since it is impossible to ascertain, as if outside the revolutionary event, from what perspective one could bear witness to, recognize as what one might also have desired, the achievement of the ideal, it is only possible to see deformation in the aftermath. This, we take it, is the paradox of those accounts that focus on the context provided by the global-ization of capital but fail to sustain the historical analysis in the light of which the conjuncture, the revolutionary moment, could be identified as such in the first place.

A further consequence of the idealization of formation and context, im-portant for what follows, is the tendency to suppose that sufficient re-sources exist for the development of socialism independent of the capitalist constitution of a material base. If it were ever imaginable, it cannot be con-ceived of today. The dilemma, suggested by those for whom the question of the contextual limitations of socialism has taken precedent over the critique of capital, is the following. (1) Socialism can grow only if it acquires re-sources of adequate scale. (2) The only such resources available for appro-priation at the level of national organization are those created by capital for its own purposes and, therefore, renewable only in those terms. (3) But the use of such resources creates a stifling dependence upon capital that is inconsistent with the imperatives of social development. Given our critique of the foundation of this position, the dilemma is not one that we should feel obliged to share, though we must nevertheless appreciate it as a predica-ment for thinking, difficult to avoid, about the prospects of socialism.

At least two problems follow from accepting the terms of this dilemma. First, there are no contemporary examples of national industrial development that can be understood comprehensively as having taken place independently of the global circuits of capital. That is, in addition to the fact that Socialist nations have faced embargoes, isolation, and military encirclement, limited access to the financial and technological resources necessary to participate in the larger circuits of value that validate all instances of large-scale production has been a crucial part of the problem those nations have faced in developing industry while maintaining viable levels of socialization. In particular, gener-ating foreign exchange, guaranteeing the integrity of national currency, and repaying foreign debt in the context of the virtually unlimited mobility of cap-ital have had at least as much impact on the internal development and social condition of domestic populations of Socialist national political economies as they have had on non-Socialist national political economies.

Contemporary capitalism is the expression of a global division and re-constitution of labor that encompasses and consolidates the world's pro-ductive capacity. It too cannot be sustained within the confines of a nation-state, as is illustrated by the fact that the vast majority of the parts in the typical American automobile are manufactured elsewhere. A socially tuned economy must be able to intersect the circuit of circulating value (capital) in favor of production, something considered merely problematic for the accumulation of capital (though obviously necessary for the mainte-nance of its productive base).[13] Yet, accumulation on a world scale denies, and continues to deny as much as possible, that opportunity, as a matter of course, to Socialist states as much as or more than it is denied to other states. Thus, the circulation of capital poses a decisive limit to social development even where it is possible to regulate—and the limitations of this process tend, as we know, to accelerate—the relationships among production, consumption, and investment.

The second problem is related to the first. The extra-national circuits of capital are not merely sources of new commodities, they also embody socialized labor on a global scale. If access to those circuits of capital, and labor, is necessary for societal development consistent with societal needs, then the horizon for any social development can only be conceived in global terms. Two familiar hypotheses follow from this. First, no national economy can provide a foundation for an autonomous society, including especially one whose project is geared to the further socialization of production and formed in anticipation of a society of the producers. Second, any discernible national crisis of socialism must be seen at the same time as a crisis of capitalism—as a feature of that conjuncture.[14]

While revolution may alter and in certain ways transcend the conditions of struggle against capital, it can only do so within the existing framework of social development, that of capital's socialization of its forces of production (labor). Otherwise its aim would be utopian rather than practical, its origin unaccountable, and its principle of organization unsustainable. The capitalist economy of labor (efficiency of cost through the socialization of production) is the concrete, historically specific, context that generates the materially oriented sociality that always makes a Socialist revolution possible as such. The New Economic Policy of the 1920s and Stalin's industrialization policies of the 1930s both shared a dependence on foreign capital (Nove 1969), not in principle but of necessity. Even China, a country with enormous resources of its own, was unable until recently to continue what had once been a relatively autonomous path of development (Mittelman 1988).

Attempts by Sweezy, Bettleheim, and other writers to reserve the term "socialism" for a state of affairs free of the contradictions of capital may be justified in the light of a still hostile climate of opinion. Yet the ideological tactic is self-defeating if, as a result, socialism is idealized beyond the historical conditions of capitalist production in (dialectical) relation to which it emerges.

Paradoxically, this does not support the sort of economically strategic delinking advocated by Samir Amin (1991). Such a delinking by a national political economy is impossible, though the link can be qualified somewhat by the actions of state. Instead, it represents a delinking only in theory, creating yet another obstacle to understanding the connection of theory to practice. Originating metatheoretically, in the confusion of the arbitrarily determined nation-state with the historically determined society, this theoretical delinking also makes obscure the changes that characterize the development of socialism and that provide opportunities for Socialist political and economic decisions.

From this perspective, the intersection of national boundaries and the circuits of capital, as was clear in the late initiatives in Eastern Europe and the Soviet Union, can be said to have precipitated a crisis. But this must be seen, if we are to think of it historically, as a moment of a perpetual crisis. In that case, it achieves its conjunctural status not at an instant of absolute time revealed uniquely to the objective eye, but in the context of political necessity and political decision. The conditions of the latter are, among other things, organizational, and have to do with the possibilities of popular mobilization in relation to any particular change in the political economies of socialism. Thus, although the external relations of socialism can and must be identified for the sake of a politics of social change, the theoretical problem of understanding (and evaluating) socialism requires reflection on the limits of theory in regard to the relationship between conjuncture and history.

The identification of socialism with capital's socialization of production expands our appreciation of the role of politics (therefore the limits of theory). The identification of capital's international division of labor as the only appropriate level at which to describe the conditions of societal formation is part of the Marxist intellectual tradition. In the United States, it is associated with world-systems theory, the original formulation of which is to be found in Immanuel Wallerstein's *The Modern World System* (1974). A volume edited by C. Chase-Dunn in 1982 attempts to locate the development of Socialist states within that global context:

> Briefly, I consider the contemporary socialist states to be important experiments in the construction of socialism—neither totalitarian nightmares nor utopias. These states represent interstices within the larger capitalist world-economy in which socialist movements have taken state power. They represent the international logic of socialism, much as labor unions and socialist parties have done in the past. They have successfully implemented some of the requisites (especially the economic ones) of socialism. However, the partial nature of these institutions and the continued strength of world capitalism, especially as it operates in the interstate system, have pushed these states in the direction of reintegration as functional parts that reproduce the logic of the capitalist world-economy. Serious socialists must confront the limitations that the still-strong dynamics of world capitalist accumulation place on national economic planning as an instrument of socialism and the powerful tendency for interstate rivalry to produce authoritarian political structures within socialist states. (p. 9)

For Chase-Dunn, socialism remains a term of struggle, neither uniquely defined as the taking of state power nor as something independent of the capitalist relations that define it as a matter of practice. But even there, the rhetoric of "system" threatens to overwhelm the sense of a dialectic. While Socialist states are said to represent the "intentional logic of socialism," that logic is, in turn, subsumed by "the logic of the capitalist world-economy" in which those states are "functional parts" and therefore tend unpolitically, therefore ahistorically, toward integration, equilibrium, and boundary maintenance. Thus, despite the obvious differences in intention between the position outlined by Chase-Dunn and that of the earlier structural-functionalists, many of the theoretical difficulties we have discussed that have to do with evaluating the Socialist experience are retained by world-systems theory.

Parenthetically, there are other reasons for rejecting the system metaphor and its idealization of the relationship between Socialist formation and global capitalist context. For example, capitalist development is not prone to equilibrium so much as prone to alternate between enforcing equilibration and enforcing both the transgression of boundaries and the desystematization of its own project. The term "reproduction" refers, then, not to the maintenance of institutions or infrastructures so much as to the very process of capitalist production understood as the complementary oppositions of forces and relations, value and prices, society and capitalist wealth. Reproduction is not something capital sets out to do so much as what makes it capital. It follows that much of what happens in the process of capitalist development, hence Socialist development, includes dissolutions as well as resolutions, transgressions of boundaries as well as the insistence upon their integrity, equilibrating moves as well as dispersals of activities only momentarily, and only politically, constituted as "functions."

For the concept of socialism, the existence of boundaries is an epiphenomenon of the relations of capitalist production and circulation. The assertion of boundaries both limits the conception of Socialist development and our understanding of the significance of the mobility of capital. Thus, boundaries, reaffirmed or constituted through the agency of capitalist development, have historically limited the unimpeded flow of capital thereby allowing some measure of autonomy, given the momentary opportunity to take time, for the development of socially attuned political economies. But the connection between forces and relations (value and price) remain a problem even under such circumstances.

That is, even in such a case, the social economy buys its time, as it buys at least some of its resources, from outside itself. One cost of this relative, momentary freedom to expand the domain of the social is the creation of an intractable debt and the corresponding threat it poses to the capacity to regulate the economic relations by which Socialist nations can be identified as at least minimally Socialist. Another cost derives from the deferral of important technological and organizational features of industrialization. This forces those nations to accept a relatively weaker global position later in exchange for the opportunity in the shorter run to construct a basis for society.

There seems to be no alternative to this predicament. On the other hand, it forms part of the constitutional dynamics of Socialist civil society and is what makes that society more volatile and capable of contributing to social change than scholarship has been willing to acknowledge. We have seen how these costs are realized and civil society manifests itself in regard to them in the political upheavals of the early 1990s. Above all, the relative consistency with which, under Socialist imperatives, the mutually transforming forces and relations of production contribute to the formation of society make even more visible the opposition of capitalist production (now taken on a global scale) to the further aspirations of any "society of the producers" (the relatively more consistent relations and forces of production provided by Socialist economic organization).

The upheavals in the USSR and Eastern Europe should not, then, be considered events *sui generis*. They should be understood, first and most generally, as representing the opposition of sociality and capitalist production on the scale of the global political economy. Despite the alarming reemergence of nationalisms, the increasingly inchoate ideological shifts and turns, and the occasional eruptions of civil disorder and conflict, these events still give voice to the only aspiration that can be truly shared, that of an end to exploitation, therefore a beginning of society. In that sense, they have more in common with movements oriented to the condition of labor, against racism, sexism, and imperialism, and for socially responsible government in the United States, than they have with whatever is represented by the contradictory expressions "free market" and "capitalist democracy." But, it must also be recognized that they have more in common with their own national histories of socialism than with the idealized bourgeois history of "free enterprise" and its "democratic revolution" with which they are increasingly said nevertheless to have an irreducible affinity.

Rethinking Socialism

The following remarks are intended briefly to explore some of the implications of the above discussion for rethinking the general problematic of socialism. Above all, any attempt to account for changes in the polities and economies of Socialist nations might do well to begin with the flight of capital from its own sites of socialization, the nations of Western industrial capitalism. This can be seen to have provided relatively free capital, on the analogy to the earlier "freeing" of labor from so-called traditional constraints on its employability. This international and now increasingly global form of capital is far less limited than before by state-supported nationally and locally determined compromises of the struggle against exploitation. These compromises, which had given determinate shape and qualification to capital and limited its capacity freely to be deployed were now confronted by precisely what they were intended to evade. They were faced, relative to their own interests, with a new foundation for capitalist power (the capacity to move) and an enormously expanded capacity of capital's representatives to reinstate, without having to account for the social, political, cultural, and locally economic consequences, the more stringent logic of the capitalist project.

This new freedom was predicated in the primary sites of capital on the continually heightened contradiction of the circulation of capital (and its tokens) with the production of goods and conditions of production that make capital possible. As a practical matter, it allowed capital to confront nations as if each was like the other (a calculable factor), that is, with a greater egalitarianism than ever before. But it also, paradoxically, reduced the availability of capital to any nation for which the social rationalization of production was a first priority. The result could only be a disruption of the overall integration of the productive system with consequences discussed below.[15]

The attempt to reckon with the increasing costs of Socialist development put pressure on Socialist economies that could only be diminished by introducing antisocial economies of labor. But this was something a Socialist government could have done only if it were willing to violate the civil imperatives of its own society. Indeed, small changes in policy for so intricate and stable a division of labor as existed, for example, in the USSR could have been expected to have exactly the sort of greater ramifications one would anticipate for any social order so like the "organic solidarity" posited a century ago by Emile Durkheim.

It may be for this reason that Mikhail Gorbachev's early attempts at *perestroika* were justified by Soviet officials (1) as a resumption of the continuing struggle for socialism, (2) as reform rather than a revolution in the social relations of production, and (3) as substituting considerations of measurable efficiency for the inefficiencies of socially practical, that is political, accountability.

The first justification held that there was to be no disruption of the relationship between the reasons people had for participating in society and what they could expect materially and socially as a result. The changes were to be understood as strictly internal and therefore technical, therefore not legitimately subject to opposition. The second held that the changes were of a medical nature, necessary to save the body but in no sense to transform it. That is, the authority of the changes was defined technocratically, in terms designed to appeal to the willingness of people in need to accept the legitimacy of those experts in positions to address that need. The third justification provided the diagnosis, thereby inviting, in principle, broader intellectual participation in the processes of decision making involved in deciding upon one or another "initiative." This, probably inadvertently but possibly not, introduced those problems associated with representation that would ultimately threaten the authoritative role of the Communist Party.

Each attempt at rationale recognized the presence of critical publics, that is a civil society, whatever their forms of organization, their media, and their established discourses, to which the state had no choice but to appeal.

Each was insufficient to account for what one might call the sociological ramifications of the disturbance in the organic solidarity of Soviet society. The result was a relative disorganization of the ideological and organizational apparatus that had mediated the relationship between civil society and the state and, consequently, an inability any longer to justify the changes to all the constituencies now mobilized without engaging in the sort of populist appeal to loyalty and trust that could only support a clearly recentralized authority above the state itself. In the light of this predicament, Gorbachev began to attend to two crucial resources, political organization as such and foreign affairs.

Once the ramifications of introducing asocial (economic) systems of accountability became evident, Gorbachev, and indeed the Soviet government, had little choice but to turn toward a total reformation of its foreign relations if it was to slow the socially disintegrating effects of economic accountability and the relative failure of legitimacy that accompanied it. This meant coming to terms with global capital—e.g., by finding ways to increase the ease with which Soviet currency could be "converted," by providing avenues of investment in contractual terms global investors could accept, given their other opportunities, and by beginning to set the stage for invidious economies of labor.

Convertibility threatened the capacity of the Soviet state to coordinate the larger dimensions of its economy, leading to pressure for increasingly less limited privatization. Better terms for investors entailed some likelihood of a drain of value from the society of the producers to what Walter Wriston, formerly of Citicorp, once called the global "financial community," leading to a need to deal, politically and economically, with unemployment, a decline in service, and insecurity on a level not previously experienced by Soviet workers. Deliberate economies of labor could only avoid negative social effects if the policies were perceived as legitimate, if workers could reasonably expect compensation or future consideration, or if political organizations such as the Communist Party, capable in principle of orienting to the interest of the society of the producers, were severely weakened. The latter, a strategy consistent with other sources of erosion of the party's legitimacy, seems likely to satisfy the new asocial requirements of accountability.

The fact that a weakening of the Communist Party entailed less political participation by the citizenry, the fact that the legitimacy of the reforms was threatened by the apparently unanticipated consequences of their attempted institution, and the fact that the capacity of the state to coordinate the Soviet economy was undermined provide the background for a host of problems addressed by Gorbachev as well as by his political competition. One serious consequence had to do with the most important initiative Gorbachev undertook: a consolidation of national resources in anticipation of further problems to come by reducing Soviet participation in the arms race and by withdrawing Soviet support for nations in the third world struggling to survive the destructiveness of capital's enjoyment of its own latest bid for freedom.

This list of problems and prospects is not intended to suggest more than that the USSR, like every other nation, could hardly have avoided dealing with global capital, and that this could only have created difficulties for its society and have had ramifications for the civil polity of its social project. To see all of this as the eruption of a democratic impulse where there had been no democracy was, we believe, mistaken. This is not to deny that there were and remain good reasons for popular protest, for challenges to the hegemony of the Communist Party, even for the expression of certain nationalistic motives. It is only to say that the attempt to redefine democracy against the already existing semi-participatory social polity of the USSR was a symptom of a greater, global, tension.

U.S. students in the 1960s tried with some success to define democracy in a society whose government, too, seemed little more than a regime, hostile to democratic values and unremittingly bureaucratic, racist, repressive, xenophobic, and warlike. Then in the United States, as in regard to the USSR, problems were identified with those aspects of society that were most unjust and least democratic. The existence of a critical public in the USSR, the fact that virtually every family in the USSR had some member in the party, and the constant attempt to politicize aspects of daily life in regard to social values, though no closer to ideal democracy than the national electoral system in the United States, provided since the 1950s a democratic aspect of Soviet socialism rooted in civil society and capable of generating change no matter what its limitations. This is not to focus on the moral quality of the Soviet experiment, but to refocus on aspects of it that have been dogmatically denied and that are crucial for understanding what the new Russia is now going through.

These are hardly novel observations. They have been made in one way or another and with various qualifications by, among others, Stephen Cohen, Moshe Lewin, and Basile Kerblay. The types of problem posed by global capital are not likely to increase the level of democracy anywhere in the world. Indeed, it appears, at the end of the G. W. Bush era, likely that the reverse will be true. No doubt the Communist Party depressed democracy even as it increased participation and social organization. Though there was exploitation, there is no doubt that the party represented, at least to an extent greater than elsewhere, social values opposed to the capitalist exploitation of labor. As a result, and regardless of what other available vehicle might better contribute to popular sovereignty, its precipitous decline remains altogether ambiguous. Given the circumstances that postcommunism is leading in the former Communist nations and republics, it seems more likely to a retreat from the project of civil society rather than to an increase in progress toward it.

Further, the historic attempt to bring relations of production more in line with an enhanced socialization of production in the USSR must itself be seen, even retrospectively, as a condition of democracy. The sort of economic accountability now fostered in the interest of global capital is hardly likely to lead to an expansion of that aspect of socialism any more than it has contributed to participation and popular sovereignty in the polities of other nations. What remains to be seen, in addition, is if and how the Socialist project, such as it is, can sustain the commitment to society, something still taken for granted by most of their citizens in the face of the mounting global attack by capital against any form of association that is not fundamentally the "society of things" about which Marx had so much of interest to say.

Notes

CHAPTER 1   INTRODUCTION: COMMUNISM, SOCIETY, AND HISTORY

1. Available evidence during the 1960s suggested that students who identified themselves as on the Left were more tolerant, open to dialogue, and more supportive of the Constitution and the Bill of Rights than students on the Right or students either in the middle or not obviously politically motivated. See the whole issue of the *Journal of Social Issues*, Vol. 23, July 1967.

2. The New Deal coupled with disappointment about the development of Soviet socialism, in particular "Stalinism," were, understandably, part of the disaffection of many on the Left; and, while not all became professional anticommunists, there were some scholars, like Seymour Martin Lipset and Neil Smelser, who could scarcely resist what was called at the time "red-baiting," as in Lipset and Smelser's perfunctory comments on and dismissal of C. Wright Mills, then the most widely read sociologist in America, in an essay on the state of American sociology (1961). But even then, the tendency was to reject revolutionary or radical reform in favor of a gradualist approach through the institutions rather than to reject socially progressive values. Stanley Aronowitz summarizes this move of ex-radicals toward the Democratic Party as based on "their claim that the highest possible progressive aspiration is incremental reform within a virtually permanent capitalist system whose framework of liberal-democratic political institutions is perfectly adequate to address the remaining, albeit residual, cultural and social problems" (2006, p. 69). What is important was not the turn against communism or Socialist values as such, but the turn of so many intellectuals against the idea of structural reform in regard to issues (e.g., growing inequality) that might have seemed urgent enough to justify a more radical approach. The assumption that piecemeal reforms would necessarily accumulate favored a gradualist approach to politics, even beyond considerations of feasibility and beliefs about what might be persuasive to large numbers of people. The assumption was nevertheless odd, given the prevailing "mass society" perspective of the social sciences. That would have indicated a greater

volatility of public opinion than could have supported the idea of an ultimately transforma-tive accumulation of reforms. It was clear then, and even clearer now, that institutional pol-itics does not produce such a sequence without something extra-institutional, and the latter is difficult to regulate according to the gradualist notion that dissent must be chosen over protest. Given Mills's influence on the "new Left" of the 1960s, his rejection of this turn must have appeared to Lipset and others as incompatible with what Talcott Parsons, in his review of Mills's *The Power Elite*, said was the proper reading of American society as a rel-atively rational system in which authority prevailed over power. But, obviously, more was at stake than theoretical differences. There was a genuine disaffection with the Left and this ran through the 1960s and beyond in the works of many of these authors. What is at issue here, however, is not whether they were justified in shifting from one set of values (social progress) to another (sustaining the institutions of democracy under capitalism) or from one strategy (radical reform) to another (gradualism), but how their discourse assimilated itself, or was assimilated by, the logic of the Cold War.

3. Lewis Feuer wrote about the dynamics of adolescence in his account of the 1960s (1969), and Talcott Parsons saw student protests at universities as effectively opposing ra-tionality (1968). For a review of the literature written soon afterward, see Brown and Goldin (1973), especially chapters 11 and 12.

4. Frances Fitzgerald's *America Revised* exposed such biases in how American history had been taught until the 1960s (1979). See also Novick (1988). There have been changes since then, but the question of relative emphasis on state or society is still much debated.

5. See Stanley Aronowitz for the effect of this context on one important activist intel-lectual's projection of a Left future (1996). His later book, *Left Turn* (2006), modifies his earlier position on radical democracy according to what he believes is feasible under pres-ent circumstances, but it still advocates the separation of the Left from its most obvious past.

6. By "misunderstanding," I do not mean to suggest that there is an alternative total characterization of communism or the Left to counter the total characterization by anticom-munists. The misunderstanding lies in assuming the validity of any such totalizing account of that history.

7. Cf. Mark Naison's *Communists in Harlem during the Depression* (1983) with Harvey Klehr's *The Heyday of American Communism* (1984). Cf. also Ottonelli (1991) and Pells (1984).

8. See George Iggers (1997) for a survey of those changes since 1975; see also Henry Abelove, Betsy Blackmar, Peter Dimock, and Jonathan Schneer (1983, originally published 1976). This book consists of interviews with many of those who influenced the new histori-ans as well as some of the latter, including E. P. Thompson, Eric Hobsbawm, Sheila Row-botham, Linda Gordon, Natalie Zemon Davis, William Appleman Williams, Staughton Lynd, David Montgomery, Herbert Gutman, Vincent Harding, John Womack, C.L.R. James, and Moshe Lewin. See also Aaron (1992), Burke (1978), Darnton (1985), Greenblatt (1994), Gunn (1992), Huet (1985), Jameson (1981), Johnson et al. (1982), Jones (1971), LaCapra (1983, 1987), Spivak (1999), Veeser (1989), and White (1973). For an account of the French contribution to post-war historiography, see Revel and Hunt (1995). For a useful, thorough, and challenging discussion of the problems of writing histories of the Nazi period from vari-ous points of view, which bears on issues discussed in this book, see Nolan (1988). Robert Rosenstone's study of the idea of history as constituted in film provides an opportunity to consider alternative approaches to imagining history that bear on the question of historical interpretation (1995, especially chapter three, entitled "Reds as History").

9. See, for a somewhat different approach to the study of Communist societies, Basile Kerblay (1983), Stephen Cohen (1986), and Moshe Lewin (1985).

10. A helpful discussion can be found in Giorgio Agamben's *State of Exception* (2005). Work by Stephen Greenblatt exemplifies the sort of history writing that situates its subject matter within society and identifies the society itself as organized in part around that very possibility. See Greenblatt (1991) and Darnton (1985) for a comprehensive look at what has

been going on at the level of theory and in regard to historiography in the human sciences. See also Stephen Greenblatt and Giles Gunn (1992). For an example, see Michael Denning's study of the Communist Party's cultural policies during the "popular front" (1998).

11. Cf. Stanley Aronowitz (2007) and Stephen Duncombe (2007). These are only the most recent entries in the two-centuries-old literature on possible Left futures. The attempt to project a new Left goes back to the beginning of modern critical movements and is represented by manifestoes, as well as records of debates and, of course, books and articles, not to mention the pamphlets and other ephemera of revolutions.

12. I co-edited a collection of papers by a number of the best contemporary writers on communism (1993). This remains fairly representative of the work being done then and now. We did not include the work of Klehr, though it is discussed along with Draper, Starobin, and other orthodox historians. Our purpose was to present a different point of view, one that was neither pro- nor anticommunist, and to bring together outstanding scholars who shared our commitment to rethinking the history of the Left in general and communism in particular. One of our criteria for selecting participants was that they be committed to describing facts about communism as they would describe another phenomenon not the subject of so heavy an agenda, which meant that they consider the CPUSA in its connection to a broader social movement itself understandable in terms of the American national context. Most of the participants seemed by their published work to be committed to these criteria. This is true of Mark Naison's comprehensive study of the work of the Communist Party in Harlem, Alan Wald's study of the political divisions among New York intellectuals who found themselves moving toward one version or another of neo-conservatism (1987), and Ellen Schrecker's accounts of McCarthyism (1986, 1998).

13. An alternative is to decide that an analysis of American society yields a sense of where the contradictions lie such that one can speak of a "Left" as making manifest the contradiction between society and such asocial manifestations as power, or between humanist values and instrumental values, etc. This assumes an analysis that highlights contradictions but not in a way that bears on our understanding of which movements are oriented to structural change and which are not, and this is what has to be specified if a focus on the idea of a Left is to have historiographical meaning—if, in other words, the Left is to be understood as indicating an aspect of basic conditions of societal change, an immanence rather than a possibility.

14. An example might be the following: We will say that doing something, for example, eating or speaking together in a conversational way, is both about its object (ingesting the food or issuing utterances) and about the social grounds of this activity being intelligible as if it is something known that someone might do under the circumstances and in this very way of doing it. In conversational speech, we talk to or about a topic, and, at the same time, display what it is to be conversational in what Blum and McHugh call a "committed" way (cf. Garfinkel 1967; Blum and McHugh 1994).

15. Parsons seems to argue that one part of history involves describing the space between structures as a movement of articulation over time (1977). While the influence of Durkheim's *Rules of Sociological Method* is evident in this (1982), Parsons's version focuses on the adaptive rather than the social aspect of articulation. In contrast, Durkheim's account of the division of labor is, as I read it, more dynamic in the sense that it speaks specifically of the relationship between the "progress of the division of labor" and the onset of social conflict. Danto's philosophy of history focuses on temporal succession by analyzing what he believes is the distinctive feature of historical writing, namely the systematic use of "narrative sentences" (2007).

16. I identify this logic with Marx's immanent critique of the defense of the capitalist mode of production. This critique is immanent, deconstructive, and dialectical in the way in which it recovers the relationship between the ostensibly simple accounts in which political economy makes its case and the more comprehensive, though ultimately contradictory account to which it is driven by the critique. The upshot of the critique is that capitalist production cannot rationalize itself in terms of its reproducibility as an ongoing affair, its

relevance to the common interest, or its capacity to maintain the grounds of capitalist wealth (cooperation on the scale of "industry" and "the society of the producers"). This is discussed in some detail in the chapter entitled "Ideology and the Metaphysics of Content."

17. Writing history is, of course, not the same as keeping records and ordering them chronologically or according to the dictates of a specifiable agenda. This sort of work is undoubtedly of great value, but it is different from the sort of history at issue here, which has to do with the ways in which accounts reflect the self-transformative aspect of society and all that is internally related to society.

18. I take it that Amartya Sen is making something of the same point when he notes that the sort of information gathered in justifying social choices tends, and this is my way of putting it, to derive from national rather than societal distributions and often lacks the quality needed to evaluate needs and resources within society as such (2002). I should add that nothing I say here bears on the issues of nationalism and nationality, which may be understood for certain purposes and in certain situations to express sociality, possibly in opposition to itself.

19. Anticommunism may well be the result of a generalization of another such logic. I suggest, in Chapter Six, that there may be a yet more general logic of exclusion behind the way in which groups and societies are graded, ethnologically, and that it may have its origins in the internal workings of society under certain conditions.

20. It is important to note that what is outside of normal practice and expectation cannot easily be communicated, which is why prophecy so often fails to convince people of the truth of its vision.

21. It is important in this regard to remember that the defense of capital begins with the proposition that societal wealth has to do with the stock of useful objects and ends with the proposition that those objects are defined not by use-value but by exchange-value and therefore monetarily. The point is that, by the logic of the defense, socialized labor under capitalist conditions (exploitation and universal exchange) is the source of wealth and, at the same time, constitutes the forces of production. From this it follows that the initial claim, which beckons toward a societal definition of wealth and then abandons it, is true only if the measure of wealth is separated from the money form of capital. In that case, the initial case made for capital, that the value it realizes is ultimately societal in effect is false because it derives from a simplification that distorts the full description of capitalist production in the interest of justifying only one feature of it, namely its distributional principle (see chapter one of the first volume of Marx's *Capital*).

22. Underproduction is a feature of that aspect of capitalism that requires the continuous infusion of wealth from noncapitalized or minimally capitalized sources (Marx refers to this as the "primitive" accumulation, not as first but as basic.) As a result, the historical accomplishment of capitalism, the constitution of abundant production, is not to be understood merely as a temporal move from precapitalist formations to capitalism, a mere succession, but a move within capitalist production from underproductive (labor-intensive) to overproductive (social-intensive) forms. In other words, it is a distorting simplification to say that capitalism succeeds feudalism if one means that it moves from one mode of production to another. Rather, it is the addition of socialized production that constitutes the capitalist revolution, and the emphasis on socialized forces shows that socialism is the fulfillment of the capitalist revolution. That is as far as abundant production based on the socialization of labor can go. This is why Marx and Engels say that it is only then that the history of society begins, with whatever tensions give it its historical quality.

23. Marx's writings, especially his political writings, offer and justify a number of robust hypotheses about limitations on political organization and action determined by the forms of social life in which people regularly participate. These remain valuable contributions to the literature on unauthorized political action, popular protest, and the informal aspects of politics. There is no over-arching theoretical approach to politics and revolution that belongs distinctively to Marx, though there are certain axioms that Marx introduced as such and that have proven valuable in this field of study. The point of my discussion of Marx's critique of

political economy is not to present an overview of his work but to illustrate how a critical dimension can be recognized in a systematic account of society.

24. To say that society is a productive force is not to model it on the image of a factory. It is to say that it becomes, at one and the same time, the creator of material wealth and the creator of itself as a system governed by a principle of mutuality. That society is or can be productive as a whole does not imply that it is nothing but the producer of material goods, just the reverse: If it is to be productive as a whole, it must be a producer of relations of cooperation under conditions of interdependence.

25. This is discussed explicitly in the third volume of *Capital*, which, in this regard, is an account of the circulation of "fictitious capital" without apparent limit, something altogether familiar to those economists particularly concerned with the effects of globalization, the rational foundation of money when the money supply is increasingly indeterminate, and the shift from productive to speculative investment (and the consequent demand for liquidity).

26. This was a point made in my 1973 book, *Collective Behavior* (with Amy Goldin). There, I tried to show that so-called "crowd" behavior and "social movements" should be seen at the outset as continuous with (and reflexive to) something else already happening. See also Blum and McHugh (1984) for an original and provocative discussion of the pedagogical fallacy of assuming that "influence" constitutes an external relation between those attempting to exercise it and those on whom it is presumably exercised.

27. This is a problem for narrative histories, which are often criticized for imposing a type of coherence on the past that belongs to an order dictated by the historian's present (see Danto, 2007, for a discussion of the problem). This is one reason why some historians have argued that historical truth resembles fictional truth in that both are subject to the criterion of plausibility (as in "this is how something plausibly described might plausibly have happened").

28. Like the distinctions between microsocial and macrosocial and the short and the long runs, the distinction between depth and structure has no clear theoretical status, nor could it have. These distinctions are always constituted within the reality they are said to be about.

29. Interests, etc., may overlap so that they need not be reduced to a single unifying disposition in this sort of analysis.

30. I am not recommending the distinction, only commenting on its use, given that one yields to the temptation to assert it in the first place.

31. See, for an account of this sort of historiography, Richard Johnson, Gregor McLennan, Bill Schwarz, and David Sutton (1982). See George Iggers (1997) for developments since the 1970s. See also Morag Shiach's "A History of Changing Definitions of 'The Popular,' " in her book, *Discourse on Popular Culture* (1989); and for a programmatic statement, see Peter Burke (1981). For a comprehensive philosophical account of aspects of historical explanation that covers some of the same literature but from a somewhat different point of view about what constitutes society from the one expressed in this book, see Christopher Lloyd (1986).

32. So, he can speak of "rebellious youth" in regard to the 1960s (p. 343). This is by now an uninformative cliché that elides many if not most of those facts which might show that it is a cliché. This tendency to characterize by cliché runs through most generational accounts, and Diggins's is no exception. The problem with an unaccountable use of generations to set up an episodic history is that it already depends on a cliché, that of "generational tensions" so that others easily follow. Diggins uses the concept as if there were a theory to back it up, and it is nowhere justified. It is not a hypothesis, rather the framework of his study, and so the validity of the study as a whole depends on assumptions that are neither stated nor justified. This is why it is fair to say it is tendentious to the idea that a Left is always more reactive than positive. The closest he comes to a concept of "generation" is where he says: "what identifies a group as belonging to a particular generation is both a shared perspective on common historical problems and a similar strategy of action taken as a result of that perspective" (p. 44). The main problem with this is that he seems to suggest, on the one hand,

that the group belongs to a particular generation because it shares something and, on the other, that it shares something because it belongs to a "particular generation."

33. On page 30, he writes that "a political phenomenon may be defined in light of its ideals." This begs the question of how it fits into society, but that is the least of its problems. Apart from duplicating the emphasis on "episodes" by particularizing "political phenomena," it asserts something almost impossible to defend, namely that such a phenomenon can be "defined in light of its ideals" and that such a definition, assuming it can be justified, is sufficient for the positive use Diggins wishes to make of it as the basis of an analysis of a complex of social facts for which the significance of "ideals" is by no means clear in any discipline. So far as the possibility of justifying the attribution of ideals to so complex "a phenomenon," one might do so empirically or by deriving them from reasonably attributable principles (of operation, of belief, etc.) such that it is clear that they are not only ideals but principles of action, which is crucial to evaluating the validity of Diggins's account. It is not just that there are differences among people attributing ideals to political movements, though that is certainly the case. It is that the empirical grounds for doing so are so undeveloped that anyone attempting to argue from ideals might be expected to at least raise the question of how the attribution is possible in the first place. If there is a legitimate question, or if the attribution cannot be justified empirically, then all that flows from it is either suspect, which I believe is the most reasonable conclusion, or of a sufficiently modest intention that one would not expect an author to have written with such forceful rhetoric that modesty is concealed, and as if what needs to be known is sufficiently known simply by the strategy of beginning with ideals, generations, and the rest.

34. "Dramatic irony" is defined in *The New Princeton Encyclopedia of Poetry and Poetics* as "a plot device according to which (a) the spectators know more than the protagonist; (b) the character reacts in a way contrary to that which is appropriate or wise; (c) characters or situations are compared or contrasted for ironic effects, such as parody; or (d) there is a marked contrast between what the character understands about his acts and what the play demonstrates about them" (1993, p. 635).

35. This would certainly have to come to terms with the vast amount of information the orthodox historians—especially Draper, Starobin, Klehr, and Diggins—have compiled as well as their interpretations of the various cases and events regularly cited by the first three authors. The most important difference is the interpretive frame of reference required by a conceptualization of society in terms of its critical aspect.

36. I mean by "paradigm," something of what Ferdinand de Saussure describes as "an associative family" in which each expression "is the point of convergence of an indefinite number of coordinated terms." What is most important here are "the two characteristics of the associative series"—indeterminate order and indefinite number" (1966, p. 126). These are part of what gives a paradigm its imperative character.

37. By "politics" in this limited context, I mean to refer to concerted activity in which something about society as a whole has become an issue, which resists cooptation as a matter of reinstating the social dimension and aim of struggle, and which has become self-reflective in a way that necessarily invokes a past as part of imagining a future that substantiates the present as something ongoing.

38. I do not mean to suggest that no such imputation could be valid, only that its validity would have to be tested against a systematic account of its ostensible instance. Mary Nolan provides a far-ranging and extremely informative discussion of some of the historiographical issues, in particular, with regard to the case of twentieth-century Germany (1988).

39. An argument might be made that an adequate account of a "context" can support differential probabilities of different anticipated outcomes. I do not disagree in principle with this, but that is not what one typically finds in the literature on communism and the Left.

40. This was the argument Stephen Cohen, and others, made about assessing Soviet society (1985, 1986). Projections based on the idea of a stasis, fueled by the idealization of totalitarianism, lead to policies that are impossible to reconcile with what we know about the

ways in which societies change and the inevitability of change. The same can be said about dispositional projections about radical movements, as in Diggins's work (1991).

41. See, for an example of studies of Russian attitudes to the aftermath of *perestroika*, M. K. Gorshkov (2005) and recent issues of the journal *Sociological Research: A Journal of Translations from Russian*. Published by M. E. Sharpe.

42. Robert Rosenstone's study of history in film (1995) shows how difficult it is to resist linear representation. See Peter Novick for a detailed account of attempts by American historians to address the question of historical objectivity in regard to the complexity of the subject matter: "My own deepest methodological commitment is to the 'overdetermination' of all activity, including thought" (1988, p. 9).

43. To indicate more concretely what my theoretical definition of the Left entails, I am identifying the political Left with socially progressive politics in which the idea of social progress includes opposing, in the name of the common good, inequality, injustice, oppression, and domination—e.g., based on wealth or prior status, and in which a question invariably arises as to the reproduction of any form of society as a definite *status quo*. In other words, for the Left, society is, in principle, inclusive without limits and it cannot be separated from either its critical aspect or its aspect of self-governance. This more concrete definition has several purposes. One is to establish the principle that distinguishes the political Left from the Democratic Party, though this distinction does not imply any necessary opposition, especially since the latter does not represent a point of view but a formally national organization relative to another such organization. The principle is that society is inclusive without limits, from which flow commitments to justice and equality and to the requirement that these be acted upon according to conditions of feasibility and the immanence of that very disposition. I have already discussed my assumption that the Left can be understood as a manifestation of the critical aspect of any instance of human affairs that can be thought of as social (including, especially for the purposes of this book, society). This is why I consider its elision in historical studies of American society to pose a significant historiographical problem for our understanding of American history.

44. If one argues that, say, rational choice is a normative ideal, the problem is how to estimate its approximation in practice. No general solution to this now exists, and it seems unlikely that one can be devised.

CHAPTER 2   HISTORY AND HISTORY'S PROBLEM

1. Thompson is trying to lay to rest the argument that the old regimes were periods of consensus, as Raymond Williams and so many other social historians have tried to do. But there is more to this than meets the eye, more than the empirical question, and more than meets the sensibility of what Thompson once called "historical logic."

2. It is possible to read "a rather different notice" as lugubrious and melodramatic in tone, as a villain might speak to an unsuspecting hero about facts yet to be disclosed on which the hero's fate will in any case depend. This effect can be achieved simply by lingering on "rather" and slightly elevating the pitch; then, "different notice" should be gradually lowered in tone and slightly sped up, the sibilance of "notice" being extended as if to be followed by sharp eye contact. Needless to say, this is not consonant with a serious reading of the passage, and so I dismiss its possibility without further comment.

3. Another mood would be possible if this were all the text there was. In that case, "we have" is the seller's monologue, the drone of the auctioneer, the tally of the accountant. So dry a series yields readily to a disturbance; so mundane a succession can easily serve as build-up to a punch line. The *succession* of voices does not allow for this though it may operate as an incidental accompaniment.

4. "Sudden" in that all principles of classification seem with this phrase to collapse, and with them the world of estates on which they were predicated.

5. There has, after all, been a long history of the posting of anonymous bills, of anonymous polemical poetry, and, more recently, malicious phone calls and mean graffiti.

CHAPTER 3 ISSUES IN THE HISTORIOGRAPHY OF COMMUNISM, PART ONE— IDENTIFYING THE PROBLEM

1. By "semiotics of discursively realized culture" I mean studies that emphasize the circulation of signs within collectivities.

2. It does not follow that representations are arbitrary or indifferent to "evidence," but only that the criteria of plausibility are in important ways not identical with the criteria usually said to apply to works that aspire to inductive quality or to the representation of "facts" as such.

3. For example, cf. Bell's bibliographical essay in the Princeton edition of *Marxian Socialism in the United States* (1967, pp. 194–201).

4. An article by Theodore Draper illustrates this attitude: "Instead of making sense of their own experience by confronting it directly, those post–New Left professors seem to want to make sense of it through the medium of an earlier generation. They have evidently turned back to the 1930s, '40s, and '50s because they are unwilling or unable to face up to their own political history" (1987, p. 29).

5. That tension between what can be written and what must somehow be denied or taken away for the sake of communication is one of the most interesting, and poignant, tropes of this attitude.

6. Draper's comment on current studies of Communist movements that attempt to illuminate the everyday lives of participants is instructive: Such details "may make a minor contribution to American social history, but they need not be politically significant or relevant to an understanding of American Communism. They cannot tell us for what ultimate ends such activities were engaged in, where the policies came from, why they were turned on and off" (1987, p. 36). But those "post–New Left historians" have tried to address precisely those questions, and it is the historiography of studies of everyday life that they have used to implement an attitude quite different from Draper's. His is precisely an attitude of desperation, and he deploys terms, even "post–New Left," intended throughout to satisfy by polemical extension the claim that he and his colleagues have settled accounts. Thus, again, he says, the study of American communism "has been taken over by a new academic generation, too young to have known what it was like to be for or against the communist movement in the 1930s or even 1950s. . . . [Now,] it is inevitably being reconsidered from different political perspectives and personal backgrounds" (1985, p. 32).

7. Again, and in a different context, Theodore Draper illustrates the point in the extreme: "Communism is codified in its canonical literature; it is at any one time what the authoritarian Party says it is" (1987, p. 34). On the other hand, not all tendencies are dispositions and not all use of the term follows the logic I have outlined. Moreover, there are insignificant uses of "disposition" that need not occupy us.

8. Draper comments, in an ugly moment of lapse, that "The new historians of American communism and the new breed of academic Marxists constitute a little-noted subdivision of the 'Yuppie social stratum' " (May 9, 1985, p. 32).

9. Lyons's book on Communists in Philadelphia relies heavily on such material (and therefore such a reified witness voice) for the substance of its accounts, as if those voice traces (like the signatures the nineteenth-century historians hoped to prove "authentic," and had in any case to debate for authenticity) were sufficient to tell the story, given their plausible arrangement by an author for whom the plausibility of arrangements of such material was and is not problematic (1982).

CHAPTER 4 ISSUES IN THE HISTORIOGRAPHY OF COMMUNISM, PART TWO—SOME PRNCIPLES OF CRITICAL ANALYSIS

1. It is not necessary to debate the issue to see that there is a difference in the following two characterizations of Eugene Dennis by two authors of different attitude and different

historiographical orientation. Joseph Starobin described Dennis at psychiatric length in his book about the American Communist Party during the 1940s and 1950s: "His voice was strangely weak, and he continually interrupted himself by throat clearing; this habit was often concealed by a Stalinesque deliberateness, a weighing of words and silences that gave an impression of greater wisdom than his opinions conveyed. He had no taste for the rough-and-tumble of either public or private debate. . . . Thus he came to personify political indecisiveness. All his political instincts ran in the direction of making his party a genuine, native political force; all his own characteristics negated these instincts. The central reasons for this contradiction lay in his tropism for Moscow, his Comintern training. Even in face-to-face conversation he seemed to believe that each 'rounded-out' phrase was being weighed in some distant balance. His indecisiveness and his Comintern mentality guaranteed that the attempt by Dennis in 1956 to rejuvenate the party on a new basis . . . would also cause him to retreat before its own implications, to suffer the fate of the 'centrist' " (1972, pp. 13–14). Compare this to Maurice Isserman's more recent characterization: "Dennis, a Communist organizer since the mid-1920s, with wide and varied experience on the West Coast, in Wisconsin, and in the Comintern's international apparatus, was being groomed for leadership in the party. He tended to side with Browder in intraleadership battles, though he displayed more independence—or, as his detractors charged, indecision—than other political committee members" (1992, pp. 23–24).

2. This distinction applies to evaluations of events in El Salvador, Nicaragua, Cuba, and other revolutionary and post-revolutionary nations—on the one hand the assumption that rebellion and resistance are instigated, and on the other that they are part of a process internal to their situation.

3. White's argument is derived from considerations on the limits and facilities of interpretation, in particular that description is descriptive and narration narrative only when their language fulfills certain requirements of sensibility analyzable as the imagination of fundamental order (as in the revelation of the whole in a part). White emphasizes, therefore, the characteristic tropes by which various historians were able to achieve explanatory affect beyond mere explanation.

4. In passing, this distinction between history and sociology excludes most of what are normally thought to define it: "structure" and "process," the study of the past and that of the present, matters of long and short duration, and descriptive accounts and the attribution of form.

5. I focus on the American literature in order to show an immanent development of critical history in the explication of an orthodoxy most rigorously expressed in the tradition of Chester I. Barnard's *The Functions of the Executive* (1945).

6. Some of Jurgen Habermas's early writing is useful for exploring this theoretical revision of the relationship between formal and informal aspects of social organization, though it remains within the rationalist tradition (1973, 1975).

7. By "polyphony" I mean many voices, none of which can complete its authority *as voice*. "Polyphony" refers to a relation among voices *constitutive of each vocalization*. This concept was introduced as part of a theory of language by Mikhail Bakhtin (1968, 1981).

8. On the other hand, a fuller account of critical history would have to address the problem posed by too easily won a familiarity with "the natives" and those perceived as "other," namely that it is precisely such events (the massacre) that allow us to appreciate what is mysterious about all events, that there is a certain "indexicality" or situation-boundness of all that happens that resists observation, summary, and account (cf. Garfinkel 1967; see, e.g., Greenblatt 1991). Without this sense, our appreciation of the "other" easily becomes sentimental and compassion for the plight of the "other" can appear presumptuous and even self-righteous. It is well known that when the "other" loses all mystery for us, we can no longer learn about ourselves from that point of view. It is that mysteriousness that reminds us of the subjectivity of our apprehension of "otherness" and, at the same time, motivates self-criticism. It is certainly permissible to attempt to make the "other" perfectly familiar, as Darnton has done, when the aim of the exercise is to reduce the tendency to denigrate; getting the joke is essential to over-

come repugnance. But the tendency to denigrate is not sufficient to make an account otherwise valid as part of a self-reflection in the historiographical project. Darnton has traded the "other's" power over us (power to mystify) for a democracy in apprehension, but he has also made it impossible to appreciate what the "otherness" of the "other" is able to teach us about ourselves.

9. The fact that these presuppositions are invalid implies that the distinction between formal and informal aspects of organization is also theoretically invalid. Not that the latter is irrelevant to the critique of the rationalist model—we have seen that it is—but that in the light of that critique, based as it is upon the further explication of the distinction, both terms, "formal" and "informal," need to be retheorized and perhaps superseded by another concept.

10. It is, of course, legitimate to use interviews for other purposes—as when the moral credibility of the interviewee encourages us to agree with his or her interpretation of events as part of asserting a moral-political bond.

CHAPTER 5 IDEOLOGY AND THE METAPHYSICS OF CONTENT

1. I say this despite disclaimers by writers like Raymond Williams, whose influence in the United States is no less important than his influence in England, and despite the persistent use of materialist language (e.g., "production" and "reproduction") in culture studies. To use that language with theoretical intent, or even heuristically, is to commit oneself to a relation of culture with material production and the intersection of circulation, and therefore to the theoretical specificities of class, labor, power, value, the contradiction of private accumulation and social production, and the contradiction of price and value within the aggregation of capitalist social relations. These are terms that allow for the distinctive conceptualization of the historical in historical materialism. Without them, one is left with "insights" secured by dangerously certain and ungoverned theory-like preconceptions.

2. Analysis appropriates what has been written without acknowledgment of that labor and with scarcely any acknowledgment of the fact that the material has standing only within an array of like materials: It is one book among many and thus partakes of the value determination that makes of that many an ordered array. Analysis is, then, parasitic to a certain labor that it takes as abstract, and takes credit for conferring value on something the value of which is already determined by the relationship among like things signaled by the fact of publication. Its appropriation is, in fact, an expropriation. Thus, the act of "reading" in analysis, for what is said about something, begins before the book is encountered; it is embodied within the society of such readers and the society of their objects. It begins within a sphere of appropriative activity that has already accumulated and deployed a multiplicity of objects of "value."

3. This extremism has, unfortunately, a rather firm position in American Marxian thought. This may account in part for the elision by some Marxist scholars, the "independent" Left, of Communist movements, parties, unions, and revolutions. The rejection itself has generated an ideology in the simplest sense of the term: Suspect groups and activities are possessed of a disposition (Leninism, Stalinism, etc.) to be no more than what they are "known" to be. They can have no history or principle of internal development beyond the unfolding of the disposition. This "sect" model, expressing as it does the hoary and anachronistic idea of primitivism, is familiar to sociologists as an ideology of superiority in the ordering of affairs. As the idea of the "crowd" and that of the "mob" came to represent, for the bourgeoisie, mass movement and popular political action—associated inevitably with the challenge of labor—so the idea of the sect came to haunt the Left, finally as an ideology of an insupportable detachment from organization that would make of theory and praxis an opposition in favor of theory.

4. In passing, it is worth noting that Roland Barthes' discussion of myth as an instance of semiosis begs this question. The operation upon the sign that accomplishes myth, its trans-

formation from sign to signifier, cannot be taken as necessary *in* thought, though it may be necessary *to* it. That reflective moment cannot have evaded the political play of the divided subjectivity it presumes without having betrayed the volatility of semiosis altogether in favor of an automatism. Transformation and reflection must involve contradiction. Therefore, they must be political accomplishments, as " 'economic" investment' is in reality a politics of social transformation and social reflection.

5. Indeed, as Marx shows, every concrete investment of wealth begs the question of the origin of wealth. In other words, for every investment, the wealth invested is the result of a "primitive accumulation."

6. The Robinsonians are correct in identifying the labor theory as a metaphysics. Marx did not disagree. His point was that capital must transform labor into labor power in order to rationalize the economy of private accumulation. The metaphysics of value is capital's practical truth, its necessary intention if it is to remain capital. The enforcement of this practical truth is capital's side of the class struggle. It becomes labor's truth and struggle only in its entailment of sociology, the society made obscure by the forcible conversion of labor into labor power.

7. "It becomes plain, that it is not the exchange of commodities which regulates the magnitude of their value; but, on the contrary, that it is the magnitude of their value which controls their exchange proportions" (Marx 1967, p. 63)

CHAPTER 6   "SOCIETY AGAINST THE STATE": THE FULLNESS OF THE PRIMITIVE

1. At one point, Clastres argues persuasively—on the basis of historical demography, contemporary ethnography, and early accounts of village life, military expeditions, and population movements—that the present sparseness of the population is not due to the continual regulation of populations of primitive communities by nature, but the result of a historical decline occasioned by the European invasion. Thus, his review of the evidence supports the conclusion that pre-Columbian America contained as many as eighty million people. The precipitous decline in the sixteenth century represents, then, the loss of one-fourth of the world's population. Present-day Indian societies are thus not instances of the historically resistant primitive but simply what remains.

2. To have already identified institution or action is either to have found something that one already knows as an instance of reason or mechanism, something about which this ambiguity is already established, or it is to have found something that one already knows is typically an occasion for reason to do its work. This might be something decisively strange. Clastres fills his account with articles that are strange, articles whose very strangeness is what we already know to be an invitation to reason.

CHAPTER 7   LEFT FUTURES

1. On this terrain, and in regard to the debate over the work of Hardt and Negri (2000), one can no longer assume that it is possible to sustain political projects predicated on the autonomy of the nation state (see also Aronowitz and Gautney 2003). "Globalization" points to the general process in which the extension of capital accumulation vitiates and then constitutes social forms as units in its projected universe of production and exchange. Given the contradictions of this process, globalization represents a perspective on one aspect of capitalist development, namely that capital is always in the process of destroying the very society it creates, whatever the scale and dimensions of its operation at any given time. We believe that any discussion of collapse would have to begin by taking this process into account.

2. This is consistent with Aijaz Ahmad's criticisms of Edward Said (1987). For some difference in emphasis, cf. Frederic Jameson (1986).

3. Critical scholarship has emphasized indigenous elements of the Communist move-ment in the United States, as elsewhere. See Brown et al. 1993. Theodore Draper's diatribes against this literature as a whole, in the pages of *The New York Review of Books*, reiterate the tired theme against the weight of evidence and with indifference to reasonable standards of historiography, that North American communism was nothing but a Soviet project, and that any attempt to complicate the picture is merely an apology for Stalinism.

CHAPTER 8   RETHINKING THE CRISIS OF SOCIALISM

1. This was advocated by Paul Lazarsfeld in the introduction to his co-edited book, *The Uses of Sociology* (1967). Lazarsfeld argued that "significant knowledge" comes primarily from contract research and that the obligation of the researcher ("professional") to the pur-suit of such knowledge is satisfied only when the "client" determines what problems need to be investigated. Talcott Parsons took a different point of view, arguing, in 1951, for the need to develop theory relatively independently of prevailing topics of research. Neverthe-less, his version of systems theory, with its emphasis on the mobilization of system compo-nents for the solution of problems and its denial of the significance of conflict to system relations, appears to be guided by the subordination of instrumental rationality to official imperatives, whatever they might be. To be sure, he attempted to build in one critical factor, legitimation; but his notion of legitimacy, as an appeal to standards and values beyond dis-cussion ("latent") assumes the same sort of consent of the governed that has always served the interests or reinforced the practices of those in positions of power. Parsons' insistence, in his famous review of C. Wright Mills' *Power Elite*, that power had been replaced, in the modern era, by "authority," merely begged the question. It was intended to reinforce his dictum that the intentions of those who ruled modern societies were the imperatives of those societies themselves, that, as he wrote in the 1930s, the problem of power has, since Hobbes, been "solved." It does not follow that all such efforts at identifying systems are skewed toward existing imperatives of management. However, this seems to have been the case with the major figures of mid-twentieth-century sociological theory. For Parsons, whose work is otherwise remarkable for its intricacy and for the comprehensiveness with which he organized his thought as a radical counter to Marxism, it is revealed in virtually all of his social commentary on student protest, race relations, and McCarthyism.

2. References to "institutional racism" and "internal colonialism" contributed construc-tively to this attempt at rethinking the relations of society according to what had once been called merely a problem. In each case, racism was reconceived as something profound in U.S. society. However, in the former, it was merely portrayed as pervasive, while in the latter it was represented as intrinsic; that is, fundamental to the preservation of relations of domina-tion (cf. Skolnick 1969; Carmichael and Hamilton 1967).

3. Harry Braverman described how industrialists took advantage of ethnic differences to undermine the sociality of workers. Easy communication among workers represented costs and potential danger—costs because interaction takes time and reinforces otherwise unac-countable decision-making at the base; danger because interaction can lead to the develop-ment of new dispositions geared to the needs of the group and in possible opposition to the goals of management (1975).

4. To get the flavor of this at its least reactionary, see, for example, C. Vann Woodward's "Freedom and the Universities," in the July 18, 1991, issue of *The New York Review of Books* (vol. 38, no. 13). See also various articles in *The New Republic*, especially in the issues of February 18, 1991, and April 15, 1991.

5. This was E. P. Thompson's project in *The Making of the English Working Class* (1963), and it preoccupies all those currently engaged in the study of "popular culture" from the points of views of race, class, gender, and condition of oppression.

6. We see this in Sartre's remarkable study, *St. Genet*, as in later writings by Roland Barthes (*The Pleasure of the Text*, 1976) and Gayatri Spivak (*In Other Worlds*, 1987). Spivak,

in particular, has made a strong case for the capacity of deconstruction to identify the possibility of voice for the subaltern as precisely what cannot be identified within the theory of the supra-altern.

7. It goes without saying that "gradualism" is the metaphysics of institutional reform. It implies that one can build, confidently, greater upon smaller gains, as if every particular socially positive change is irreversible, thereby allowing politics to proceed confident in the permanence of its past accomplishments. The fallacy of the irreversibility of reform, its utopianism, has been thoroughly exposed by events in two countries that had once been particularly susceptible to it, the United States and England. However helpful this may be in clearing the air, it is by no means an unmitigated blessing. The exposure of the fact that reforms are only as durable as the movements that give rise to or substantiate them tends to suggest either that reform is impossible or that only the power of reason (in practice always the reason of power) can administer change according to clearly defined human values. When all is futile or all is power, politics tends to identify its task neither as a historical one nor as one that lends itself to democracy. The resurgence of technocratic and neo-Fascist ideologies among formerly liberal politicians—e.g., in regard to education, welfare, city administration—represents a likely outcome of a utopian cycle in which the gradualist metaphysics of reform is first asserted as the only valid politics, then exposed as invalid because its failure is that of the only valid politics, then denied for its political irrealism as part of a more general denial of the viability and meaningfulness of politics as such.

8. What we are attempting to identify here is a tendency within a range of Left analyses that, whatever else it has to offer, risks entering uncritically into a rhetorical climate that denies even the discursive possibility of recognizing the relationship of politics to history. Paradoxically, this tendency surfaces even in self-critically theoretical efforts to rethink the history of the relation of socialism to capitalism, such as those of Laclau, Mouffe and Laclau, Jean Cohen, and Guatarri and Negri. All seem to have in common a reluctance to apply the same self-critical methodology to the history of the Left.

It is also prevalent in certain strategies whose Leftism is defined within the limited confines of what Theodore Lowi discussed as the liberal tradition: for example, that most desperate strategy promoted by Michael Harrington in the name of democratic socialism throughout the 1970s and 1980s—limited work within, and never beyond, the more liberal portion of the mainstream of the Democratic Party. In this, Harrington sought alignment with and recognition from institutions hostile in principle to the Left. Only the force of his remarkable personality could have sustained the trick of getting liberal Democrats to focus on the content of their liberalism; certainly this could not have formed the basis for a social movement, nor could it have provided a Left strategy that could be democratic in its own forms of implementation. Effective work within the Democratic Party could only have been possible for elites from the Left having special access not available to others, and a quiescent mass of people willing to wait for the benefits of changes devised through the good offices of those elites. This helps explain Harrington's continued hostility, from the 1960s on, to grass roots movements, indigenous movements of resistance in the Third World, the Jackson campaign, and other activities that, by their nature, could only disturb the peace required for the limited institution-based work of modifying small elements of public policy.

9. That is, given the abstraction of site, to what extent do the events made evident by the abstraction conform to the critical relation between the sociality of productive activity and the irrepressible expansiveness of exchange. If they can be described in those terms, and this is always arguable, then it is reasonable to retain a sense of Socialist continuity. Notice that emancipation in the utopian sense implied by Habermas's early work, cannot be a criterion for evaluating the Socialist disposition of any momentarily identifiable socialism. Notice also that the problematic of democracy is built into the dialectic of sociality, as one aspect—reference to what people do together—of the negation of capitalist exchange by the sociality of productive effort. When democracy, emancipation, and similar idealizations are taken as criteria for judging the success or failure of socialism, socialism can no more meet those standards than any other imaginable instance of society. The use of the term "totalitarianism" is

derived from precisely this sort of ahistorical idealism—first, uncritically, the standards, then the application, finally the judgment—though it is often defended on inductive grounds.

10. There was, however, prior to *perestroika*, a literature that provided evidence of civil society in the USSR even though it was not theorized as such (cf. Friedgut 1979; Hahn 1988).

11. The modern society of an "organic solidarity" of irreducibly divided labor was an intrinsic feature of capitalist production on a national scale. While this hypothesis is identified with Marx's critique of capital, it is at least implicit in most classical social theory, from Maine, Durkheim, and Toennies, to Parsons.

12. The terms "civil society," "state," and "the people" must have different referents when socialism provides the frame of reference for their use.

13. The literature on Fordism and post-Fordism provides one version of the analysis of capitalism in the context of globalization (cf. Aglietta 1987; Lipietz 1987; Harvey 1989). "Fordism" is taken from Gramsci's analysis of capitalism in the United States. It refers to the attempt to coordinate labor and consumption by rationalizing the costs of socializing production through the sales of goods to the agents of production while degrading concrete labor in the production process itself (1971, p. 309). As the mobility of capital increased, opportunities for investment opened that did not need to accept such costs and therefore had no need to form such a compromise of economic interest. As a result, the Fordist principle gave way to a renewed separation of production and consumption, with a corresponding weakening of labor as a national political force, on an international and then global scale.

14. Thus, the costs of socialization are mitigated by pressure within national capitals for an increase in capital's freedom to move beyond established legally restrictive political boundaries. This, in addition to the contradiction of price (realization of value) and value (social conditions of production seen from the point of view of the reproduction of capital), constitutes one part of the global intersection of national interests that comprises the globally critical relation of capitalism and socialism.

15. This freedom itself, it must be remembered, expresses the more generalized aspects of the constitutive crisis of capitalism. The conditions under which capital circulates (providing resources for investment) are always somewhat at odds with the conditions under which goods are produced and the conditions under which the social organization of production is reproduced as a whole. Exchange proceeds (and expands) only to the extent to which it achieves a rationality suitable to calculation and therefore only if it presents conditions under which all things are comparable. Because of this, the normal tensions between the conditions of investment (exchange) and the conditions of production become acutely contradictory when exchange is universalized and rationalized as a circuit (circulation), and production is sufficiently integrated (socialized) that its external investment requirements cannot be reliably met. What is contradictory at the primary sites of "advanced capitalism" has, at other sites, for societies of production, a dual character. On the one hand, it presents them with a wealth of available capital that they are not organized enough to accept; on the other hand, it constitutes a decisive interference with the marginal economy of investment on which they had always had no choice but to rely. Thus, the USSR, like any other national economy, required at least marginal income from foreign trade. So long as this trade was mediated politically (by treaties and special arrangements between governments) rather than subject to the thoroughly speculative movements of capital Marx called "circulation," it provided at least some stability of marginally necessary resources for the Soviet political economy. Once capital's mobility was transformed from one essentially impeded by states to one essentially free of states, access to capital was no longer manageable by national agencies of economic coordination. Given the character of a social economy, however, a failure of the need for a reliable source of extra investment to be met was, under those circumstances, bound to unsettle the political economy and, of course, the relationship between state and civil society.

Bibliography

Aaron, Daniel. 1992. *Writers on the Left: Episodes in American Literary Communism.* New York: Columbia University Press.

Abalove, Henry, Betsy Blackmar, Peter Dimock, and Jonathan Schneer, eds. 1983. *Visions of History.* New York: Pantheon Books.

Abraham, D. 1981. *The Collapse of the Weimar Republic: Political Economy and Crisis.* Princeton: Princeton University Press. (Rev. ed., Holmes & Meier, 1986).

Agamben, Giorgio. 2005. *State of Exception.* Chicago: Chicago University Press.

Aglietta, M. 1987. *A Theory of Capitalist Regulation: The U.S. Experience.* London: Verso.

Ahmad, Aijaz. Fall 1987. "Jameson's Rhetoric of Otherness and the 'National Allegory.'" *Social Text* 3–25.

————. 1992. *In Theory.* London: Verso.

Almond, Abraham. 1954. *The Appeals of Communism.* Princeton: Princeton University Press.

Amin, Samir. 1991. "The Issue of Democracy in the Contemporary Third World." *Socialism and Democracy* 12:83–104.

Anderson, P. 1983. *Arguments within English Marxism.* London: Verso.

Aronowitz, Stanley. 1993. "The Situation of the Left in the United States." *Socialist Review* 93:5–79.

————. 1996. *The Death and Rebirth of American Radicalism.* New York: Routledge.

————. 2006. *Left Turn: Forging a New Political Future.* Boulder, CO: Paradigm Press.

Aronowitz, Stanley, and Heather Gautney, eds. 2003. *Implicating Empire: Globalization and Resistance in the 21st Century World Order.* New York: Basic Books.

Bakhtin, Mikhail. 1968. *Rabelais and His World,* translated by H. Iswolsky. Cambridge: MIT Press.

————. 1981. *The Dialogic Imagination,* translated by C. Emerson and M. Holquist, edited by M. Holquist. University of Texas Press.

Barnard, Chester I. 1945. *The Functions of the Executive*. Cambridge, MA: Harvard University Press.

Barthes, R. 1976. *Pleasure of the Text*. New York: Hill and Wang.

Bell, D. 1967 (originally published in 1952). *Marxian Socialism in the United States*. Princeton: Princeton University Press.

Bellknap, Michael. 1977. *Cold War Political Justice: The Smith Act, the Communist Party, and American Civil Liberties*. Westport, CT: Greenwood Press.

Bentley, Eric, ed. 1971. *Thirty Years of Treason: Excerpts from the Hearings of the House Committee on Un-American Activities, 1938–1968*. New York: Viking Press.

Bettleheim, C. 1975. *The Transition to Socialist Economy*. Atlantic Highlands: Humanities Press.

Bittner, E. 1965. "The Concept of Organization." *Social Research* 32:230–55.

Bhaskar, Roy. 1986. *Scientific Realism and Human Emancipation*. London: Verso.

Blum, A. 1974. *Theorizing*. London: Heinemann.

Blum, A., and P. McHugh. 1984. *Self Reflection in the Arts and Sciences*. Atlantic Highlands: Humanities Press.

Blum, A., M. E. Brown, F. Dallmayr, M. Roche, and K. Wolff. 1987. *Self-Reflection in the Human Sciences*. Edmonton: University of Edmonton Press.

Bologh, R. W. 1979. *Dialectical Phenomenology: Marx's Method*. Boston: Routledge & Kegan Paul.

Braudel, F. 1980. *On History*. Chicago: Univ. of Chicago Press.

Braverman, H. 1975. *Labor and Monopoly Capital*. New York: Monthly Review Press.

Brown, Michael E. Spring 1978. "Ethnography and Ideology: the New City and the Myth of the Primary." *Journal of Comparative Urban Research* 6.2:54–69.

———. 1978. "*Society Against the State*: The Fullness of the Primitive." *October* 6:61–75.

———. 1979. "The Politics of Anti-Theater." *Social Text* 1:157–68.

———. 1979. "Sociology as Critical Theory" in *Theoretical Perspectives in Sociology*, edited by Scott McNall, pp. 251–76. New York: St. Martin's Press.

———. 1986. *The Production of Society: A Marxian Foundation for Social Theory*. Totowa, NJ: Rowman and Littlefield.

———. 1993. "The History of the History of U.S. Communism" in *New Studies in the Politics and Culture of U.S.*, edited by Michael E. Brown, Randy Martin, Frank Rosengarten, and George Snedeker, pp. 15–44. New York: Monthly Review.

Brown, M. E., and Amy Goldin. 1973. *Collective Behavior*. Pacific Palisades, CA: Goodyear.

Burke, Peter. 1978. *Popular Culture in Early Modern Europe*. New York: New York University Press.

———. 1981. "People's History or Total History?" in *People's History and Socialist Theory*, edited by R. Samuel. London: Routledge and Kegan Paul.

Butler, Judith, Ernesto Laclau, and Slavoj Zizek. 2000. *Contingency, Hegemony, Universality: Contemporary Dialogues on the Left*. London: Verso.

Carmichael, S., and C. V. Hamilton. 1967. *Black Power*. New York: Random House.

Chase-Dunn, C., ed. 1982. *Socialist States in the World System*. Beverly Hills: Sage.

Clastres, P. 1977. *Society Against the State*, translated by Robert Hurley and Abe Stein. New York: Urizen Press.

Cliff, T. 1974. *State Capitalism in Russia*. London: Pluto Press.

Cochran, Bert. 1979. *Labor and Communism: The Conflict that Shaped American Unions*. Princeton: Princeton University Press.

Cohen, G. A. 1978. *Karl Marx's Theory of History: A Defense*. Princeton: Princeton University Press.

Cohen, Jean L. 1987. *Class and Civil Society: The Limits of Marxian Critical Theory*. Amherst: University of Massachusetts Press.

Cohen, Jean L., and Andrew Arato. 1992. *Civil Society and Political Theory*. Cambridge: MIT Press.

Cohen, Stephen F. 1985. *Sovieticus: American Perceptions and Soviet Realities*. New York: Norton.

———. 1986. "America's Russia: Can the Soviet Union Change?" *Socialism and Democracy* 3:5–16.

Corpus, Duane J., and Rachel Scharfman. Fall 2007. "Editors' Introduction: Historical Reflections on Religion and Politics after 9/11." *Radical History Review* 99:1–17.

Danto, Arthur. 2007. *Narration and Knowledge: Including the Integral Text of Analytical Philosophy of History*. New York: Columbia University Press.

Darnton, Robert. 1985. *The Great Cat Massacre and Other Episodes in French Cultural History*. New York: Vintage.

Dawley, Alan. 1991. *Struggles for Justice: Social Responsibility and the Liberal State*. Cambridge: Belknap Press.

Deleuze, G., and F. Guatarri. 1983. *Anti-Oedipus: Capitalism and Schizophrenia*. Minneapolis: University of Minnesota Press.

———. 1987. *A Thousand Plateaus: Capitalism and Schizophrenia*. Minneapolis: University of Minnesota Press.

Denning, Michael. 1996. *The Cultural Front: The Laboring of American Culture in the Twentieth Century*. London: Verso.

Diamond, Stanley. 1974. *In Search of the Primitive: A Critique of Civilization*. Transaction Books.

Diggins, John Patrick. 1991. *The Rise and Fall of the American Left*. New York: Norton.

Draper, Theodore. 1957, republished 1981. *The Roots of American Communism*. New York: Viking.

———. 1960. *American Communism and Soviet Russia*. New York: Viking.

———. August 15, 1985. "Revisiting American Communism: An Exchange," in *New York Review*.

———. January 26, 1987. "The Myth of the Communist Professors: The Class Struggle," *The New Republic*, 29–36.

———. January 13, 1994. "The Life of the Party." *The New York Review of Books* XLI:1 and 2:45–51.

Drucker, Peter. 1994. *Max Schachtman and His Left: A Socialist's Odyssey through the "American Century."* Atlantic Highlands: Humanities Press.

Dubofsky, Melvyn. 1994. *The State and Labor in Modern America*. Chapel Hill: University of North Carolina Press.

Duncombe, Stephen. 2007. *Dream: Re-imagining Progressive Politics in an Age of Fantasy*. New York: The New Press.

Durkheim, Emile. 1933. *The Division of Labor in Society*, translated by George Simpson. New York: The Free Press.

———. 1982. *The Rules of Sociological Method*, translated by W. D. Halls and edited by Steven Lukes. New York: The Free Press.

Feher, F., A. Heller, and G. Markus. 1983. *Dictatorship over Needs*. New York: St. Martin's Press.

Feuer, Lewis. 1969. *The Conflict of Generations*. New York: Basic Books.

Field, Mark G. 1987. "The Contemporary Soviet Family: Problems, Issues, Perspectives" in *Soviet Society under Gorbachev*, edited by Friedberg and Isham, pp. 3–29. London: M. E. Sharpe, Inc.

Fishbein, Leslie. 1982. *Rebels in Bohemia: The Radicals of the Masses, 1911–1917*. Chapel Hill: North Carolina Press.

Fitzgerald, Frances. 1979. *America Revised: History Schoolbooks in the Twentieth Century*. Little, Brown, and Co.

Fitzpatrick, Sheila, ed. 1984. *Cultural Revolution in Russia, 1928–1931*. Bloomington: Indiana University Press.

Foley, Barbara. 1993. *Radical Representations: Politics and Form in U.S. Proletarian Fiction, 1929–1941*. Durham: Duke University Press.

Foner, Eric. 2002. *Who Owns History: Rethinking the Past in a Changing World*. New York: Hill and Wang.

Fried, Albert. 1997. *Communism in America: A History in Documents*. New York: Columbia University Press.

Friedberg, Maurice, and Heyward Isham, eds. 1987. *Soviet Society under Gorbachev*. London: M. E. Sharpe, Inc.

Friedgut, T. 1979. *Political Participation in the USSR*. Princeton: Princeton University Press.

Garfinkel, Harold. 1967. *Studies in Ethnomethodology*. Englewood Cliffs: Prentice-Hall.

———. 2002. *Ethnomethodology's Program: Working out Durkheim's Aphorism*. Lanham, MD: Rowman and Littlefield.

Geertz, Clifford. 2000. *Available Light: Anthropological Reflections on Philosophical Topics*. Princeton: Princeton University Press.

Goffman, E. 1961. *Asylums*. Englewood Cliffs: Prentice-Hall.

———. 1963. *Stigma*. Englewood Cliffs: Prentice-Hall.

Goldfield, Michael. December 1989. "Worker Insurgency, Radical Organization, and New Deal Labor Legislation." *American Political Science* 83.4:1257–82.

Goldfield, Michael, and Melvin Rothenberg. 1980. *The Myth of Capitalism Reborn: A Marxist Critique of Theories of Capitalist Restoration in the U.S.S.R.* New York: Line of March Publications.

Gornick, Vivian. 1977. *The Romance of American Communism*. New York: Basic Books.

Gorshkov, M. K. 2005. "Perestroika through the Eyes of Russians: Twenty Years Later." *Sociological Research: A Journal of Translations from Russian*. (M. E. Sharpe) 44.6: complete issue.

Gramsci, A. 1971. *Selections from the Prison Notebooks*. New York: International Publishers.

Greenblatt, Stephen. 1991. *Marvelous Possession: The Wonder of the New World*. Chicago: University of Chicago Press.

Greenblatt, Stephen, and Giles Gunn. 1992. *Redrawing the Boundaries: The Transformation of English and American Literary Studies*. New York: The Modern Language Association of America.

Griffith, Robert, and Athan Theoharis. 1974. *The Specter: Original Essays on the Cold War and the Origins of McCarthyism*. New Viewpoints.

Guattari, F., and T. Negri. 1990. *Communists Like Us*. New York: Semiotexte.

Gutmann, Amy. 2003. *Identity in Democracy*. Princeton: Princeton University Press.

Habermas, J. 1970. *Toward a Rational Society*. Boston: Beacon Press.

———. 1971. *Knowledge and Human Interest*. Boston: Beacon Press.

———. 1973. *Theory and Practice*. Boston: Beacon Press.

———. 1975. *Legitimation Crisis*. Boston: Beacon Press.

Hahn, J. 1988. *Soviet Grassroots: Citizen Participation in Local Soviet Government*. Princeton: Princeton University Press.

Hallas, Duncan. 1985. *The Comintern*. New York: Bookmarks.

Hampshire, Stuart. 2000. *Justice Is Conflict*. Princeton: Princeton University Press.

Hardt, Michael, and Antonio Negri. 2000. *Empire*. Cambridge, MA: Harvard University Press.

Harvey, David. 1989. *The Condition of Postmodernity*. Cambridge, MA: Blackwell.

———. 2006. *The Limits to Capital*. London: Verso.

Hegel, G.W.F. 1977. *The Phenomenology of Mind*, translated by J. B. Baillie. Atlantic Highlands: Humanities Press.

Hemmingway, Andrew. 2002. *Artists on the Left: American Artists and the Communist Movement, 1926–1956*. New Haven, CT: Yale University Press.

Hobsbawm, Eric. 1984. "Marho Interview" in *Visions of History*, pp. 27–46. New York: Pantheon.

———. 1959. *Primitive Rebels*. Manchester: Manchester University Press.

Horne, Gerald. 1988. *Communist Front? The Civil Rights Congress, 1946–1956.* Bethlehem, PA: Associated University Press.

Hough, Jerry F. 1977. *The Soviet Union and Social Science Theory.* Cambridge, MA: Harvard University Press.

Howe, Irving, and Lewis Coser. 1957. *The American Communist Party: A Critical History, 1919–1957.* Boston: Beacon Press.

———. 1974. *The American Communist Party: A Critical History.* Cambridge: Da Capo.

Huet, M. H. Fall 1985. "La Signature de L'Histoire." *Modern Language Notes*, pp. 715–27.

Iggers, George G. 1997. *Historiography in the Twentieth Century.* Wesleyan: Wesleyan University Press.

Isserman, M. 1982. *Which Side Were You On? The American Communist Party during the Second World War.* Wesleyan: Wesleyan University Press.

———. 1987. *If I Had a Hammer . . . : The Death of the Old Left and the Birth of the New Left.* New York: Basic Books.

Jaffe, Phillip. 1975. *The Rise and Fall of American Communism.* New York: Horizon Press.

Jameson, Fredric. 1981. *The Political Unconscious: Narrative as a Socially Symbolic Act.* Ithaca: Cornell University Press.

———. Fall 1986. "Third-World Literature in the Era of Multinational Capitalism." *Social Text* 15:65–88.

Johanningsmeier, Edward P. 1994. *Forging American Communism: The Life of William Z. Foster.* Princeton: Princeton University Press.

Johnson, Richard, Gregor McLennan, Bill Schwarz, and David Sutton, eds. 1982. *Making Histories: Studies in History Writing and Politics.* Minneapolis: University of Minnesota Press.

Jones, G. S. 1971. *Outcast London.* Oxford: Oxford University Press.

Keeran, R. 1980. *The Communist Party and the Auto Workers Unions.* Bloomington: Indiana University Press.

Kelley, Robin D. G. 1990. *Hammer and Hoe: Alabama Communists during the Great Depression.* Chapel Hill: North Carolina University Press.

Kerblay, Basile. 1983. *Modern Soviet Society.* New York: Pantheon.

Klehr, Harvey. 1984. *The Heyday of American Communism: The Depression Decade.* New York: Basic Books.

———. 1988. *Far Left of Center: The American Radical Left Today.* Newark: Transaction.

Klehr, Harvey, and John Haynes. 1992. *The American Communist Movement: Storming Heaven Itself.* Twayne.

Klehr, Harvey, John Haynes, and F. I. Firsov. 1995. *The Secret World of American Communism.* New Haven, CT: Yale University Press.

———. 1996. *Red Scare or Red Menace? American Communism and Anticommunism in the Cold War Era.* Chicago: Ivan R. Dee.

Klehr, Harvey, and Kyril Anderson. 1998. *The Soviet World of American Communism.* New Haven, CT: Yale University Press.

Kolko, Gabriel. 1976. *Main Currents in Modern American History.* New York: Harper & Row.

Kornblum, W. 1974. *Blue Collar Community.* Chicago: University of Chicago Press.

Kutulas, Judy. 1995. *The Long War: The Intellectual People's Front and Anti-Stalinism, 1930–1940.* Durham, NC: Duke University Press.

LaCapra, Dominick. 1983. *Rethinking Intellectual History: Texts, Contexts, Language.* Ithaca: Cornell University Press.

———. 1987. *History, Politics, and the Novel.* Ithaca: Cornell University Press.

Laclau, Ernesto. 1990. *New Reflections on the Revolution of Our Times.* London: Verso.

———, ed. 1994. *The Making of Political Identities.* London: Verso.

Laclau, Ernesto, and Chantal Mouffe. 1985. *Hegemony and Socialist Strategy.* London: Verso.

Laibman, David. 2007. *Deep History*. Albany: State University of New York Press.

Lane, David. 1978. *Politics and Society in the USSR*. London: Martin Robertson.

Laslett, J. M., and S. M. Lipset, eds. 1974. *Failure of a Dream? Essays in the History of American Socialism*. Garden City: Anchor Press/Doubleday.

Latour, Bruno. 2005. *Reassembling the Social: An Introduction to Actor-Network-Theory*. Oxford: Oxford University Press.

Lazarsfeld, P., W. Sewell, and H. Wilensky, eds. 1967. *The Uses of Sociology*. New York: Basic Books.

Lee, Anthony. 1999. *Painting on the Left: Diego Rivera, Radical Politics, and San Francisco's Public Murals*. Berkeley: University of California Press.

Lefebvre, H. 1971. *Everyday Life in the Modern World*. New York: Harper and Row.

Levenstein, Harvey. 1981. *Communism, Anticommunism, and the CIO*. Westport, CT: Greenwood Press.

Lévi-Strauss, Claude. 1961. *Tristes Tropiques*, translated by John Russell. Criterion Books.

Levine, Andrew. 1984. *Arguing for Socialism*. Boston: Routledge & Kegan Paul.

Lewin, M. 1985. *The Making of the Soviet System*. New York: Pantheon.

Lipietz, A. 1987. *Mirages and Miracles: The Crisis of Global Fordism*. London: Verso.

Lipset, Seymour Martin, and Neil Smelser. March 1961. "Change and Controversy in Recent American Sociology." *British Journal of Sociology*. Reprinted by the Institute of Industrial Relations, Reprint No. 164, Berkeley, 1961.

Lipsitz, George. 1994. *Rainbow at Midnight: Labor and Culture in the 1940s*. Champaigne: University of Illinois Press.

Lloyd, Christopher. 1986. *Explanation in Social History*. Boston: Basil Blackwell.

Lyons, P. 1982. *Philadelphia Communists, 1936–1956*. Philadelphia: Temple University Press.

March, J., and H. Simon. 1958. *Organizations*. New York: Wiley.

Marcuse, Herbert. 1964. *One Dimensional Man*. Boston: Beacon Press.

Marquardt, Virginia. Spring 1993. "Art on the Political Front in America: From *The Liberator* to *Art Front*." *Art Journal* 52.1:72–81.

Marquit, Irwin. 1994. "Ideological Basis of the Organizational Crisis of Marxist-Leninism in the United States." *Rethinking Marxism* 7:116–31.

Martin, R. 1988. "Democratic Features of Socialism's Two Cultures." *Socialism and Democracy* 7:121–37.

Marx, K. 1967. *Capital*, Volume I. New York: International Publishers.

———. 1968. *Theories of Surplus Value*, Part II. Moscow: Progress Publishers.

———. 1977. *Capital, Volume One*, translated by Ben Fowkes. New York: Vintage.

———. 1978. *The German Ideology*. Excerpt in *The Marx-Engels Reader*, Second Edition, edited by R. C. Tucker. New York: Norton.

———. 1981. *Capital*, Volume III. Middlesex: Penguin.

McNall, S., ed. 1979. *Theoretical Perspectives in Sociology*. New York: St. Martin's Press.

Mills, C. Wright. 1956. *The Power Elite*. London: Oxford.

Milton, David. 1982. *The Politics of U. S. Labor: From the Great Depression to the New Deal*. New York: Monthly Review Press.

Mischler, Paul. 1999. *Raising Reds: The Young Pioneers, Radical Summer Camps, and Communist Political Culture in the United States*. New York: Columbia University Press.

Mittelman, J. 1988. *Out From Underdevelopment*. New York: St. Martin's Press.

Mouffe, Chantal, ed., 1992. *Dimensions of Radical Democracy*. London: Verso.

———. 1993. *The Return of the Political*. London: Verso.

Mouffe, C., and E. Laclau. 1985. *Hegemony and Socialist Strategy*. London: Verso.

Murphy, F. James. 1991. *The Proletarian Movement: The Controversy over Leftism in Literature*. Champaigne: University of Illinois Press.

Naison, M. 1983. *Communists in Harlem during the Depression*. Champaigne: University of Illinois Press.

Nekola, Charlotte, and Paula Rabinowitz, eds. 1987. *Writing Red: An Anthology of American Women Writers, 1939–1940*. New York: Feminist Press.

Nicolaus, Martin. 1975. *Restoration of Capitalism in the USSR*. New York: Liberator Press.

Nolan, Mary. Spring/Summer 1988. "The *Historikerstreit* and Social History." *New German Critique* 44:51–80.

Nove, A. 1969. *An Economic History of the USSR*. London: Penguin.

———. 1986. *Marxism and "Really Existing Socialism."* London: Harwood.

Novick, Peter. 1988. *That Noble Dream: The "Objectivity Question" and the American Historical Profession*. Cambridge: Cambridge University Press.

Ottanelli, Fraser. 1991. *The Communist Party of the United States: From the Depression to World War II*. Piscataway: Rutgers University Press.

Parenti, Michael. 1985. *Inventing Reality: Politics and the Mass Media*. New York: St. Martin's Press.

Parsons, Talcott. 1949 (1937). *The Structure of Social Action*. Glencoe, IL: Free Press.

———. 1951. *The Social System*. Glencoe, IL: Free Press.

———. 1960. "Social Strains in American" *Structure and Process in Modern Societies*. Glencoe, IL: Free Press, pp. 226–47.

———. November 1965. "Full Citizenship for the Negro American?" *Daedalus*, pp. 1009–54.

———. 1965. "Youth in the Context of American Society" in *The Challenge of Youth*, edited by E. Erikson, pp. 110–42. New York: Anchor.

———. Fall 1968. "The Academic System: A Sociologist's View." *The Public Interest* 173–97.

———. 1977. *The Evolution of Societies*. Englewood Cliffs: Prentice-Hall.

Pells, Richard. 1984. *Radical Visions and American Dreams: Culture and Social Thought in the Depression Years*. Wesleyan: Wesleyan University Press.

Poulantzas, Nicos. 1975. *Classes in Contemporary Capitalism*. London: New Left Books.

Preminger, Alex, and T.V.F. Brogan, eds.1993. *The New Princeton Encyclopedia of Poetry and Poetics*. Princeton: Princeton University Press.

Przeworski, A. 1986. "Material Interests, Class Compromise, and the Transition to Socialism," in *Analytical Marxism*, edited by John Romer, pp. 162–88. Cambridge, UK: Cambridge University Press.

Putnam, Hillary. 2002. *The Collapse of the Fact/Value Dichotomy and Other Essays*. Cambridge, MA: Harvard University Press.

Rabinowitz, Paula. 1991. *Labor and Desire: Women's Revolutionary Fiction in Depression America*. Chapel Hill: University of North Carolina Press.

Radosh, Ronald. March 2, 1982. "Why American Communism Failed." *Voice*.

Revel, Jacques, and Lynn Hunt, eds. 1995. *Histories: French Constructions of the Past*. New York: The New Press.

Rosenstone, Robert A. 1995. *Visions of the Past: The Challenge of Film to Our Idea of History*. Cambridge, MA: Harvard University Press.

Rude, G. 1964. *The Crowd in History*. New York: Wiley.

Ryan, James. 1997. *Earl Browder: The Failure of American Communism*. Tuscaloosa: University of Alabama Press.

Said, Edward. 1979. *Orientalism*. New York: Vintage.

———. 1994. *Culture and Imperialism*. New York: Vintage.

Samuel, R., ed. 1981. *People's History and Socialist Theory*. London: Routledge & Kegan Paul.

Sartre, Jean-Paul. 1974. *St. Genet*. New York: Mentor.

———. 1976. *Critique of Dialectical Reason*. London: Verso.

Saussure, Ferdinand de. 1966. *Course in General Linguistics*. New York: McGraw-Hill.

Schiller, Herbert I. 1973. *The Mind Managers*. Boston: Beacon Press.

Schrecker, Ellen. 1986. *No Ivory Tower: McCarthyism and the Universities*. Oxford, UK: Oxford University Press.

———. 1998. *Many are the Crimes: McCarthyism in America*. Boston: Little, Brown.

Schutz, A. 1967. *The Phenomenology of the Social World*. Evanston: Northwestern University Press.

Schwartz, Lawrence. 1980. *Marxism and Culture: The CPUSA and Aesthetics in the1930s*. Port Washington, NY: Kenikat Press.

Sen, Amartya. 2002. *Rationality and Freedom*. Cambridge, MA: Harvard University Press.

Shaffrer, Robert. May–June 1979. "Women and the Communist Party, U.S.A., 1930–1940." *Socialist Review* 9:73–118.

Shakhnazarov, G. 1974. *The Role of the Communist Party in Socialist Society*. Moscow: Novosti Press Agency Publishing House.

Shannon, David. 1959. *The Decline of American Communism: A History of the Communist Party of the United States Since 1945*. New York: Harcourt Brace.

Shiach, Morag. 1989. *Discourse on Popular Culture*. Stanford: Stanford University Press.

Simon, Herbert. 1983. *Reason in Human Affairs*. Stanford University Press.

Skolnick, J. 1969. *The Politics of Protest*. New York: Ballantine.

Smelser, N. 1963. *Theory of Collective Behavior*. New York: Free Press.

Spivak, G. Fall 1985. Lecture at the City University of New York. Summarized by Randy Martin in *Socialism and Democracy*, Spring/Summer 1986, 2:92–95.

———. 1987. *In Other Worlds*. New York: Routledge.

———. 1999. *A Critique of Postcolonial Reason: Toward a History of the Vanishing Present*. Cambridge, MA: Harvard University Press.

Starobin, J. R. 1972. *American Communism in Crisis, 1943–1957*. Berkeley: University of California Press.

Suttles, G. 1968. *The Social Order of the Slum*. Chicago: University of Chicago Press.

Sweezy, Paul. 1980. *Post-Revolutionary Society*. New York: Monthly Review.

———. June 1994. "The Triumph of Financial Capital." *Monthly Review* 46.2:1–11.

Szajkowski, B. 1982. *The Establishment of Marxist Regimes*. London: Butterworth Scientific.

Szymanski, Albert. 1979. *Is the Red Flag Flying? The Political Economy of the Soviet Union*. Boston: Zed Press.

Taylor, Brandon. 1991 (Vol. 1), 1992 (Vol. 2). *Art and Literature under the Bolsheviks*, Volumes 1 and 2 . London: Pluto Press.

Thompson, E. P. 1963. *The Making of the English Working Class*. New York: Knopf.

———. 1975. "The Crime of Anonymity" in *Albion's Fatal Tree*, edited by D. Hay et al., pp. 255–344. New York: Pantheon.

———. 1978. *The Poverty of Theory*. New York: Monthly Review Press.

———. 1984. "Marho Interview" in *Visions of History*, pp. 3–25. New York: Pantheon.

Tucker, Robert, ed. 1977. *Stalinism: Essays in Historical Interpretation*. New York: Norton.

Veeser, H. Aram, ed. 1989. *The New Historicism*. London and New York: Routledge Chapman and Hill.

Wald, A. 1987. *The New York Intellectuals: The Rise and Decline of the Anti-Stalinist Left from the 1930s to the 1980s*. Chapel Hill: University of North Carolina Press.

———. 2007. *Trinity of Passion: The Literary Left and the Antifascist Crusade*. Chapel Hill: University of North Carolina Press.

Wallerstein, Immanuel. 1974. *The Modern World System*. New York: Academic Press.

———. May 1994. "Review of *The End of The Cold War* and *Beyond the Cold War*" in *Contemporary Sociology* 23.3:385.

———. 1995. *After Liberalism*. The New Press.

Weber, Max. 1947. *The Theory of Social and Economic Organization*, edited by Talcott Parsons. Glencoe, IL: Free Press.

White, H. 1973. *Metahistory*. Baltimore: Johns Hopkins University Press.

Wilentz, S. June 1985. "Red Herrings Revisited: Theodore Draper Blows His Cool." *Voice Literary Supplement*.

————. August 15, 1985. "Response to Draper," in "Revisiting American Communism: An Exchange" in *New York Review*.

Williams, R. 1977. *Marxism and Literature*. Oxford: Oxford University Press.

————. 1980. *Problems in Materialism and Culture*. London: Verso.

Zizek, Slavoj. 2001. *Did Somebody Say Totalitarianism?* London: Verso.

Zurrier, Rebecca. 1985. *Art for The Masses: A Radical Magazine and Its Graphics, 1911–1917*. New Haven, CT: Yale University Art Gallery.

Index

Michael E. Brown is Professor in the Department of Sociology and Anthropology at Northeastern University and former Professor of Sociology at Queens College and the Graduate School of the City University of New York. He is author of *Collective Behavior* (with Amy Goldman) and *The Production of Society* as well as the co-editor (with Randy Martin, Frank Rosengarten, and George Snedeker) of *Recent Studies in the Politics and Culture of U.S. Communism.*